THE
TEST
OF BATTLE

THE
TEST
OF BATTLE

The American Expeditionary Forces in the Meuse-
Argonne Campaign

PAUL F. BRAIM

DELAWARE
Newark: University of Delaware Press
London and Toronto: Associated University Presses

Associated University Presses
440 Forsgate Drive
Cranbury, NJ 08512

Associated University Presses
25 Sicilian Avenue
London WC1A 2QH, England

Associated University Presses
2133 Royal Windsor Drive
Unit 1
Mississauga, Ontario
Canada L5J 1K5

The paper used in this publication meets the requirements
of the American National Standard for Permanence of Paper
for Printed Library Materials Z39.48-1984.

Library of Congress Cataloging-in-Publication Data

Braim, Paul F., 1926–
  The test of battle.

  Bibliography: p.
  Includes index.
  1. Argonne, Battle of the, 1918.   2. United States.
Army.   American Expeditionary Forces—History—World
War, 1914–1918.   I. Title.
D545.A63B73   1987   940.4'34   85-40991
ISBN 0-87413-301-7 (alk. paper)

Printed in the United States of America

To my beloved wife, Barbara

who has correlated names, locations, and events in this text until she has learned more about the Meuse-Argonne campaign than she really cared to know.

CONTENTS

Foreword		9
Preface		15
Acknowledgments		19
1	Europe Chooses War	23
2	1917—The Year of Hope and Despair	30
3	America Sends an Army to France	35
4	The Americans Move into the Line	59
5	The First American Offensive—St. Mihiel	75
6	The AEF Accepts the Challenge: The Meuse-Argonne	87
7	The Test of Battle: Fighting through to Victory	113
8	In Retrospect	144
Appendixes		171
	1. Definitions of Military Terms, Abbreviations, and Symbols	173
	2. Time Spent in Training and Combat	176
	3. Status of Divisions on the Western Front, 11 November 1918	177
	4. Division Days on the Line in France	178
	5. Distance Advanced against Fire	179
	6. Awards for Valor, Aggregated by Division	180
	7. Casualties, Aggregated by Division	181
	8. Prisoners of War, Aggregated by Division	182
	9. Consolidation of Performance Factors	183
	10. Responses of 728 Veterans of the Meuse-Argonne Campaign to Army Service Experiences Questionnaires	184
Notes		185
Bibliography		203
Index		221

FOREWORD

During the earliest months of American belligerency in 1917 the United States government had to answer a most important question: What military support should it contribute to the cause of the Allies? This decision had to be consistent with the larger political goals to which President Wilson had committed the nation. His aim was to create a situation in which both the Central Powers and the Entente Powers would have to agree to a peace settlement of American design. Wilson had in mind a peace that would not be much more acceptable to the principal leaders of the Allies than to those of the enemy coalition. He wanted to forge a new world order based on a league of nations—a far cry from the future envisioned in the competing collections of secret treaties that bound together the two European coalitions.

Whatever the outcome of peacemaking, the first task was to defeat the Central Powers; to achieve this end the United States had to make a significant contribution to the war on land as well as on the sea. If the Central Powers met defeat, particularly a truly catastrophic one, they would be unable to resist whatever was offered in the postwar settlement. Wilson calculated further that the war would have been so devastating that the victors would probably have suffered almost as much as the vanquished. Given the exhaustion of both European coalitions, the United States, reaching the apogee of its power as Europe reached its nadir, could reasonably expect to dominate a peace settlement however unpalatable in diverse ways to the Allies.

The problem for President Wilson was how to make a significant contribution to the defeat of the Central Powers on land, while at the same time maintaining broad freedom of action to proceed as he wished after the war came to an end. In essence, France and Britain wanted the United States to supply troops as individuals or in small units to serve as replacements for depleted European armies. The United States would ship personnel; the European armies would do the rest. This approach would ensure

9

efficacious American assistance at the earliest possible moment and lead to the earliest possible decision.

To propositions of this nature the American military leaders returned a definitive rejection. They were fully prepared to concentrate American forces on the western front, because the decision was sure to take place in that theater and because the United States could exert maximum pressure more quickly and more effectively there than anywhere else, but the conception of "amalgamating" American soldiers into European armies never received serious consideration in Washington. The American people would never have permitted it; the Army was unalterably opposed to any such course; and it might well have had deleterious consequences for Wilson's peace plans.

Instead of amalgamation the President chose to mobilize a strong independent army, one that would operate in its own sector of the western front, under its own commanders, according to its own doctrine, and with its own services of supply. Such an army, after making a considerable and perhaps even a decisive contribution to victory, would surely enhance the American bargaining position at the postwar peace congress.

The decision to field an independent American army entailed considerable risk. The situation in Europe was quite desperate. After all, the Germans had resumed unrestricted submarine warfare on the high seas against neutral and noncombatant shipping, although it would almost certainly lead to American belligerency, because they were convinced that they could force a decision before the unprepared Americans would exercise much influence on the outcome. Despite these portents the Americans did not diverge from the decision to mobilize and deploy an independent army. Given their low level of preparedness, in April 1917 the United States could not hope to undertake land operations on a truly independent basis until 1919, and perhaps not even until 1920. Nevertheless, even after the many reverses of 1917—the French defeat on the western front, the British failure to force a breakthrough on the Somme, the collapse of Russia, and the terrible rout of the Italian army at Caporetto—the United States unswervingly adhered to the concept of an independent army. It was an unavoidable concession to the exigencies of both the domestic political situation and the imperatives of the plan to create a league of nations.

A remarkable effort was made to begin the mobilization of a great independent army during 1917, but as 1918 began it was evident that the end of the process lay very far in the future. Only a few troops had been shipped to France, and it was obviously unfeasible to occupy an independent sector for many months.

Developments during the early months of 1918 thoroughly compromised the rational American plan to field an independent army. When

Germany failed to win by using submarines in 1917, the German army was concentrated in France in the desperate hope of achieving a decision on land before the Americans could put in enough resources to ensure an ultimate victory for the Entente. The German assault began on 21 March 1918, and it did not cease until 18 July, when the Allies gained the initiative. During the emergency the United States agreed to ship only front-line troops, an expedient that militated against the early formation of an independent army because it cut off the flow of support units. Moreover, the Commander of the American Expeditionary Forces, General John J. Pershing, agreed to the temporary brigading of American divisions with French and British counterparts, under European command, to gain experience in quiet sectors, although some American divisions saw service during the defensive battles of March–July 1918. This process further disrupted training and other activities essential to the creation of an independent army.

Although the massive German attacks bent the Allied front, it did not break, and General Ferdinand Foch, the generalissimo, assumed the offensive as soon as the German attacks were stopped. Shortly thereafter the impatient Pershing was allowed to form the American First Army, although it lacked many of the normal components of such an organization. It was quite a far cry from an independent force.

The First Army conducted its first operation, a kind of rehearsal for more difficult service, against a huge salient at St.-Mihiel near the right of the active front in a largely quiet area. Pershing intended not only to reduce the salient but to move north and east against vital rail lines, deemed essential to the continuing supply of the German units fighting all along the front. If these communications were interdicted, the First Army would make a vital contribution to the final decision—just what had been intended, even if the First Army was but a pale shadow of the force that had been contemplated earlier. Unfortunately Foch, now a marshal of France, decided to restrict the attack on the St.-Mihiel salient. Pershing received orders to reduce the salient, but then break off the advance. He was then to move the First Army westward to the Meuse-Argonne sector, where it would cooperate with French units in attacks coordinated with those of the British and the Belgians to the north. The Franco-American elements would move northward and the British and Belgians eastward, displacing the entire German line.

The attack on the St.-Mihiel salient, which took place on 14–16 September 1918, proved most successful, but in retrospect it does not appear as impressive as was claimed at the time. The German high command decided not to fight for the salient, but to withdraw, a means of shortening the line. This retrograde movement began just before the Americans jumped off. In effect the First Army simply speeded up the German evacuation. A more experienced force might have captured most of the retreating defenders, but they were able to escape with much of their equipment.

The stage was thus set for rapid deployment to the Meuse-Argonne sector. It had to be accomplished in a mere ten days, because the big push was scheduled for 26 September. Although the Americans would not encounter the better German divisions in France, they would have to fight in very difficult terrain that favored the defense. It would be a severe test indeed for the fledgling American troops—far from the degree of readiness for combat that had been envisioned earlier. This premature operation stemmed from the unexpected circumstances that materialized in 1918—first the German offensive and then the Allied counteroffensive. These events thoroughly disrupted Pershing's preparations to field an independent army and also forced extensive combat operations long before the Americans were fully prepared for them.

Although the American army ultimately gained its objectives in the Meuse-Argonne campaign, the victory came only after ghastly losses in blood and treasure and agonizing delay. Shortly afterwards the German army collapsed completely, and diplomatic negotiations led swiftly to the armistice of 11 November 1918. This outcome obscured much of the real history of the Meuse-Argonne campaign. Certain Europeans on both sides of the conflict raised questions then and later about the effectiveness of the American operations, but these criticisms were either ignored or dismissed as sour grapes. Consequently military historians have never really provided a fully comprehensive and authoritative history of the campaign.

Colonel Paul F. Braim (Ret.) has set himself the task of preparing a detailed and objective campaign history of the Meuse-Argonne operations. To this task he brings broad experience as a career army officer and expertise in the methods of the professional historian. In his civilian guise he is Dr. Paul F. Braim; this study began as a doctoral dissertation at the University of Delaware. It moves well beyond the collection of myths, half-truths, and downright misconceptions that until now have colored our perceptions of this important event.

Perhaps Colonel Braim's principal accomplishment is to have asked the right questions and to have approached his task without debilitating preconceptions. Other scholars are bound to contest his findings, which of necessity constitute the beginning rather than the end of a full professional inquiry into the topic. They are nevertheless a crucial turning point; all future accounts must necessarily depart from this one, a pioneering enterprise. Colonel Braim has used scholarly techniques that greatly enhance the utility of his work. He has walked the terrain, applying the skills of an expert combat soldier in following the battles. He has made a diligent examination of many extant records. He has also consulted a panel of historians who have offered previous assessments of the American army's performance during 1918, allowing him to measure his results against prevailing viewpoints.

In conducting this investigation Colonel Braim always retains an awareness of the necessarily desperate conditions that obtained on the battlefield—those extraordinary pressures that manufacture "the fog of war." Awareness of the unexampled confusion that prevails on the modern battlefield greatly strengthens the cogency of this professional estimate.

For all these reasons it is a privilege to commend this volume to those concerned about the American participation in the Great War of 1914–1918. It moves well past previous authorities; it should exercise significant influence on future evaluations of the American Expeditionary Forces.

DAVID F. TRASK
Washington, D.C.
November 1985

PREFACE

Sixty-seven years have passed since the guns fell silent on the western front in France. The "war to end all wars" halted—for a score of years—but did not end! The American Expeditionary Forces Headquarters wrote their after-action reports, and their operational directives and administrative papers were diligently correlated and stored in Washington, D.C. Most of the records and reports of the major Allied and Central Powers were likewise collected. Many of the senior commanders, both the victorious and the defeated, rushed from the battlefield into print, claiming, in their memoirs, credit for victory or giving excuse for defeat. Called the "Battle of the Memoirists," these literary struggles continued into the 1930s. The leaders of the victorious European armies generally downgraded the efforts of the United States on the Western Front, while the former American commanders jabbed at each other with ever more intense criticism. The defeated German military found solace in accusing their politicians of having given them a "stab in the back."

The issues of "The Great War" became obscured and relatively forgotten with the onset of World War II; subsequently, studies of the Second World War took precedence. The official narrative history of the First World War, which was being drafted by the Historical Division of the United States War Department, was canceled in 1948. A few scholars, however, continued to labor to record the events of World War I and to stress its relationship to contemporary world problems. They have called for additional studies of the accumulations of archival material that are resting in relative obscurity in the national libraries and archives of the former contesting powers.

This work attempts to summarize and analyze a portion of that material connected with the participation of the American Expeditionary Forces (AEF) in the Meuse-Argonne campaign, the greatest test of battle that the American Army had undergone up to that time. The manner in which the Army of the United States rapidly expanded to twenty times its prewar strength and met the tremendous challenge of the Meuse-Argonne, pro-

15

vides an understanding of the capabilities and limits of a free society to fight a modern war with little preparation, and suggests some lessons of value regarding military preparedness and coalition warfare.

In undertaking this study, I posed some basic questions: Why did the AEF undertake such a difficult task? Were the Americans sufficently trained to meet the challenge? Was American military leadership as poor as some of our Allies charged, or as inspired as some participating officers claimed? How was the Meuse-Argonne campaign planned and conducted? How did the campaign turn out? What was gained; was the hard-won success worth the cost? What failings, mistakes, and inadequacies are revealed, and what lessons can be derived from that campaign? Finally, was the campaign a decisive contribution to the Allied victory?

The archival material of the AEF, through which I waded, contains a wealth of orders, reports, maps, records, diaries, letters and memorabilia to permit a researcher to gain an appreciation of the challenges that the AEF faced. Reconnoitering the restrictive terrain of the Meuse-Argonne, I gained an empathy with those who fought there. I acquired new information and opinions from a number of scholars who were knowledgeable about that campaign. Talking to veterans of the fighting, and reading their notes, letters, and memorabilia, gave me a sense of communion with that event—that awful delight experienced by an historian as he lifts one corner of the shroud of time that obscures a great event.

During research, I found my opinions forming on both sides of most of the questions I had posed earlier. It became apparent that there were wide variations in the experience, ability, and aggressiveness of the American military leaders. However, the opportunity to take aggressive action was not presented in the same way to each leader, and some military leaders were burdened by tremendous missions, which the resources they commanded could in no way fulfill. In assessing the plans, problems, successes, and failures of the AEF in the Meuse-Argonne, I found no "Great Captains" in the American roster; nor did I find any fools or scoundrels for condemnation—although some leaders had been condemned by being removed from their commands during the battle. What I discovered was a hard-working group of relatively inexperienced leaders, struggling mightily with a most unique and challenging set of battlefield management requirements, which taxed their resources and capabilities to the limit. This story bears telling, and its lessons should be learned, for it was a noble struggle, the like of which our militarily unprepared society has been required to undertake again and again.

To relate the story of the Meuse-Argonne campaign, it is necessary to refer to the annotated maps convenient to the narrative. Tabular information is provided in appendixes. Military abbreviations and symbols used are explained in Appendix 1. The opinions of veterans of the First World

War were gained from interviews and from a review of the responses of World War I veterans to a Military Service Experiences Questionnaire issued by the Military History Institute (MHI) of the United States Army.

I wish to thank, in the first instance, Dr. David F. Trask, the chief historian of the United States Army's Military History Center, who suggested that the Meuse-Argonne campaign needed further scholarly research, and offered guidance on unresolved matters related to it.

I am eternally grateful to Dr. James M. Merrill, distinguished professor emeritus of the University of Delaware, whose unfailing support and encouragement were sustaining and inspiring during the long, often-interrupted work on this history. My deep appreciation must also be·expressed to Doctors George F. Frick, Raymond C. Callahan, and Gerald M. Straka of the University of Delaware, who reviewed the manuscript and gave the author many hours of guidance, evaluation, and encouragement. My indebtedness is also acknowledged to Mr. Charles Shaunessey, who guided my research through the old army records of the National Archives. I also received aid and guidance from Colonel Harold M. Hannon and Major James W. Rainey of the Department of History, United States Military Academy. Colonel Donald P. Shaw and Colonel Rod Paschall, directors of the United States Army's Military History Institute, were most helpful, as was Dr. Richard J. Sommers, the institute's archivist, and Dr. Jay Luvaas, the Harold K. Johnson Visiting Professor of Military History. Captain Jonathan M. House of the Combat Studies Institute, United States Army Command and General Staff College, gave me expert assistance. Mr. Peter Simkins of the British Imperial War Museum deserves much thanks for providing me with expert opinion on the British armies of the period. Mr. Norman Iorio, superintendent of the United States Military Cemetery at Romagne, assisted my reconnaissance of the battle area. Colonel Joseph Whitehorne of the United States Army's Center of Military History also gave me valuable planning assistance. Among the many scholars who provided me information and informed opinion, I cite Donald Smythe of John Carroll University. From his two-volume biography of General Pershing and from my discussions with him, I gained a deeper insight into my subject than I got from any other single source. Appreciation is offered here to all the scholars who gave of their time and expertise in responding to my queries. Their names are in the bibliography, and their opinions are reflected throughout this book.

The text of this study was typed and proofread by the patient and skilled labors of Charles Cook; a thorough and very painful editorial "scrub" of the text was made by Harvey C. Fenimore, Jr. To both, my appreciation. It must be said, however, that the responsibility for the material and conclusions presented herein is solely that of this author.

ACKNOWLEDGMENTS

Appreciation is expressed to the Head of the Department of History of the United States Military Academy, West Point, New York for permission to reproduce the maps from the U.S.M.A. text, *The Great War* (West Point: U.S.M.A., 1979).

Appreciation is also expressed to the director of The U.S. Army's Military History Institute, Carlisle Barracks, Pennsylvania for permission to reproduce selected photographs from the *Terrain Studies* of the American Battle Monuments Commission (Washington: GPO, 1931) held in the institute's archives.

THE
TEST
OF BATTLE

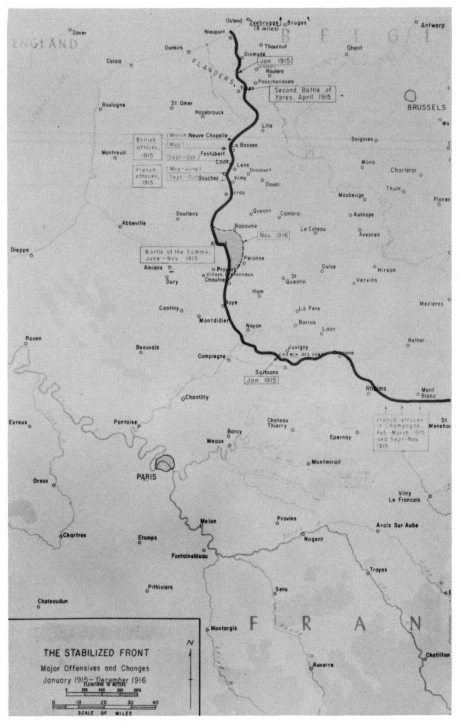

Map 1. The Stabilized Front, 1915–1917. *(From Department of History, United States Military Academy, map to accompany interim text,* **The Great War.** *West Point: U.S.M.A., 1979.)*

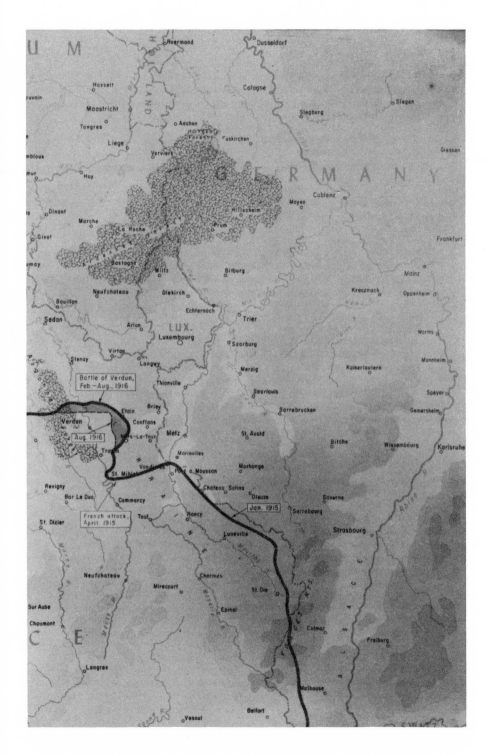

1

EUROPE CHOOSES WAR

Europe went to war in 1914 with enthusiasm, self-confidence, and "righteousness" on both sides of the contest. Political leaders were nearly unanimous in their readiness to go to war to resolve power relationships; their military chiefs were equally ready to fight and certain of quick and relatively painless victory. That element of the citizenry which was politically aware—the educated, affluent intelligentsia—was "up" for a war, a war that would provide high adventure and fulfillment to their hopes for personal ennoblement. The lower classes of Europe, who would carry the terrible burden of the war on both sides, were less publicly articulate, but they were, in almost all European countries, gaining in political consciousness and developing nationalistic ideologies.[1] The approach of the "Age of the Common Citizen" was shaking all the monarchical systems of Europe, even as population growth produced pressures for geographic changes to reflect new power positions. Few political or military leaders, or savants, appreciated the destructive power that modern weaponry and an industrial society were even then able to deliver upon a fixed battlefield.[2]

Among the more significant improvements in the implements of war that were developed during the latter half of the nineteenth century were an effective semi-automatic, breech-loading rifle with magazine feeding. This increased the average rate of fire of the rifleman from about four shots to thirty shots per minute. The rifling in the barrel and the precision manufacture of bullets markedly increased the killing range of the rifle under combat conditions. Smokeless powder came into general use late in the nineteenth century, as did the most effective mass killer, the machine gun, although the latter was only used as an "emergency" support weapon by most Western armies prior to the First World War. Lighter artillery pieces, with improved breech mechanisms and a more lethal exploding shell, had been developed, which quintupled artillery effectiveness against troops in the open or in uncovered fortifications.[3]

Scientific developments in the civil arena also contributed to enhancing the efficiency of combat. The telephone improved command and control by allowing instantaneous communication between headquarters; it also permitted artillery to fire an indirect parabola from emplacements in the rear, directed by a "forward observer" with a telephone. The tremendous increase in railroad mileage allowed armies to move hundreds of miles in one day and provided munitions and sustenance for millions during periods of intense combat.[4] Colonel Trevor N. Dupuy, in his text *The Evolution of Weapons and Warfare,* graphically illustrated a tenfold increase in the lethality of weapons during this period.[5]

With regard to strategy and tactics in this era, Dr. Theodore Ropp in *War in the Modern World* has pointed out that there was very little change from the parade ground methods of past centuries.[6] The warning of amateur strategist Ivan Bloch as early as 1898 that "war has become impossible except at the price of suicide" was heeded by few. Reports from military observers on the terrible effectiveness of modern weaponry during the Russo-Japanese War (1904)—in which each side took one quarter million casualties—were also generally ignored.[7] The armies of "The Triple Entente" (to be called in this text the "Allies") were confident of the moral superiority of "l'offensive à l'outrance" (offensive to the utmost). And they moved to war in varicolored uniforms, the better to be seen by their commanders—and, of course, by the enemy. The Germans, who directed the "Central Powers" (the Triple Alliance less Italy) in the war, had a better military system. They used the ground in attack and defense better than did their enemies, and they wore a dull field grey.[8]

A minor Balkan incident (the murder of the Austrian Archduke) precipitated a worldwide conflagration. The Great War was undertaken by the major powers of Europe with a verve and spirit almost romantic in character—a gladness to be about an exciting, important new crusade. Poets "sang" of the thrill of the contest, while even philosophers justified the commitment. The political crisis of the summer of 1914 also provoked a powerful momentum toward war: the massive mobilization and counter-mobilization of millions of men within the shrinking time-distances in Europe. Like a "genie" let out of a bottle, preparations for defense of the homeland quickly grew beyond human authority to prevent their spillover into a clash of arms.[9]

Six million men were mobilized in the heat of a very warm summer across the face of Europe. Germany deployed 1,500,000 against France, which moved 1,000,000 to her own eastern border. Britain readied over 100,000 men to deploy to the continent north of the French deployment.

Russia called up 1,400,000; Germany sent 500,000 to the east to oppose them, while Austria moved 500,000 against the Serbs and the Russians.[10]

As we have noted, the armies of Europe, excepting only the German, were not trained or equipped, nor were their leaders prepared to fight and sustain their forces on a modern battlefield. The Germans, having been devastatingly victorious in their previous continental war (the Franco-Prussian War of 1870–1871), were enabled by their growing industrial and demographic might to adopt an expansionist foreign policy, which required a strong military force. The German general staff system, devised and dominated by Prussians, was the most efficient in the world, a superbly effective agency for directing modern armies. The appreciation of the effectiveness of the machine gun by the Germans, and their infusion of machine gun teams into the forward elements of their armies, gave them a considerable superiority in killing power over that of their enemies.[11]

All the armies of Europe had developed war plans based upon mobilization rates and, except for the British, on conscription. Each of the war plans of the European powers, including those of the minor European states, assumed the martial superiority of its forces; all plans consisted of a bold, short offensive thrust. None succeeded—though the Germans did come very close to victory. Called "The Schlieffen Plan," the German war plan was drawn up by Count von Schlieffen, chief of the Great General Staff in 1905. It called for a wide turning movement on the western front, with the major force sweeping through the low countries and northern France to trap the French in a cul-de-sac.

The European war plans were developed by planners with some rudimentary knowledge of the plans of presumed enemies; however, all assumed the ability of their forces to delay or defeat enemy thrusts with minor forces, while their own offensives were striking decisive blows in their enemies' rear. The French strategic plan (Plan XVII) called for an offensive in Lorraine. It was, by chance, so complementary to that of the Germans as to have brought about near-fatal results to the French.

One month after the murder of the Archduke, Austria-Hungary declared war on Serbia (28 July 1914). On 29 July Austria bombarded Belgrade. Russia began mobilizing on 30 July. Germany demanded that Russia cease mobilizing, then mobilized herself on 1 August. France did as well on that date. Germany then went to war with France and Russia. When Germany demanded free passage against Belgium, then moved into Belgium on 3 August, Britain declared war on Germany (4 April 1914). The other powers of the Triple Alliance and Triple Entente then exchanged formal declarations of war, except Italy, which voided her obligations to the Triple Alliance.

On the western front, the forces were nearly evenly matched: eighty-seven German divisions were opposed by sixty-two French, seven Belgian, and seven British divisions. The Infantry division, the standard independent fighting unit of all modern armies, numbered about eighteen thousand soldiers in European armies in 1914. Later attrition lowered this figure to twelve to fifteen thousand. A cavalry division had five thousand to six thousand troops. But, the Germans had more modern artillery, more and better automatic weapons with forward elements, better mobility and logistics, better discipline, and better commanders than their foes.

The German drive swept through Belgium and northwestern France like a great scythe. The momentum of the German strategic envelopment finally was attenuated, with the spearhead of the German advance only some forty miles from Paris. The French, and their British allies, countered this advance with a strategic penetration of their own, which forced the Germans back and brought about a stalemate.[13] Called the "Miracle of the Marne," the Allied victory was due more to luck than to martial skill and courage. Both sides were experiencing coordination problems. Subsequent attempts by each to envelop the flanks of the opposing forces caused a rapid surge of the battle line north to the English Channel near Dunkerque. This "race to the sea" was a tie, and resulted in a stabilized situation all along the front, from the channel to Switzerland. Frontal attacks by both sides were repeated throughout the remainder of 1914 with heavy losses, as each side made maximum use of artillery, barbed wire, and the very lethal machine gun. Modern weaponry had established the primacy of defense in war![14]

During 1915, the major European powers attempted to gain maneuverability in a strategic sense, by launching offensives in other theaters. The Germans launched a major offensive on the Russian Front and gained a momentous victory at Tannenberg, wiping out or capturing nearly one half the Russian Army and expelling it from East Prussia.[15] The British attempted a bold amphibious operation in the Dardanelles, which failed because of inept execution, with heavy casualties. They gained some security for their Suez lifeline by the seizure of German colonies in Africa.[16] In 1915, Italy entered the war on the side of the Allies; it bloodied its armies against the Austrians in the Isonzo region.[17] Along the western front, the Allies made a series of limited attacks in Artois and Champagne without causing much change in the line. "Attrition" had become the accepted method for fighting the war on the western front, as the leaders of both the Entente and Central Powers found themselves unable to devise techniques which would allow for extensive maneuvers in offensive operations.[18] The Allies, in particular, were experiencing coordination problems between their "cooperating" military forces.

1916 was the year the major powers of Europe sacrificed a whole generation of their young men in attempts to prevail over their enemies through attrition. "God was," as Hanson Baldwin said, "on the side of the big factories as well as the big battalions."[19] Previously unimagined tonnages of artillery ammunition were poured on the opposing trenches, and massed armies of conscripts were thrown against barbed wire and machine guns. The Germans attempted to bleed the French white at Verdun, and they succeeded in killing more than half a million French, while suffering nearly half a million casualties of their own in failing to gain that vital area. Following the denouement of that battle, the British Expeditionary Force (BEF), with French assistance, launched their own major offensive in the area of the Somme River during the summer and fall of 1916. An immense artillery preparation of seven-days duration turned the battlefield into a wasteland of carnage and spoilage. Over the resulting rubble the British attacked in waves, "the men in each, almost shoulder to shoulder in symmetrical, well-dressed alignment . . . at a slow walk. . . ."[20] At the end of this Allied offensive, the Germans had lost 650,000 men, while British losses were 420,000 (60,000 in a single day) and French losses were 200,000. The end of the year 1916 found the fighting lines on the western front in practically the same positions as they had been at the beginning of the year. Map 1 (immediately preceding chapter 1) shows the trace of the battle line and the campaigns in this period.

On the sea, the British lost an unique opportunity to destroy the German high seas fleet at Jutland, largely because of their excessive caution. The British, however, forced the German fleet back into harbor, from which it never again emerged in force.[22] Meanwhile, submarine warfare was beginning to take a heavy toll on Allied shipping, while the Allied blockade was producing significant shortages of food in the homelands of the Central powers.[23] A Russian offensive in Eastern Europe in the spring and summer of 1916 resulted in temporary success, which was turned around by the Germans and Austrians, resulting in losses approximating a million men on each side of the line. On the Italian front, the fighting surged back and forth through the Isonzo and Trentino regions with no significant gains and with heavy losses being taken by both Italian and Austrian forces. By the end of the year, all the major contestants had reached a state of near exhaustion of their manpower, and food supplies at home were nearing critically low levels.[24]

Politicians and articulate persons of the bodies politic, on both sides, clamored in anguish and anger against the sterile tactics and the bloody operations that had taken place.[25] Writers, scholars, and other savants have since criticized the lack of strategic innovation on the western front during this period. It has been, and remains today, popular to condemn those responsible for prosecuting the Great War, because they were not able to do so in a less bloody fashion. Hanson Baldwin made the point, however, that millions of men fighting in a relatively small, confined area, using weapons of mass destruction are necessarily committed to the strategy of "attrition." Trevor Dupuy has also excused the generals from full responsibility for the carnage that industrial society brought to the battlefield in 1914.[26] However, C. S. Forester, in his text, *The General,* incisively castigated the unimaginative, tradition-bound "Colonel Blimps," whose refusal to try new strategies caused the loss of the "flower of the nations."[27] It was industrial technology that developed the weapons of mass destruction. It was also industrialization that allowed for large armies to replace those slaughtered.

In fact, there were tactical innovations made by both contestants. Lieutenant General Wilhelm Balck, a student of battle tactics who commanded on the western front in World War I, in his text, *The Development of Tactics—World War,* detailed the important changes that were being made by both sides during the stalemate.[28] The massing of artillery, which reached a density of one gun per four meters of front line, forced the development of a system of multiple connecting entrenchments by both sides. The trench line nearest the enemy was lightly occupied, often abandoned during enemy "drumfire." A second line of entrenchments, beyond the observed fire of the enemy, contained the major defensive force. A third line, out of artillery range, with deep, covered bunkers, housed the reserve. The area between these lines was defended by machine-gun and trench-mortar pillboxes, camouflaged and mutually supporting. When the Allies attacked, the Germans surrendered the first trench, then contained the thrust by flanking fire from bypassed pillboxes and trench groupments, while the reserve moved along connecting trenches to swiftly attack the penetration, also in flank. The Allies, according to Balck, were less flexible, more inclined to fight for their sacred land, but their defenses gradually came to resemble those of the Germans.[29]

In his text *If Germany Attacks: The Battle in Depth in the West,* Captain Graeme C. Wynne (British Army) credited the German General von Lossberg with another defensive innovation in late 1915: Siting the second, the "main defensive line" on the reverse (rear) slope of ground to protect this line from the devastation of increasingly accurate direct-fire weapons of the enemy! Wynne also noted that the Germans learned in 1916–1917 to disperse their bunker locations and to move reserves out of deep entrenchments when under fire, as "these were only deathtraps."[30]

In the attack, both sides learned to move their infantry closely behind rolling barrages of artillery. By 1917, the Germans had begun relying on short-range attacks to avoid the disorganization which inevitably occurred when the attacking elements made a deep advance. After seizing a single trench system, the German troops immediately assumed a defensive posture, dug in, reorganized, then moved again if no counterattack came.

Balck said they learned that a deep penetration was often lost because attacking troops had become disorganized when the inevitable counterattack came. He charged the failure of the French offensive of 1917 to the attempt to make too deep a penetration—as well as to the fact that the Germans knew the attack was coming and were prepared for it.[31] A technique to gain surprise in attack was learned late in 1917 by both contestants—and by the Americans in 1918: the use of short, violent artillery preparatory fires, rather than the long "drumfire" of the artillery defenders had come to expect.

Despite these innovations, the stalemate and the carnage continued throughout 1917. The British strategist General Sir Frederick Maurice said of this stalemate: "It took the French and British four years to recover from the initial mistakes of (French) Plan XVII."[32] The long stalemate, eventually taught the Germans to develop bypass tactics, while the Allies turned to the tank to effect the rupture of enemy defenses.

2

1917—THE YEAR OF HOPE AND DESPAIR

When the embattled Europeans faced the dawn of 1917, the third year of total war, they saw yet another stalemate on most of the battlefronts of the world.On the map of Western Europe, a 376-mile trench system ran from the North Sea southeast to the border of Switzerland. Much of the area on both sides of this jagged scar was plowed and pockmarked from intensive shelling and equally feverish digging, and the earth had been poisoned by the carnage. Rain and mud were constant companions of the soldiers. After three heartbreaking years of a war of attrition, the armies on both sides were depleted and the civilian manpower pool exhausted. The great vulnerability of soldiers attacking across the battlefields was illustrated by the millions of dead lying "over the top," deaths incurred in driving the battle lines an insignificant distance east or west. Gas was regularly used, and the tank had made its appearance. The effectiveness of the internal combustion engine had not yet been fully realized on the battlefield, neither in tank operations nor in the air; but truck convoys were a regular feature of the extensive logistics systems, interspersed with animal and human carriers, delivering hundreds of thousands of tons of material and supplies to the front. Patrols and raids into "no man's land" were sporadic activities, designed to capture prisoners and to determine the location and nature of enemy activity. Preparations for offensives were usually easy to discover because they required the movement of masses of men and supplies forward preceding each operation.

The turn of the year was a time for the military and political leaders of both coalitions to revise their aims and strategies. The Germans made the decision to go on the defensive on the western front, to withdraw from vulnerable salients, and to attack in the east to eliminate Russia from the war. Following Russia's elimination, their plan was to concentrate all their forces for a swift victory in the west, before American power could make a significant difference in Allied strength. To aid in this plan, the Germans persuaded their Austrian allies to undertake another offensive, one designed to drive the Italians out of the war.[1]

In the Allied coalition, a "star" arose, promising early victory—the French General Robert Nivelle. A dynamic personality, Nivelle proclaimed that the philosophy of the pre-world war French armies would serve again as a model for success: offensive actions, carried out violently and without regard for the casualties incurred! Despite high-level objections and fears that this philosophy would produce even greater human carnage, Nivelle's spirit finally gained him the support of the new French War Minister, Paul Painleve. He (Nivelle) also convinced the new British Prime Minister, Lloyd George, that a violent offensive would rupture the German lines and allow for a deep strategic penetration that would end the war.[2] This impending Allied offensive was widely discussed in Allied capitals and even in French newspapers; it was, thus, no surprise to the Germans. To strengthen their defenses, the Germans made a strategic withdrawal from 25 February to 5 April 1917, abandoning the Noyon salient and establishing the "Hindenburg Line," centered on strong defenses across the center of France from Arras south to the Aisne River. Those actions also freed a large number of front-line divisions to provide a German reserve. In conducting their withdrawal, the Germans devastated the areas they left behind, destroying homes, railroads, and roads, even poisoning wells. While such actions were militarily sound, they further incensed the Allies, and even turned neutral opinion against the German cause.[3]

Refusing to admit that the German strategic withdrawal had made an Allied offensive less likely of success, Nivelle urged the British to conduct a "spoiling attack" with the intention of drawing reserves away from the Aisne area. On 9 April 1917, the British launched a series of attacks in the vicinity of Arras. The attacks had some initial success, but they gained little ground and caused scant shifting of German reserves. Furthermore, these attacks caused very high losses among the British and Canadian forces, already weakened by the mass casualties of 1916.[4]

On 16 April 1917, an unusually cold and snowy morning, Nivelle launched his grand offensive, labeled the "Second Battle of the Aisne."[5] (Map 1 shows the location of the Nivelle offensive of 1917.) Attacking with a force of 1,200,000 men supported by 7,000 artillery pieces, the French assaulted the Hindenburg Line along a forty-mile front between Soissons and Rheims; the main attack was aimed at the Chemin des Dames, a series of wooded, rocky ridges paralleling the front. After that objective was seized, the attackers were to conduct a deep exploitation drive. Just before the attack—unfortunate for the French—German aviators seized control of the sky from Allied aviation; the German airmen then helped to direct artillery fire, which played havoc with Allied columns of infantry, artillery, and tanks. The Allied artillery barrages rolled forward too fast for the advancing infantry, which found itself caught in well-laid German machine gun fire from the flanks. French gallantry in the face of murderous fire enabled the attackers to take the ridge of the Chemin des Dames, but the attack stopped after four days of fighting, and proceeded no further despite repeated assaults. The Germans, from their deep system of elastic defenses, launched strong counterattacks.

Result: The Nivelle offensive was a colossal failure! The French lost approximately 190,000 men. German losses were considerably lighter. Although these losses were of no greater magnitude than those of previous years, the bold promises of success in this battle, of strategic penetration, and of victory—a promise so evidently unfulfilled—devastated French morale. Mutiny broke out and spread rapidly among French troops. Mutinous actions by relatively large groups occurred in at least fifty-four French divisions. The French line facing the Germans quickly became "combat ineffective." Their defenses uncovered, the French nation was in mortal danger. General Nivelle was replaced by General Henri Pétain. A cautious and wise campaigner, he first set about restoring the confidence of the "poilu" in the ranks. He listened to their complaints, provided them with better living conditions, and had them remain on the defensive. Unique is the fact that the French were able to censor all public information on the mutiny, successfully withholding knowledge of it from the enemy—something they had never been able to do before and were seldom able to accomplish again.[6]

The French armies in disorder, it became the British lot to launch attacks with weary and weakened forces to prevent the Germans from taking advantage of the Allied turmoil. Despite parlimentary opposition, General Douglas Haig, the commander of the BEF, launched a strong drive in the alluvial mud of Flanders. In a strategic sense, it worked. The attention of General Erich Ludendorff, the German quartermaster general and *de facto* commander of the armies of the Central Powers in the West, was fully engaged by the resumption of offensive operations by the British. To facilitate this offensive from the Ypres Salient, the British Second Army was given the mission of seizing the dominating terrain, the Messines ridge complex. Careful preparations led to a successful, set-piece attack. After a seventeen-day artillery preparation, the Second Army, on 7 June 1917, detonated a mine containing one million pounds of explosives under the Messines ridge and executed a well-planned attack. Surprise was complete, and the British gained the ridge position quickly. Casualties were relatively high (17,000 for the British and 25,000 for the Germans). Nonetheless, this clear-cut victory restored Allied morale; it was particularly cheered in Britain. On 31 July 1917, the BEF, accompanied by the French First Army, launched its main offensive in the vicinity of

Ypres, following a thirteen-day intensive bombardment. The low ground in the Flanders area, sodden with rain, had become an almost impassable quagmire. The British forces struggled forward slowly in the mud from July through November, with high casualties. Then, another horror of war emerged: mustard gas was used by the Germans for the first time! German aircraft were also becoming very effective in strafing attacks, employing machine guns mounted on their airplanes. The taking of Passchendaele ridge on 6 November, with great casualties for the British, ended the offensive. The casualties from Passchendaele caused post-war British history books to depict the horror of offensive operations against entrenched troops—a horror that was to affect British political and military decisions throughout World War II. The Ypres offensive cost the British 300,000 casualties, while German losses were estimated at 260,000. The offensive gained a strip of ground five miles deep.[7]

Stubborn as ever, despite such losses, Haig continued to conduct small offensive operations through the rest of 1917, a series culminating in the very successful attack by massed tanks at Cambrai on 20 November 1917. This attack opened a five-mile salient into the German lines—a salient not exploited by the British, who were not prepared to follow up such a success. The salient was subsequently eliminated by German counterattacks. When the year ended on the western front, the battle lines remained little changed from their locations at the end of the previous year, despite huge intervening losses.[8]

On the eastern front, Russian operations in 1917 were severely hampered by political turmoil at home. In March, a revolution forced the abdication of the czar. That event was followed by an outbreak of street fighting, in which soldiers joined the rebellious workers. Soon the Russian armies, weakened by defections from their ranks and a lack of direction from headquarters, were retreating from the line of contact with the Germans on the Baltic.

The new Russian regime (the Provisional Government) pledged to continue to wage war against the Central Powers.[9] Under the leadership of Alexander Kerensky, the Russians gathered their forces for an offensive in the summer of 1917. The troops were led by the new Chief of Staff, Alexei Brusilov, the most capable general in the theater. Employing surprise, together with an unprecedented amount of advance planning, Brusilov's July offensive resulted in some initial success. But the heart was not in the Russian soldiers to fight. A German counterattack on 19 July 1917 resulted in the retaking of all the area previously gained northwest of Leningrad. The German offensive accelerated in the autumn; the opposing Russian forces were either in disarray or nonexistent. The Germans, attacking in the north toward Leningrad and as far south as the Pripet marshes, were only limited in their advances by their inability to supply their forces, which were moving great distances.[10] During this period, the German forces employed new tactics for swift penetration, for the bypassing of strong points, and for the coordination of infantry movements with artillery fire. Called "Hutier tactics" for their inventor, General Oscar von Hutier, these shock assaults were the basis for the "Blitzkrieg tactics" of the Germans during World War II.[11]

In October 1917, the Kerensky government, in a state of near chaos, abandoned Petrograd (St. Petersburg) for Moscow, and the Bolsheviks began to take over power in the major cities. The final revolution of 7 November 1917 established the Bolsheviks as the ruling power in Russia, under Lenin and Trotsky—that duo began dickering with the Germans for a peace treaty. On 15 December 1917, after Bolshevik delaying tactics failed to stop the advance of the German armies, an armistice was agreed upon, effectively taking Russia out of the war.[12]

Meanwhile, the Italians had been driven backward in 1917 by an Austro-German offensive, which culminated in the battle of Caporetto during October and November of 1917. The Italian line was penetrated by means of the new Hutier tactics. A disastrous withdrawal, followed all the way to the Piave River, the Italians suffering over 700,000 losses (including 400,000 desertions). The defeat caused the Allies to send eleven divisions to Italy from other theaters; it also forced them to form a supreme war council in an attempt to provide unity for the Allied military effort.[13]

The only significant military successes for the Allies that year were gained by the British in Palestine. David Lloyd George, the British prime minister, gave his support for a British-led offensive in Palestine in 1917 by directing a significant diversion of manpower and munitions to that theater. In that British offensive, General Edmund Allenby drove the Turks back along the Mediterranean and entered Jerusalem in triumph on 9 December 1917.[14] The other land theaters were of little significance to the Allied global situation.

In May 1917, the British instituted the "convoy system" to protect their shipping. Supported by Lloyd George and the American Admiral William Sims, and opposed by most of the British admiralty, the convoy system quickly ended excessive losses in Allied shipping, and considerably eased the Allied supply situation at the front and at home.[15] The reinforcement of the Allied blockade by American warships, followed by raids on German bases, further reduced German supplies and adversely affected morale on their home front. The entry of the United States into the war on 6 April 1917 had little effect on the fighting fronts, because United States forces were not engaged in significant land battles during 1917. The tremendous wealth and industrial power of the United States, however, brought an immediate reinforcement to the Allies' war efforts and to the sustenance of their people.[16]

3

AMERICA SENDS AN ARMY TO FRANCE

Some apologists for the German cause have argued that the United States was never "neutral in thought as well as action"—a condition of sentiment called for by President Wilson as the European war began in August 1914.[1] It is true that major American industries quickly turned to producing material of war for the Entente Powers. The Allies were also able to float huge loans in the United States, and foodstuffs from America assured the survival of their peoples. One could argue that the United States was trading with all customers who called for our goods; the Central Powers were unable to trade with us because of their location and the domination of the seas by Great Britain. It is also true that all American sentiment was not with the Entente Powers. In his text, *The Wars of America,* historian Robert Leckie says:

> Others who were of German descent naturally echoed the Kaiser's cry that Germany must have her place in the sun, while those of Irish blood, remembering Albion's crimes against Erin, prayed to see her humbled. The heartland of America, meanwhile, the home of isolationism and of the Progressive Movement, raised the banners of strict neutrality. . . . Immigrants to America, many of whom could be described as refugees from European militarism, turned their backs with a scornful "plague on both your houses," while Socialists and their sympathizers frankly rejoiced in the *Gotterdammerung* of the dynasties. . . . In all, the great bulk of the American people, especially the working men, were neutral.[2]

As the war in Europe entered its second year, ever closer association with the Entente markets, and with their propaganda, was causing Americans to identify emotionally with the Allies. It was primarily the widely publicized sinking of merchant ships by German submarines, whose submarine crews made little or no attempt to rescue survivors, that was turning America against Germany. The sinking of the British passenger liner *Lusitania* on 7 May 1915, with the loss of 1,198 lives including those of 128 Americans, raised American anger against the "Hun" and ended her "neutrality in spirit." President Wilson's sharp note of protest only temporarily limited German submarine activities. Meanwhile German espionage operations in America were exposed in our press. On 7 December 1915, Wilson laid before the Congress a comprehensive plan for improving national defense; then the President toured the nation urging increased military preparedness. On 3 June 1916, Congress passed the National Defense Act. It provided for the immediate expansion of the Regular Army to 175,000 men, and, in increments, to 223,000 over a five-year period. For the Regular Army, seven infantry and two cavalry divisions were authorized. Each division was then provided with a signal battalion, an aero squadron, larger medical detachments, and administration and supply elements. The act also authorized a National Guard of 450,000 and established an Officers Reserve Training Corps at universities, colleges, and military encampments. It contained provisions for governmental assistance for industrial preparedness for the production of wartime materials.[3]

Woodrow Wilson was reelected in November 1916 by a slim margin; his party's slogan was, "He kept us out of war."[4] Although the victorious president called for a "peace without victory," two events turned him into a strong supporter of the Allies: While the German Chancellery talked of a peaceful settlement, Wilson learned that the Kaiser had secretly ordered the resumption of unrestricted submarine warfare on 1 February 1917. That same month, the British informed our government of the "Zimmerman telegram," to Mexico from the German government offering generous terms for Mexico's going to war with the United States as an ally of Germany.[5] America's outrage thundered in the press and in civic halls, and the "preparedness program" took to the streets on parade. When two American ships were torpedoed in March 1917, President Wilson sadly prepared his request to Congress for a declaration of war. War was declared on Germany on 6 April 1917.[6]

Despite the authorizations of the National Defense Act of 1916, most of which were awaiting implementation, the onset of the war found the United States, as in all previous wars, unprepared both politically and militarily. A host of difficult problems descended upon American leaders and their small staffs in Washington—problems that required immediate resolution by the Congress, and, in many cases, by executive directives. Although Abraham Lincoln had enacted economic regulations under his "war powers," there was no precedent for organizing the entire nation for war. Business and transportation had to be coordinated to supply the burgeoning army at home and abroad and to provide major war material and sustenance for America's allies. These requirements called for a significant increase in the authority of the executive branch of government, for bipartisanship in legislative affairs, and for the ability of civil and military leaders to organize and think in broad and bold terms for the unparalleled effort to be made. It required civilians appointed from industry and academe to make decisions on political-military matters, a field in which they were totally inexperienced. It required the promulgation of policies and directives that limited, severely, the constitutional rights of private citizens.[7]

The War Department Headquarters (which had been limited by act of Congress to a total of nineteen officers) was no more ready to direct the military build-up than were the civil agencies of the United States. Only a small contingency plan for military expansion existed. The staff of the Army War College at Fort McNair in Washington, D.C. had, in 1915, drawn up a "concept plan" for a million-man army. The plan had received little attention until the declaration of war; then it was seized upon by the War Department as the basis for a military build-up. This was the very thin reed on which the War Department had to lean for the expansion of the army![8]

In April 1917, the Regular Army of the United States totalled 133,000 enlisted men and 9,000 officers; an additional 67,000 National Guard troops had been federalized and were on active duty along the Mexican border. No units larger than a regiment (2,000 men) were active. One machine gun company, of six weapons, had become organic to each infantry regiment in 1916.[9]

On 18 May 1917, with the enthusiastic recommendation of the Congress of the United States, the president signed the Selective Service Act, making the entire manpower of the United States available to prosecute the war against the Central Powers. The act called for the immediate raising of the Regular Army and National Guard to their final strengths authorized by the National Defense Act of 1916. On 3 July the President called the entire National Guard to federal service. The first draft registration, on 5 June 1917, produced ten million young men for service. Through subsequent registration acts, nearly half of our male population, or approximately twenty-six million, were registered for the draft. Of these, some 4,800,000 were called into the armed forces, the Army receiving a total of four million inductees. The Army's total strength at the highest point, the time of the Armistice, was 3,865,000, of which 200,000 were officers.[10]

The draft functioned very smoothly, with few protests and little difficulty in meeting the increasingly large cells made upon the system. It is worth noting that 69 percent of the men called up for induction were considered physically fit for service—a much higher percentage than that found acceptable in Allied countries. This country could easily have fielded an army of ten million men without calling upon any of the deferred or exempted elements of our male population.[11]

Equipping a large, modern army was a far greater problem than manning it. Except for a stock of 600,000 Springfield rifles (model 1903), the army had no relatively modern weapons or equipment. For field artillery support, the army could only muster a total of 600 three-inch guns, subsequently discarded except for training purposes. Despite the tremendous expansion of the American armaments industry, only one hundred artillery pieces manufactured in the United States reached our troops in France before the armistice. The American Army adopted and procured the French 75- and 155-millimeter artillery weapons. The prewar army had only a few tanks for testing purposes, and fifty-five aircraft, most of which were considered unsafe for combat flying. Tanks and aircraft were loaned or purchased from France.[12]

Lacking equipment, housing, and even officers, the inductees moved to army posts and camps for training. To increase the Regular Army, infantry divisions designated the 1st through the 20th were organized, mostly at old army posts. The National Guard divisions called to the colors formed infantry divisions numbered 26 to 42. A national army was created, consisting of volunteers, the majority of the drafted men, and newly commissioned officers. These were housed in sixteen new divisional camps, the divisions designated numbers 76 to 93 (some numbers were not used). Besides the divisional camps, many special camps were constructed for the training of officers and enlisted specialists in artillery, engineering, the signal corps, the tank corps, the aviation service, and the chemical warfare service. Because most of the divisions (Regular, National Guard, and National Army) ultimately were filled by draftees, the army abolished divisional distinctions by the type of service in July 1918. Fifty-five divisions were activated, of which forty-two served in France.[13]

The War Department plan called for six months of training for each new soldier at one of these home bases, generally the one nearest to his point of induction. That was to be followed by two months of training in France and one month of experience in a quiet sector of the front before a serviceman entered into battle. As the build-up accelerated, however, training periods for a great many of the troops were much shorter.

England and France sent eight hundred officers and noncommissioned officers to the United States to assist in training the American Army. These advisers were distributed to various divisional and special camps throughout the United States. They, and subsequent liaison groups and visiting Allied specialists, urged the adoption of their tactical concepts for the fighting of the war, whenever they were not pressing even more vigorously for the integration of American troops into Allied armies. Adding to the training pressures the Americans experienced through their allies was the belief expressed by British and French military and political leaders until practically the end of the war, that the United States could never raise, equip, and sufficiently train an American army to take the field prior to the decisive time at which the tide of war would turn. The British and French also believed the American Officer Corps could not be expanded sufficiently, nor was its regular component capable of leading large forces in modern war.[14]

The pressure from the Allies in these regards paralleled the thinking of many American military and political leaders immediately prior to America's entry into the war. In response to French Marshal Joffre's suggestion that the Americans send a single division to France to bolster Allied morale, the War Department adopted a plan for gathering a division of twelve thousand men from existing regular units. They cautioned, however, against "the early dispatch of any expeditionary force to France," because of the lack of American training and capability in modern warfare.[15] This attitude, echoed throughout the army hierarchy, was based on the fear that poor performances by untrained masses of American soldiers would deplete Allied morale, while raising the morale of the Germans.[16]

There is little evidence that President Wilson even considered the commitment of an army force to the war in Europe prior to the last days of March 1917. It appears to have been the last priority among his decisions. We were going to war to ensure freedom of the seas: he agreed we should send a naval force to cooperate with Britain to destroy the submarine menace. He also agreed with Walter Hines Page, United States ambassador to Great Britain, that we must help the Allies with loans and supplies. But he rebuked the War Department staff in March 1917 for their eagerness to "get in" on plans for fighting the war.[17] As late as 19 March 1917, Colonel Edward M. House, President Wilson's adviser, wrote him on this matter: "No one looks with favor upon our raising a large army at the moment, believing it would be better if we permit volunteers to enlist in the Allied armies." House believed, as did others among Wilson's advisers, that the role for America, if it came to war, primarily would be to provide industrial and economic aid, and that military aid should be provided only as needed by our allies.[18]

Major James Rainey, of the United States Army, who did a comprehensive study of the development and training of the American Expeditionary Forces (AEF) believed that President Wilson's tilt toward fielding the AEF came shortly after our entry into the war, as he (Wilson) realized that the weight of American political influence in the postwar world would likely be related to the degree of our participation in the fighting, the victory, and the sacrifice. Wilson may have been influenced in reaching this conclusion by his adviser, Herbert Hoover, who, as early as 13 February 1917, stated:

> Our terms of peace will probably run counter to most of the European proposals, and our weight in the accomplishment of our ideals will be

greatly in proportion to the strength which we can throw into the scale.[19]

Wilson was certainly thinking of an American army in France in the late days of March. In his private discussions with *New York World* reporter Frank I. Cobb the evening before his war message to Congress, Cobb remembers Wilson agonizing over the need for "illiberalism at home in order to support our men at the front."[20]

Certainly Wilson came around to wanting an American army in France upon calling for a declaration of war. Shortly after the approval of the declaration, he played an active role in selecting a commander-in-chief for the American Expeditionary Forces. Of the seven major generals on active duty in 1917, one, Major General Frederick Funston, had died on 19 February.[21] Four were too old and relatively infirm. Another, Major General Leonard Wood, who was very popular with the American people and with Congress, was an active Republican, who had criticized the administration's lack of courage in not standing up to the Germans. The remaining general, Major General John J. Pershing, was a fine commander who had carried out a difficult political-military task in Mexico. He was selected to head the AEF.

Major General John J. Pershing was a "regular" officer with thirty-one years of military service. A graduate of the United States Military Academy who had held the esteemed cadet rank of first captain, Pershing had extensive small-unit combat experience pacifying Indians and Filipinos. His military nickname was "Black Jack," a reference to his early duties commanding black soldiers. A taciturn disciplinarian, he had commanded American Army units on the Mexican border from 1915 to 1917 and had pursued the bandit Pancho Villa into Mexico. His service also included duty as military attaché in Tokyo during the Russo-Japanese War. He had been promoted by President Theodore Roosevelt from captain to brigadier general over 862 more senior officers. When selected to lead the AEF in May 1917, he was the junior of six major generals in the Army, at age fifty-six. Within three weeks, he was on his way to France, with orders, dated 27 May 1917, from Secretary of War Newton D. Baker to form, train, and commit to battle the AEF under his command. These orders had been approved by President Wilson. The key paragraph in these orders read:

In military operations against the Imperial German Government you are directed to cooperate with the forces of the other countries employed against the enemy; but in so doing, the underlying idea must be kept in view that the forces of the United States are a separate and distinct component of the combined forces, the identity of which must be preserved. This fundamental rule is subject to such minor exceptions in particular circumstances as your judgment may approve.[22]

Pershing was "vested with all necessary authority to carry on the war vigorously in harmony with the spirit of these instructions and toward a victorious conclusion."[23] Such a charter "made Pershing almost czar" with respect to the American effort in France, according to one of Pershing's biographers, Frank Vandiver.[24] However, these simply stated instructions were challenged by our allies—by means of diplomatic and, later, direct disagreements—and executing them was a greater personal struggle for Pershing than operating against the enemy.

On 14 June 1917, General Pershing and his small, hand-picked staff arrived in France, beginning the American commitment to the war on the western front.[25] Charged by the War Department with recommending an organization to fight the war in Europe, Pershing quickly shook off the enthusiastic welcoming and introductory celebrations, settled into his temporary headquartrs in Paris, and put his staff to work. The units of the U.S. 1st Division began arriving on 26 June 1917, and moved to Gondrecourt to begin training.[26]

When General Pershing departed for France, the War Department Headquarters had formed no definite plans for the military effort required of America. After Pershing's planning staff studied the military situation in brief, Pershing cabled the War Department on 6 July 1917: "Plans should contemplate sending over at least one million men by next May."[27] However, the War Department had sent its own board of officers to Europe (the Baker Board) to study and recommend the size and organization of the force to be committed to Europe. Not to be upstaged by this group, Pershing directed the members of the War Department Board and his AEF staff to consider together the plans proposed by his (AEF) Operations Section. The picture shows General Pershing surrounded by the members of the AEF Staff and the Baker Board. Many of these would become commanders of major U.S. organizations as the war progressed.[28] The AEF plans were subsequently adopted. Known as the General Organization Project, the report dated 10 July 1917 stated:

> It is evident that a force of about a million is the smallest unit which in modern war will be a complete, well-balanced, and independent fighting organization. It is taken as the force which may be expected to reach France in time for offensive in 1918 and as a unit and basis of organizations. Plans for the future should be based, especially with reference to manufacture of material, artillery, and aviation on three times this force, that is, at least three million men. Such a program . . . should be completed within two years.[29]

The messages began a relationship between AEF Headquarters and the War Department, which, under the pressures of frequent program changes and lagging communications, grew more hostile by the month. One of

General Pershing standing in center, with members of AEF staff and those of War Department Baker Board. *(From U.S. Army Signal Corps Photo, archives of U.S. Army Military History Institute, Carlisle Barracks, Pennsylvania.)*

Pershing's earliest recommendations, supported by reports from United States military missions, was to increase the size, firepower, and staying power (ability to absorb casualties) of the American division. The War Department Headquarters melded these recommendations into an organization called the "square division," larger than most corps had been in the Civil War and twice the size of contemporary British, French, and German divisions. It was composed of two infantry brigades (each with 8500 personnel), one artillery brigade (one heavy artillery and two light artillery regiments with a total of seventy-two guns), a combat engineer regiment, three machine-gun battalions, plus signal and administrative units. Totalling 28,000 personnel, the division was strong (260 machine guns), but unwieldy and slow in reaction, maneuver, and movement by foot. It was found necessary to equip the soldiers of these divisions with the British Lee-Enfield rifle; the armory in Springfield, Massachusetts, which had been providing the army's standard weapon (the 1903 Model Springfield) was unable to manufacture the quantity of rifles which the wartime army required. After these huge divisions were organized and into encampments, it was discovered that the great number of personnel in each unit provoked problems in command and control for their inexperienced leaders. Furthermore, reorganizing the national guard and regular army divisions according to the new table of organization and equipment created extreme organizational turbulence at the very time that most organizations were being called to the colors.[30]

General Pershing's AEF staff met with the Baker Board on 11 July 1917 to discuss the type of artillery to be provided for the AEF. Disagreeing with the Baker Board's recommendations for a light general support weapon, the AEF staff argued for the French 155-millimeter (six-inch) gun. For direct support of maneuver units, the AEF desired the French 75-millimeter cannon. Their argument was that these weapons would provide the weight of firepower needed, and they could be made available from French sources much sooner than weapons produced in the United States. The artillery matter was settled as the AEF staff wished.[31]

As the pace of mobilization increased, the War Department Headquarters was quickly "swamped" in paperwork. A functional reorganization of the War Department Headquarters had been made in 1904, under the vigorous leadership of Secretary of War Elihu Root; however, the department still consisted of a very small staff supporting the chief of staff and a number of semi-independent bureaus (such as that of the Adjutant General). These bureaus were, theoretically, under the direction of the chief of staff; actually, they carried on direct relationships with Congress and with the executive agencies. The small War Department general staff of nineteen officers was also involved in War College instruction; some staff officers had their offices at the War College at Fort McNair, across town from the War Department headquarters in the State, War, and Navy Building.[32] In rapid order, four officers held the titles of chief of staff or acting chief of staff during 1917—the fourth one, Major General Peyton C. March, finally received the permanent appointment and the rank of full general (four stars) on 20 May 1918.[33] Prior to March's assumption of the duty of acting chief of staff on 1 March 1918, the War Department continued its peacetime procedures at its leisurely pace, including an eight-hour day for most of its staff. Consequently, even after the declaration of war, papers and messages piled up in the department's message center and in the halls outside departmental offices. The first series of complaints that Pershing and his staff registered was that their messages and requests were not refused—they just were not answered at all.[34]

The question of the number of men to be shipped to fill the AEF grew to become an increasingly difficult decision. The War Department staff could never catch up with the demands of the AEF for thousands more than the numbers previously scheduled—a problem exacerbated by the increasing demands of the Allies for American replacements. Allied requests often caused political agreements, at the highest U.S. executive levels, for the provision of numbers of American troops that the training and transport system could in no way provide. March's first cable to Pershing (in March 1918) stated that he would ensure that at least two divisions per month were sent to the AEF. This would mean a force of 56,000 men in divisional units and an additional 36,000 men as support troops per month. However, Pershing had already agreed with the British (in January 1918) to bring six additional divisons in British transport—these divisions were to be trained by the British and committed to the AEF after the completion of their training.[35]

Additional pressures came upon the War Department from the Congress. On 12 December 1917, the Senate Military Affairs Committee began hearings on the progress of American military preparations. Its chairman, Senator Chamberlain (D/Oregon) announced, "The military establishment of America has fallen down." Secretary of War Baker remained placid throughout the hearings, despite demands in the press for his resignation. But he and General March worked tirelessly to improve the quality and timeliness of departmental affairs.[36]

It was obvious to Secretary Baker and General March that the AEF Headquarters did not appreciate the problems with which the War Department was wrestling in matching limited resources to increasing demands. It was equally obvious to General Pershing that the War Department had failed to comprehend the enormity of his task—to organize a million-man theater of operations, while receiving, training, equipping, and sustaining those early arrivals who were to flesh out the basic organizational structure itself. On 15 March 1918, General March cabled Pershing suggesting a resolution to the attitudinal problem between their headquarters: an exchange of thirty officers between the two headquarters, to be followed by subsequent reassignment exchanges. The AEF staff was suspicious—Pershing's Chief of Staff, Harbord, suggested it was a prelude to March's taking over the AEF. Only one exchange was half-heartedly effected by the AEF.[37]

The heart of the problem was the degree of control over the AEF and its commander to be exercised by the chief of staff of the army. Pershing was promoted to full general (four stars) on 6 October 1917. The Army Chief of Staff was still a two-star general. An early confrontation occurred on the matter of temporary promotions to general officer. In March 1918, General March requested Pershing's recommendations for such promotions. Pershing responded with ten names. The list for Senate confirmation contained only half of Pershing's recommendations. It contained names of officers in the United States considered by March to be most deserving of promotion, and it contained names of a few officers in the AEF (such as Colonel Douglas MacArthur) not recommended by Pershing. Pershing exploded! In cables to March and Baker, he disapproved of the list and demanded that confirmation be withheld until he sent additional recommendations. March fired a cable in return: "There will be no change in the nominations already sent to the Senate." Pershing let the matter drop for the time, but bad relations continued between the two leaders and between their headquarters, and the problem resurfaced again and again.[38] Morale among the hard-working officers in the War Department was low; they were publicly called "slackers" by newsmen, who should have known better. Most hoped to escape to France, and many of the more capable succeeded.

Immediately after their arrival in France, Pershing and his small personal staff examined the organization of the British and French headquarters. Pershing approved a functional staff system for the AEF, modeled primarily upon that of the French, with some attachments and sophistications based upon the fact that the American organization had to interact with the British and French forces as well as French civil departments and agencies.

Initially, the AEF planning staff was divided into three sections: operations, intelligence, and administration. Upon moving to their permanent headquarters at Chaumont, a more operationally oriented staff organization was effected. This AEF Headquarters organization was based on a chief of staff and a four-way division of staff responsibilities among assistant chiefs, according to function: that is, one staff agency was assigned responsibility for all matters having to do with personnel (labeled G–1); one dealt with intelligence (G–2); one with operations and training (G–3) (training was later separated into its own staff function, G–5); and a final staff function dealt with supply and sustenance (G–4). Technical organizations and staffs, such as engineering and medical agencies, abounded in association with these four, later five, primary staff functions. As the staffs grew and their procedures became relatively standardized, the management of the war began to take on the appearance, for the American Army, of a large business operation, as it had been for the Allies for the past three-and-a-half years.[39]

Keeping uppermost in his mind that the United States would field a separate military force on the western front, General Pershing gained the approval of the Allies for the Americans to develop that force and its support in the Lorraine Sector, generally the area southeast of Verdun to the Swiss border. After he opened his headquarters at Chaumont, Pershing worked to establish the organizational and structural foundations of the American Expeditionary Forces in France. This sector was a relatively quiet portion of the line. However, because of its location, close to German communication complexes and resource areas, it could pose a tremendous threat to the entire German front, a great salient north and west of this area, if an American offensive were launched from there. It was also an excellent region for the establishment of the infrastructure necessary to support the AEF in field from the ports and bases in the rear. While the British were generally established in the north of France, close to the English Channel ports for their support, and the French were established athwart the center of the fighting line, their location protecting the bulk of their vital installations and the capital city of Paris, the area south of the French was relatively unencumbered by active Allied military installations. With improvements in the ports and throughput systems, it could function as an American operational area, based on the southwestern ports of France. It was upon this skein that Pershing and his growing staff built the complex organization of the American Expeditionary Forces in France.[40]

Out of supply activities an organization grew to manage the line of communications functions from the ports to the rear boundaries of the combat forces. This was initially called the "services of the rear." It was divided into nine base sections for the receipt of supplies (each with one or more port complexes), an intermediate section in the center of the area for storage, classification, and transshipment of supplies, and an advance section for the distribution of supplies to the combat forces in the zone of operations. Later this agency was called the "services of supply" (SOS). Organizing these logistical activities while coordinating the throughput of supplies and personnel with the French created many problems and bottlenecks. The organization became so large and its functions so complex as American divisions arrived in the country that suggestions were made to the secretary of war, and ultimately to the president, that this agency be taken out from under General Pershing's personal supervision and made a separate organization, coequal with the AEF. This matter is taken up again in chapter 4.[41]

With respect to training for battle, Pershing and most of the regular officers of the "old army" believed in the efficacy of the well-trained soldier using his rifle and bayonet. The "regulars" were certain that the mass citizen army, formed by conscription with little professional leavening, would require extensive training and experience prior to undertaking combat operations. Pershing saw this training requirement as being largely the responsibility of the War Department and of the continental training establishment in the United States.[42]

In his thesis on the training of the AEF, James Rainey incisively summarized the difficulties under which this training was undertaken and recorded the failure of the leadership to develop and coordinate an offensive doctrine that could have been translated into effective training for operations in France.[43] Rainey argued persuasively that the army's only experience with large-scale offensive operations came from Civil War days; this experience had faded from living memory and from the texts and regulations relating to contemporary military operations. He opined that the experience of the Regular Army was largely of small-unit operations and cantonment administration; this argument was reinforced by Pershing's own opinion of the army's residual capabilities, and it was further agreed upon by many of the "memoirists" who wrote their judgments immediately after the war.[44] On the other hand, Irving B. Holley, professor of history at Duke University, argued that a good bit of preparation for the high command of large armies had been gained by the regular officers through the army school system; some of the regulars also had had the opportunity to observe foreign armies in "modern" operations.[45] It is true that most regular officers had gone to the line or staff school at Fort Leavenworth; fewer (only 4.7 percent) had attended the highest military school, the Army War College.[46] This schooling had prepared the few for high command and staff duties, but none had any such experience. Rainey's argument that the Army had a "small unit mentality" that adversely affected its ability to develop a system of training for modern warfare appears to be a fair assessment of the regular officer establishment.[47]

While Pershing expected the War Department to provide training guidance and doctrine appropriate to the battlefields of World War I, the department was unprepared for developing this doctrine, and clearly deferred to Pershing to provide recommendations in this regard. Pershing responded to their requests for guidance with a strong statement, the essence of which was that "the rifle and the bayonet remain the supreme weapons of the infantry soldier and . . . the ultimate success of the Army depends upon their proper use in open warfare."[48]

Pershing believed that the three years of trench warfare on the western front had established a "mind set" among the Allied commanders, which was defensive in nature, and accepted attrition in attack, without seeking alternatives that would accomplish the same military objectives with fewer casualties. He felt that the Allied generals had become accustomed to moving their troops directly from trench to trench, placing increasing amounts of heavy fire forward of their advancing soldiers to protect them, to destroy enemy positions, and to attenuate the enemy's strength. He believed that the Allies were too concerned with the defensive firepower of the machine gun, with absence of flanks that could be turned, and that aggressiveness in attack was no longer demanded by Allied commanders.[49] Pershing's observations convinced him that an "offensive spirit" was still the essential element necessary for victory on the western front. He was adamant that a self-confident individual soldier, skilled with the rifle and the bayonet, could advance against enemy positions with bold maneuvers and forward movements on the modern battlefield. This philosophy he expressed in training guidance and in cables to the War Department.[50] War Department offensive doctrine was embodied largely in the Infantry Drill Regulations of 1911, as revised in 1917. Both the 1911 edition and the 1917 revision contained the statement that:

> machine guns must be considered weapons of emergency . . . of great value at critical though infrequent periods of an engagement. . . . Machine guns should not be assigned to the firing line of an attack. When attacking a hostile armed with machine guns . . . infantry must silence them before it can advance. . . . An infantry command should concentrate a large number of rifles on each gun in turn, until it has silenced it.[51]

One could, perhaps, blame bureaucratic indolence for the department's failure to change the Infantry Drill Regulations, despite the tremendous increase in the amount and lethality of firepower (particularly of machine guns) that had been displayed during three years of the world war. It is more difficult to explain Pershing's insistence upon "open warfare" maneuver for attacking arrays of machine guns in a limited zone of advance without open flanks. His observations and those of his staff of the fighting in his front yard should have caused him to modify his precept, or to explain "open warfare" as a later stage of advance. Professor Russell Weigley of Temple University, author of several military histories and studies, has expressed amazement at Pershing's failure in this regard, and at his (Pershing's) apparent inability to change his prewar convictions in the light of his observations as commander-in-chief of the AEF.[52] The author David Kennedy, in his text *Over Here: The First World War and American Society*, has also criticized Pershing for having "overlooked" the firepower of machine guns and artillery in emphasizing maneuver over firepower. Rainey, however, stated that the problem was greater—that of defining an appropriate modern offensive doctrine, a problem which even the Allies had not solved. Some observers, even within Pershing's own staff, argued that the effects of modern firepower had reduced infantry maneuver to short movements from one covered position to another. The result, Rainey stated, "was that no clear and positive explication of the tactics of open warfare was ever published."[53]

The influence of Allied doctrine, which could be called "cautious offense," was considerable, especially upon American military missions and early liaison groups. After all, the Allies had had considerable combat experience in modern warfare, and we had none. Allied offensive doctrine was translated into War Department tactical instructions despite Pershing's insistence upon open warfare. The AEF staff then reproduced the War Department Instructions as their own guidance to AEF organizations, at the same time as AEF spokesmen were criticizing Allied tactics. Obviously, the AEF headquarters, which was becoming a large agency, was not functioning in harmony.[54]

With respect to the training given American units in France, AEF inspectors reported to Pershing that the training being presented by French instructors in the line and in AEF schools continued to emphasize defensive and trench warfare. On 4 July 1918, the AEF Chief of Training, Colonel H. B. Fiske, reported that he had come into possession of a "secret" memorandum of the French General Headquarters instructing French commanders to impregnate American units with French methods and doctrine. The Fiske Report (enclosing the French secret memorandum) made the point that:

> The offensive spirit of the French and British armies has largely disappeared as a result of their severe losses. Close association with beaten forces lowers the morale of the best troops. Our young officers and men are prone to take the tone and tactics of those with whom they are associated. Whatever they are learning that is false or unsuited for us will be hard to eradicate later. . . . The French do not like the rifle, do not know how to use it, and their infantry is consequently too dependent upon powerful artillery support. Their infantry lacks aggressiveness and discipline. The British infantry lacks initiative and resource.

Colonel Fiske's report ends by recommending that American training in France be emancipated from Allied supervision. Pershing annotated the report with handwritten guidance to his chief of staff: "This is entirely my own view." He went on to direct that the AEF should work out a means by which American forces could be advised of the falseness, the "heresies" of French doctrine.[55]

There is evidence that, as the Americans gained direct combat experience in 1918, the AEF staff was gradually forming a new tactic for the offensive, which muted their "open warfare" ideal with an appreciation of the realities of the power of defensive weaponry. An example of a mutational approach to "open warfare" was revealed in a study by the AEF Deputy G–3, Lieutenant Colonel Hugh A. Drum: "Since, on the Western Front, open warfare will occur only in periods, followed by long periods of trench warfare, the ideal organization is that best suited for offensive trench warfare."[56] Such conclusions also led to a reconsideration of the square (heavy) division originally advocated by the AEF. Many commanders and staff officers felt that the heavy division (with two brigades, each of two regiments) was too large for offensive warfare. However, in the aforementioned study, Lieutenant Colonel Drum wrote that the war of mass and attrition would continue to require heavy divisions, since "the gaining of ground counts for little; it is the ruining of the enemy's main army that will end the struggle."[57] Major General Hunter Liggett, commanding I Corps, and considered the most perceptive of AEF commanders, groped for a solution to the problem of applying open warfare to the western front. In a letter to Colonel Fox Connor (AEF G–3) on 9 April 1918, he wrote:

> I am enclosing a copy of a memo which I have drawn up . . . upon some practical line for open warfare offensive and defensive. I can find nothing in the mass of literature I have received which teaches this, to me, essential question.[58]

Some scholars who have studied Pershing's theories have concluded that his insistence upon "open warfare tactics," despite evidence that such tactics were more theoretical than practical, was an attempt to infuse and maintain an offensive spirit within the AEF.[59] It appears that even Pershing came to doubt his emphasis on open-warfare maneuver. On 7 August 1918, he instructed his Chief of Staff, Major General James McAndrews, to make a study of the whole question of attack against machine guns and artillery, opining that, "perhaps, we are losing too many men." The resulting study promulgated to the AEF on 5 September 1918 (just prior to the initiation of the St.-Mihiel campaign) delineated the difference between "trench warfare" and "open warfare" in the following terms: Trench warfare is characterized by "regulation of space and time by higher command down to the smallest units . . . little initiative . . . by the individual soldier." Open warfare is "irregular formations, scouts preceding the assaulting waves, and a high degree of individual initiative. . . . Primary reliance upon the infantry's own firepower to enable it to get forward."[60] The reader of these instructions can only conclude that the emphasis upon open warfare was modified by the realization that strong supporting fire and slow movement may be necessary in assaulting well-defended fortifications, and that "open warfare" was a condition that occurs after the penetration of trenches. Russell Weigley argued that Pershing had concluded, by this time, that no real alternative remained except a strategy that aimed at destroying the German armies by grinding them into ruin.[61]

A greater training problem than that caused by uncertain tactics was the extreme personnel turbulence taking place within army units in the United States. Divisions forming and training were frequently stripped of thousands of their troops to fill units deploying according to an ever-more-accelerated schedule. These units were then refilled with new draftees. This turnover required the repetition of basic training in the units. It also "gutted" unit integrity and provided little time for subordinate commanders to get to know their men or to gain experience in leading their troops. Senior commanders and staff officers were absent, often on trips, attending boards, and busy with school details. In the build-up of the AEF, which increased in geometric progression to a three-million-man force, insufficient attention was given to the need for establishing supporting organizations, staffs, and housekeeping, and labor elements. Thus, when the base support requirements became imperative, combat units were further stripped of civil specialists and technically qualified personnel to perform such functions—functions necessary to the equipping, sustaining, and processing of the combat units overseas and toward the front.

The personnel chaos was compounded by an uneven flow of recruits from the draft levies. Adding to all this turmoil was the inadequacy of training facilities and the scarcity of weapons, equipment, and ammunition for training.[62] Rainey characterized the turnover as "personnel rapes." He cited as an example the experience of the 78th Division. In November 1917, this division was filled with personnel beginning training in the United States. Frequent personnel levies so reduced their numbers that by January 1918 the units were at one-third strength. The division was only at 50 percent strength in April, but by June 1918 it had been filled, largely with new recruits; it then sailed for Europe.[63]

The absence of modern weapons for training is well recorded in the 28th Division's "Official History":

Rifles, automatic rifles, trench mortars, 37, 75, 155 millimeter guns used in combat were not secured until the Division reached France. We had

one bayonet for every third man, which meant changing for drill. For
several months we used improvised wooden guns for machine gun work.
The one 37 millimeter gun in camp was a novelty. The Division had but a
few gas masks, which made training slow and difficult.[64]

The chart in Appendix 2 depicts the period of time that each of the forty-
two AEF divisions spent in the United States, in the rear of the line, in the
battle line, and in combat. The graphics show that, except for divisions
deployed in 1917, each had at least six months in the United States—
adequate time to complete a four-month unit training program. The personnel turmoil described above, however, ensured that few had gained the
requisite individual and unit training upon their arrival in France.

Pershing was aware of the poor state of training of the divisions arriving
in France in 1918. Earlier, he had encouraged the War Department to form
a central training committee to manage all training and training facilities.
His recommendation was rejected by the War Department, largely because of the pressure of combat branch and technical staff specialists, who
argued for their traditional training and school prerogatives.[65] Rather than
agree to the creation of a new training-management body, the War Department expanded the existing War College Division Training Committee.
Major General John F. Morrison was recalled from duty in France at
Pershing's recommendation and appointed to head this training committee
as the army director of training.[66] Although Morrison came from the AEF,
Pershing was never satisfied with the War Department Training Committee's efforts to inculcate the tactics of "open warfare" into training in the
United States. He wrote in his memoirs, "training continued defective,
being usually limited to trench warfare."[67] Pershing's criticism also reflected the opinion of many in the AEF that the War Department was
being influenced unduly by Allied officers and their theories. These suspicions were confirmed when French and British military attachés on duty
in the United States were "attached" to the training committee of the War
Department.[68]

Pershing had previously attempted to divide the training being given on
both sides of the ocean, to offset the limited maneuvering area available in
France, by tasking the War Department to concentrate on long-range
marksmanship training and "open warfare" in training in the United
States. This recommendation, which he had made on 19 October 1917,
also involved Pershing's acceptance of the responsibility for providing
"trench warfare" training in France. Using the trenches already available
in France, American units could gain realistic acclimatization to the conditions of trench warfare.[69] The War Department accepted Pershing's recommendations; however, their later directives indicated that "trench warfare"
would be taught by division commanders in the United States under the

special instruction of their British and French advisers. "Open warfare" was not neglected in training instructions, but it was only mentioned in general terms. Pershing protested this deficiency in War Department training guidance, and the War Department promised to place greater emphasis on "open warfare" training.[70]

A major task for the new AEF Headquarters was the training of American forces in France. It was recognized that the divisions shipped to the combat zone would require area training and acclimatization to the theater of war and to the nature of the combat there. It was agreed between the AEF and the Allied headquarters that American divisions, on their arrival, would be placed in association with "veteran" French divisions—to be trained and to receive orientations, subsequently to take their place "in the line" as the final phase of their training.

The training was to be accomplished in three phases: The first phase was to consist of familiarization and retraining with the weapons being used in theater, followed by tactical exercises in the training areas up to the division level, where the terrain permitted. The second phase embraced a one-month tour by infantry battalions and like units of supporting arms in the trenches under French regimental command. During this phase, commanders were to be stationed with the French and British units to observe operations under fire. The third phase was to consist of division-level exercises by the combined arms of infantry, artillery, and aviation, operating as teams. Following these exercises, each division was to go into the line, under its own commanders, as part of a French corps.[71]

To supplement this divisional training, Pershing directed the establishment of a broad program of schooling for gunners, specialists, and officers in France. The program, developed by the assistant chief of staff for training (G–5) and approved by Pershing, would set up schools beginning at the corps level to serve the needs of the divisions and supporting troops for specialist training. Each corps would be assigned a training division to conduct its training. (Each corps would also have a replacement division to process replacements forward and to reassign returnees.) The training division would conduct the in-country training of troops received from the replacement division. This division would also train soldiers to become noncommissioned officers. Each corps would form an infantry school to give tactical and weapons training to rifle company commanders, machine gun unit commanders, and commanders of mortar units. Each corps would also organize an artillery school to instruct officers and enlisted men in artillery instrumentation, communications, firing, ranging, and targeting; an engineer school to train engineer company and platoon commanders, sappers, and pioneers; a cavalry school to train personnel in mounted service; a gas school that would train all arms and services in the use of and defense against gas; a signal school that would train communications NCOs and signal company and platoon commanders; a corps sanitary school that would train ambulance and field-hospital officers. The corps aeronautical school would have a combat aviation course and a combat balloon course. Finally, each corps would also have a field officer's school that would train majors and lieutenant colonels—their training would include visits to all other schools of the corps.[72]

At the Army level, schools would consist of a general staff college, which would train officers for staff work. Army line schools would train company and battery commanders for infantry, artillery, engineer, and signal units. The line schools would also provide familiarization and re-fresher training for captains, majors, and lieutenant colonels of all arms of the service. An officer candidates school would be established to train soldiers to become officers. An anti-aircraft school would be opened to teach the employment of artillery and machine guns in an anti-aircraft role. The army artillery school would train officers and men in heavy artillery, trench artillery, and railroad artillery. The army signal school would train personnel in telephone and telegraph, radio, visual, and carrier pigeon communications. It would also train personnel in communication system operations. The army aeronautic school would train pilots and balloonists and would also train infantry and artillery observers for flying duties. The army sanitary school would give courses in greater depth (than those at the corps level) to hospital and medical personnel on health matters. The army engineer school would be designed to give courses in bridging, mining, searchlight employment, ranging, topography, camouflage, sapper (tunneling and mining), and pioneer (basic engineer) schooling—all at a higher level than that of the corps schools. The army infantry specialists center was established to train personnel in conducting training in mus-ketry, use of the bayonet, sniping, automatic weapons firing, throwing grenades, trench mortars, and 37 mm cannon firing. The army center of information would establish conferences and demonstrations for generals and colonels of all arms. The army tank school was designed to train tankers and tank commanders. The army gas school was designed to provide training in chemical warfare and in defenses against chemical operations.

In addition, in each army corps, the replacement division would set up a training center to retrain infantrymen as cooks and bakers, clerks, me-chanics, saddlers and horseshoers, stable sergeants, drivers and packers, chauffeurs, telephone operators and telegraph and radio operators—skills needed for services within the rear areas at the various headquarters.[73]

This great complex of schools was based on the extensive systems of the British and French. Its establishment was, for the most part, fully accom-plished. Three of the corps established school systems; these were turned over to Army G–5 as the corps became involved in battle. All the planned army schools were opened and operational, except the cavalry school; experience proved that it was not needed. In addition, an American expeditionary forces university and a bandmasters' school were founded. The initial cadre of instructors was almost entirely French, with a leavening of British officers, and few Americans. The irony in this situation is that the Americans were forced by shortages of qualified instructors to rely on the Allies, with whose training philosophies they disagreed.

It was Pershing's intention to make up for the deficiencies in knowledge of his officers and men and to achieve the "standards of West Point" in the AEF. He insisted that all commanders and their general staff officers attend the line or staff courses. Furthermore, he drove his trainers to establish his "open warfare" philosophy in the schools and to replace the Allied instructors as soon as possible. Even with minimum American staffing, the school system severely taxed the officer strength in theater. The initial instructor quota especially was a heavy cut in the officer strength of the 1st Division—the only one in country at the time of the activation of the school system. This drawdown of personnel was very detrimental to the division's preparations for imminent operations.[74]

By his insistence on training before combat and his inspections and reports, Pershing got his training and school systems. The drain on combat strength was criticized by division commanders, by the Allies, and even, finally, by Secretary of War Baker, who allowed that training could be shortened and still be effective in time of war, since proximity to the area of combat made troops eager to learn.[75] After the first sessions of the AEF school program, the quality of the students attending declined rapidly. Busy and harassed commanders preparing their units for combat quite naturally sent officers and men whom they could most afford to lose. A good man sent to school was lost at a critical time—and maybe lost forever, assigned to the school faculty or to a higher staff job.[76]

Deficiencies also existed in the instruction. AEF inspectors repeatedly noted that the schools were not presenting approved instruction in an informative manner, and especially that "open warfare" tactics were not being taught. The AEF staff was certain this was caused by the omnipresence of Allied officers on the faculties. James Rainey, however, showed that even senior American officers lecturing at the schools put emphasis on the attack and defense of fortified positions and had little to say about "open warfare."[77] There is, on the other hand, ample evidence that the Allied officers maintained a patronizing attitude in conducting their instruction. The French high command provided this guidance to their officers who were detailed to instruct and act as liaison to the AEF: "Recognize the delicate nature of this association, but ensure the correctness of instruction!" The American hierarchy was found, in many instances, to be in agreement with the French assessment of "correct" battlefield tactics.[78]

The AEF school system continued throughout the war, despite the intensity of combat. The general staff college at Langres graduated 537 officers before the Armistice. Courses were three months in length. The line (tactical) school, also at Langres, came to serve as a preparatory course for the staff college, receiving officers of less military experience for a three-month, low-level tactical course. The line school had four sessions before the end of the war and graduated 488 officers. With respect to officer candidate schools, these were organized at Langres, San Saumur, and Mailly. They were under pressure to produce officers because of the heavy losses of officers caused by the Meuse-Argonne fighting. Casualties among platoon and company commanders were particularly heavy. The total number of men commissioned from officer candidate schools in France was 6,895 infantry, 2,384 artillery, 1,332 engineers and 536 signal officers—all quickly absorbed into AEF units.

To meet the increasing demands for officers, several of the three-month courses had to be shortened. The schools established by three of the corps were deemed to be adequate for training all the officers and noncommissioned officers in the replacement system. These schools, altogether, graduated 15,916 officers and 21,330 noncommissioned officers for a total of 37,246. The courses at all of the schools were entirely too short for the nature of the training; under the circumstances, they constituted a reasonable compromise between the demand for haste and the compelling demand for the preparation of soldiers for battle.[79]

With respect to the organizational training of the deployed divisions, only the 1st Division (the first in France) went through the entire three-phase program, as prescribed by the AEF and as represcribed by Pershing after inspection of that division's training.[80] After coming out of the trenches in March 1918, the 1st Division underwent refresher training. Still, after nearly a year in training and in battle, this division was found to be too much "trench-oriented" by AEF G–5 inspectors. The main problem, as Rainey stated, was that "open warfare" training, as it was explained by the AEF, was inapplicable to the fighting conditions in France in 1918—at least as the 1st Division had seen these conditions.[81]

The training of the next three American divisions to arrive was directed according to the model of the 1st Division's training. The great German drive beginning on 21 March 1918, however, eliminated the third phase of the training of these divisions. Instead, they were committed to blunt the German drive; then they remained operationally committed, despite Pershing's desire to disengage them for more training. As the divisions gained combat experience, they modified, considerably, the AEF directives in their training guidance. Under the pressure of the circumstances that prevailed in April 1918 which demanded the early combat commitment of arriving divisions, Pershing himself shortened the division training to a four-week "first phase" program of individual and small-unit training.[82]

As shown in the chart in Appendix 2, the twenty-nine divisions committed to battle averaged two months in France before entering the line; six had one-and-a-half months of preparation (the 5th, 6th, 35th, 81st, 88th, and 82d); and two (the 29th and 37th) entered the line after only one month overseas. Again, it must be noted that much of this "training" time was spent moving, reorganizing, drawing supplies, and performing routine camp duties and prescribed details. Since the divisions conducted their own training in accordance with a general army directive, it is understandable that little more was done than the firing of assigned weapons. A problem which impacted on large unit training was the fact that elements of a division were often billeted in small towns spread over a ten-mile area. Bringing them together for training was difficult and time consuming.[83] The divisions that were rushed over in British transports from January through March 1918 and were trained with the British suffered the additional problem of having been filled with recruits just before deployment. Their commanders were hard-pressed, as were their British trainers, to teach them even the rudiments of individual combat before they were moved into the trenches. AEF inspectors reported that the training given by the British was poor, fragmented, boring, and, as with that provided by the French, contrary to AEF offensive doctrine.[84] As a result, Pershing decided that divisions arriving in the summer of 1918 would be trained by the AEF itself. The need to commit the divisions arriving that summer to the ongoing battles made their training short and rudimentary, though the AEF Headquarters had planned otherwise.[85]

Most of the historians with whom I have corresponded thought the Americans were better trained than the Allies credited them to be, but none took the position that the AEF was well or properly trained. Russell Weigley supported Rainey's conclusion that the training emphasized was inappropriate to the combat the Americans faced.[86] Jay Luvaas, a noted military historian, agreed with them, and he added the opinion that time limitations precluded adequate training, whatever had been the emphasis, a view echoed by Theodore Ropp, professor of history at Duke University.[87] General Theodore Conway, who served under World War I veteran officers, said those veterans believed training had been inadequate.[88] The British authors who responded to my queries all characterized American training as inappropriate—even as they also criticized the United States for tarrying too long in a training mode in France.[89] Dr. James Stokesbury, a Canadian author, gave a more kindly but still critical opinion of the quality of American training.[90]

It seems logical to conclude that the chief problem was a lack of time to conduct training. The attempt to create the base of a three-million-man army in a few months caused such personnel turbulence that training had to be sacrificed to the more visible requirements of bringing troops into the line. Although AEF training/tactical guidance was unclear and inappropriate to the battlefield, it was not followed where it differed from combat requirements as perceived by those closest to the fighting. Pershing and his staff were aware of the uneven state of training in units committed to combat—they were forced to overlook the fact that some soldiers were not sufficiently trained to kill and defend themselves. Former Infantry Private Edmund Seiser, Headquarters Company, 316th Infantry Regiment, 79th Division, stated that he had not seen a rifle or a pistol until he reported to the 79th Division, and then, almost immediately, he was sent on to an outpost. Corporal William Sibley, Company B, 109th Infantry Regiment, 28th Infantry Division, in the Argonne Forest, stated that replacements arrived in the forest wearing white civilian shirts. They said they had had only two weeks in the army before they left the United States. Private Frank Groves, Company H, 28th Infantry Regiment, 1st Infantry Division, stated, "Our training did nothing to equip us to take care of ourselves in combat. Training in the U.S. was not realistic. Training in France was nonexistent." With regard to AEF schools, Lieutenant Colonel Merritt Pratt (who served as a junior officer in Company G, 131st Infantry Regiment of the 33rd Division in the Meuse-Argonne fighting) said that the AEF schools gave inadequate and uninteresting training.[91] Perhaps some of these comments can be discounted because of the long time that has elapsed since the experience. However, the training system which brought relatively untrained men to the front should be condemned. In Pershing's behalf, his frequent complaints to the War Department about the receipt of untrained or partially trained men should be noted. The AEF's training programs, however, did not take full advantage of the time available to make up training deficiencies. It appears that, in the rush of great events, the problems of receiving untrained men and officers were either forgotten, or that attempts to train these men were overtaken by more pressing business.

4

THE AMERICANS MOVE INTO THE LINE

When the representatives of the Allies met at Rapallo, Italy, in November 1917 to coordinate their future operations, it was agreed that the strategies and tactics they had employed previously had resulted in unacceptable losses, and that the societies supporting the conflict on the Allied side could not continue to sustain this kind of attrition. The French Army was still unstable as a result of the mutinies of 1917, and that entire nation was in a defeatist mood. The British were strained, but they had borne their losses better. General Allenby's victory in Palestine had helped British morale. The tank and the airplane were just beginning to show some promise—and the Americans, young, exuberant, and physically larger than their European allies, were supposed to be arriving soon. It was decided that victory had to wait for the production of more tanks and the arrival of the Americans.[1]

Realizing, at that late hour, the need for better international coordination of their war efforts, the Allies formed a Supreme War Council. The purpose of the new body was to effect improved military coordination on the western front. It was to overwatch the general conduct of the war, approve war plans submitted by national military commanders, and make recommendations to the national governments for the conduct of the war. National military commanders were to remain responsible to their own governments. The council was to consist of the prime minister and a member of the government of each of the great powers whose armies were on the western front. The council proposed to meet at least monthly. One military representative from each of the great powers would form a committee of technical advisers to the council. These would be in permanent, day-to-day session, to advise the council. The permanent military representatives appointed to the council were: for France, General Ferdinand Foch; for Great Britain, General Sir Henry Wilson; and for Italy, General

Luigi Cadorna. The question of American representation on the council was a delicate one. The United States was in the war in a "cooperative status" with the Allies. The American government had no treaty of alliance, and it had made no pledges regarding Allied war aims.

The idea of a war council as a policy and decision making body did not sit well with the commander of the British Army, and a good many British political figures opposed it also. President Wilson, however, cabled his approval, strengthening the new council's political status. The American president, with the advice of the secretary of war, then appointed Major General Tasker M. Bliss, the chief of staff of the United States Army, as the permanent military representative on the council. Ignoring Allied entreaties, President Wilson avoided the issue of appointing a political representative to the council.[2]

The peril that all the Allies recognized was the likelihood that Russia would be forced out of the war shortly, and that the full weight of the Central Powers could then be turned against the western front before the Americans arrived to balance the Central Powers' forces. On the other side of the line, the Central Powers were equally concerned with heavy losses. Acute food shortages had lowered morale at home. But their military leaders were confident that, by the rapid shifting of forces from the east to the western front, they could gather sufficient forces to gain a final victory before the Americans could arrive in sufficient numbers. In fact, Hindenburg and Ludendorff confidently promised the Kaiser that victory would come with one more gigantic offensive on the western front. By dint of good staff work, the Germans were able to pull some fifty-six of their divisions from the eastern front prior to the end of the war with Russia. They then trained them in the new "Hutier tactics" in preparation for moving them as "shock troops" to the western front. Additional divisions were being readied for dispatch to the western front as Ludendorff, the virtual commander of the forces of the Central Powers, prepared his "spring offensive."[3]

The Allies pressed the query: Where are the Americans? The 1st Division had completed its training in the rear and had assumed a defensive position "in the Vosges," a quiet sector of the line, on 21 October 1917. On 3 November, a German raid caught them unprepared; three American soldiers were killed, five were wounded, and twelve captured—the first American casualties in the war.[4] By the end of 1917, four American divisions were in France; two more were on the way over. A total of 9,804 officers and 165,080 men were assigned to the AEF. Pershing continued to emphasize training, and the organization of a balanced, self-sustaining force, including a sizable administrative and logistical support complex. The small number of American combat forces compared to support forces was very disappointing to the Allies. Their entreaties for assignment of individuals and small units of American infantrymen as fillers in their armies now took on more strident tones.[5]

The AEF staff was also reflecting the pressure on its commander. An AEF staff study, done in November 1917, indicated that the situation might become grave for the Allies if the bulk of the eighty German and Austrian divisions remaining on the eastern front were committed into battle in the west, adding to the strength of those in France. It was agreed at GHQ-AEF (apparently, also by Pershing) that the situation might arise in which units of the AEF might have to be used to reinforce the armies of the Allies, as a last, desperate resort. But, the study concluded, the Allies should be able to stop the enemy without American reinforcement if "they held firm and secured unity of action." The situation and its prospects in no way justified curtailing plans to form an army under the American flag, the study concluded.[6]

Allied proposals for the integration of American troops into their armies were nothing new; they had begun in April 1917, as soon as it was apparent that America intended to field a ground force in France. The Joffre-Vivani visit to the United States in May 1917 was the occasion for Marshall Joseph Joffre (the former commander-in-chief of French forces) to suggest a French-American partnership, with the French acting as the seniors in leading the Americans in battle. (This proposal was never presented officially.) A British proposal to draft Americans into British battalions (presented by British Major General G. T. M. Bridges in April 1917) was quickly rejected by the American government.[7] Late in 1917, the Allies tried to gain "Yankee" reinforcements through General Bliss, the American member on the Supreme War Council; Bliss was sympathetic to their plight, but, nonetheless, supported a separate American Army.[8]

In December, the British Ambassador to the United States, Lord Reading, carried a proposal to President Wilson's adviser, Colonel Edward House for reconsideration of the "amalgamation" of American companies or battalions within British divisions. This appeal stressed the return of those units to American command, "if later desired." It had the personal support of Lloyd George, the British prime minister. House queried Pershing, who emphatically rejected it as yet another attempt to subvert the build-up of an American Army. House supported Pershing, but the political pressures continued. On 25 December 1917, the War Department cabled that both France and England were pressing for amalgamation. Pershing answered that "no emergency exists which would warrant putting our companies and battalions into British and French units."[9]

In January 1918, Pershing made two positive responses to this continuing pressure. Marshal Pétain and Pershing agreed that the program for moving American divisions into the line should be expedited. Pershing also agreed to a British plan to expedite the shipment of American troops to France for training and service with the British, using British ships. Pershing insisted that the units involved would be trained for major independent operations and that they be returned to the American command when called for. The agreement, concluded on 30 January 1918, involved six American divisions; it was called the "Six Division Plan." The British agreed on the ultimate return of American divisions, but their later complaints showed that they expected to employ these divisions indefinitely.[10]

The Allies increased their pressure on Pershing by means of the Supreme War Council's approval, on 12 January 1918, of Note #12, drafted by their military representatives. This note stated that France could only be successfully defended if "British and French forces are maintained at their present aggregate strength, and receive the expected reinforcement of not less than two American divisions per month."[11] Pershing chose the occasion of this memo to send a cable of bitter complaint to the secretary of war regarding the failure of the War Department to provide even the numbers of personnel previously agreed upon. The winter of 1917–1918 being one of the coldest on record, he also castigated the War Department for its failure to provide the troops with adequate winter clothing.[12]

The increasing German threat eventually led to ever increasing American combat force commitments being made to the Allies. By recalling some divisions from Italy and more from the east, General Ludendorff assembled more than 3.5 million men on the western front by the spring of 1918. Approximately two hundred German divisions faced one hundred sixty-nine Allied division equivalents. The location of the front lines in 1918 and the offensives of 1918 may be followed on Map 8 (immediately following chapter 8). The Germans assembled sixty-two of their best divisions along the Somme. Their plan was to split the Allied forces at their juncture and to roll the British back against the English Channel, with the hope, thereby, of taking them out of the war. The principle on which Ludendorff's offensive was based was to defeat the British, the stronger force, first. Then, the less capable force, the French, would fall easily to the might of German arms. The area of the juncture of the Allied armies, the Aisne-Marne region of France, was also viewed by the Allies as a point of great significance. They were not deceived about German intentions; in fact, all along the line it was known that a "spring offensive" was due, and, generally, it was appreciated that its purpose was to split the Allied forces from their cooperative but fragile union. Viewing the growing disparity between Allied forces and their reinforcing enemy (potentially, a disadvantage in numbers of two to one) the French prodded Pershing to put the other American divisions in France into the line.[13] On 19 January 1918, the 1st Division took over a sector north of Toul. By the agreement of Generals Pershing and Pétain, this sector was to be expanded to include an American corps, then the American Army. The 26th United States Division ended its training and entered the line in the Chemin-des-Dames sector on 8 February 1918; on 21 February, the 42nd Division entered the French line near Luneville. The 2nd Division was brigaded with the French in the Verdun area on 18 March 1918.[14]

Despite the obvious threat to the juncture point of their combined forces, neither General Haig nor General Pétain would do more than give each other assurances that each would reinforce the other in the event of attack in his sector. The tendency to concentrate reserves, such as there were, near the center of the mass of each army was a natural command action. Thus, the area of the juncture, athwart the left flank of the Fifth French Army where it joined the Third British Army (the Amiens sector), was weakly manned, and, considering the manning that had been established in the trench warfare of the time, relatively overextended.

The Germans, having trained their troops to attack closely following a rolling barrage of artillery, struck on the morning of 21 March 1918, after a short but intensive artillery barrage that was heavy in gas and smoke. Aided also by a thick fog, small groups of highly trained "shock troops" rushed forward, bypassing centers of Allied resistance, they seized vital terrain. The swift movement of the "shock troops" surprised the defenders; the Germans drove through the positions of the Fifth French Army and the right wing of the BEF—gaining the banks of the Somme River in the first forty-eight hours. As he had promised, General Haig shifted British forces to reinforce his right flank, and he tardily dispatched two divisions to the command of the Fifth French Army. The German attack was temporarily halted, the result of elasticity of the Allied defenses, the shifting of their reserves, and the exhaustion of the leading German divisions.[15]

The Allies, however, were frightened by this attack. It was far more violent, more successful, and more strategically threatening than anything that had occurred since the Battle of the Frontiers in 1914. The Germans had advanced forty miles in eight days. They had taken 70,000 prisoners. Allied casualties exceeded 200,000. But German casualties were as high, and their "shock divisions" were decimated. The giant "Paris gun" began lobbing shells into Paris, while Lloyd George and his staff hurried over from London to consult with their counterparts about the new situation.[16]

It was agreed by the British and French, and seconded by Pershing, that General Ferdinand Foch (later Marshal) would be given the role of "coordinator" of all Allied armies; he would be responsible for "strategic direction," controlling the general reserves of both forces and the commitment of those reserves. Pétain and Haig reluctantly surrendered control of their reserves; by so doing, they took another step toward a coalition command.[17]

On 9 April 1918, the Germans struck again, this time along the Lys River in the British sector of Flanders, north of their Amiens salient. Following an intensive bombardment, eight German divisions attacked along the south bank of the Lys, broke through a Portuguese division, and reached open country beyond the British trenches. Foch refused Haig reinforcements, sensing the British would hold. Haig gave his "backs to the wall" order, and the British held. The Germans held the Passchendaele Ridge, but little else of value. British losses were high—305,000; but German losses reached 350,000.[18] A third German offensive struck the French Fifth and Sixth Armies in the Aisne region, south of the first penetration. The drive broke through their defenses on the Chemin-des-Dames on 27 May and gained twenty miles the first day. Three days later, the German forces stood on the banks of the Marne River at Chateau-Thierry, less than fifty miles from Paris—a position that they had not been able to reach since the early days of 1914.

In this crisis, the Allies renewed their pressures for American replacements for their forces. On 27 March Lloyd George requested of President Wilson that three hundred thousand men be shipped at the earliest moment and that trained divisions in France be put into the line immediately. "We are at the crisis of the war," he cabled.[19] Wilson showed his mettle by refusing to throw "our troops in to stop up that hole." He passed Lloyd George's request on to Secretary Baker in Paris.[20] At the same time, the Supreme War Council was pressing Pershing to approve immediate, temporary amalgamation of his troops with those of the Allies. On 28 March, the permanent military representatives (including General Bliss) recommended to the Supreme War Council, meeting at Douellens, that all plans for the shipment of Americans to France be altered, and that for the foreseeable future, only infantry and machine gun units be shipped. This recommendation was approved and promulgated as Joint Note 18. Pershing, after remonstrating with General Bliss, gained Secretary Baker's approval of a message to President Wilson regarding Joint Note Eighteen. They recommended that the president approve the shipment of only infantry and machine gun units in the emergency, with the following provisos:

> These units to be under the direction of the Commander in Chief of the AEF. He will use these . . . to render the greatest military assistance . . . keeping in mind always the determination of this government to have its . . . forces collected . . . into an American Army.[21]

The President approved this response.

Hearing that the Douellens conference had also appointed Foch as coordinator of the Allied armies, Pershing (who considered Foch's position to be that of supreme commander) motored to Foch's headquarters and made a historic commitment: "Infantry, artillery, aviation; all that we have are yours. Use them as you wish!"[22] Pershing's agreement to provide all his forces meant, according to his memoirs, that he would provide the five divisions of the American forces then in France. This would have given the Allies the equivalent, as Pershing saw it, of ten of their own divisions. However, the Supreme War Council's requests for infantry and machine gun troops had resulted in the War Department's being directed to dispatch these troops without their accompanying support. Pershing's return cable stressed that:

> Americans must not lose sight of the purpose to build up divisions and corps of their own . . . must avoid the tendency to incorporate our infantry into British divisions where it will be used up and never relieved.[23]

Pershing recommended that the infantry in two divisions be sent by British shipping and that two be sent by American shipping, but that present plans should go no farther than this shipment of infantry without supportive arms. By return message, Secretary Baker relayed the president's concurrence with Pershing's interpretation of the American commitment and restressed Pershing's authority to decide questions of American cooperation or replacement.[24] These agreements threw the War Department's plans, still in the stages of development and partial execution, into a "cocked hat." Infantry and machine gun personnel would have to be pulled out of four divisions, to be shipped in a relatively semi-trained or untrained state during April and May of 1918. Furthermore, the British government in the person of Lloyd George, chose to assume that the dispatch of infantry and machine gunners was to be continued for succeeding months. The terrible losses of the early spring, as the German army drove to the banks of the Marne for the second time in the war, also caused General Foch to appeal to French Prime Minister Clemenceau for his representation to the American president that additional infantry and machine gun personnel (at the rate of one hundred twenty thousand per month) be provided on a continuing basis. Accompanying this political pressure, great personal pressures were brought to bear upon General Pershing at a meeting of the Supreme War Council at Sarcus (General Foch's headquarters) on 27 April 1918. General Bliss also attended that meeting, representing the United States. Bliss was more inclined toward immediate support for the Allies, and less worried about the ultimate results of such action, than was Pershing. In his *Memoirs,* Foch speaks of a ready accord regarding the need for the shipment of American infantry and machine gunners. Pershing's description (in his *Experiences*) records a bit more acrimony at that meeting, especially when he discovered that the British had apparently gained President Wilson's prior agreement to the shipment of only infantry and machine gun troops for an additional four months. (Pershing, himself, had been apprised of this presidential agreement only a few days before and he had hastened to object to the continuation of such shipments.) After much discussion, it was agreed to continue shipments of machine gunners only for the month of May, and to reconsider the matter later in the light of the Allied situation.[25] Pershing followed this agreement with a cable to the secretary of war, requesting that plans be developed for a one-and-one-half-million-man army in France as soon as possible. The War Department replied that 1,500,000 was an impossible number of men to draft, because such large numbers of men could not be housed, trained, or shipped by any configuration of existing resources.[26]

At the meeting of the Supreme War Council on 1 and 2 May 1918 at Abbeville, the Allied leaders insisted on continuing the shipment of only infantry and machine gunners for the month of June. The French complained at that meeting that no provision had been made, thus far, for a diversion of those forces shipped by British tonnage to serve with the French Army. Premier Clemenceau made a strong statement protesting the fact that all of the infantry and machine gunners had gone thus far to the British, and he demanded that the French receive the same number (120,000) in June. Clemenceau also stated that, "there are close to 400,000 Americans in France at present, but only five divisions, or about 125,000 men can be considered as combatants. This is not a satisfactory proportion."[27] Pershing responded that, in his opinion, the best way to help the Allied forces was by the quick formation of an American army. At this point, Foch said: "You are willing to risk our being driven back to the Loire?" Pershing said: "Yes, I am going to take that risk. Moreover, the time may come when the American Army will have to stand the brunt of this war, and it is not wise to fritter away our resources in this manner." Pershing recorded that all five of the Allied party attacked him with all the force and prestige of their high positions. He finally stated, with the greatest possible emphasis, "Gentlemen, I have thought this problem over very deliberately and will not be coerced." Others present have claimed that Pershing accompanied this statement by pounding on the table. The council adjourned for the day to take up the matter of American reinforcements on 2 May.[28]

The next day at the Abbeville conference, Lloyd George made the strongest appeal yet propounded by the British:

> If the United States does not come to our aid, then perhaps the enemy's calculations will be correct. If France and Great Britain should have to yield, their defeat would be honourable for they would have fought to their last man, while the United States would have to stop without having put into the line more men than little Belgium.[29]

Pershing agreed to continue the shipment of one hundred twenty thousand American infantry and machine gunners for June and to reconsider the need for such shipment in July. He gained from this session the agreement of the Supreme War Council that an American Army should be formed as early as possible, under its own commander and its own flag. It was also agreed that any tonnage over and above that necessary to ship the required numbers of infantry and machine gunners would be devoted to bringing over such other troops as the AEF commander would determine necessary. Pershing gained some flexibility in this commitment, allowing him additional personnel for in-theater support and administration.[30]

Pershing's commitment of the best American divisions to the western front at the Marne River helped sustain the fragile Allied defenses. By the night of 31 May 1918, the motorized machine gun battalion of the United States' 3rd Division was dug in at Chateau-Thierry; it helped to hold that bridgehead over the Marne. The rest of the division also took up positions along that river. On 1 June, the 2nd Division took up positions north of the Marne, west of Chateau-Thierry, protecting the main route to Paris. Ludendorff, convinced that he was on the brink of a breakthrough, threw his reserves against the hastily deployed Americans. For the first days in June, the issue was in doubt at the highest headquarters—but not on the line. The Americans had stiffened the Allied defenses; their aggressiveness had inspired the wary French. Together, they stopped the German offensive cold!

Meanwhile, the 1st Division, in the first American offensive operation of the war, attacked on 28 May 1918 and seized Cantigny and commanding ground at the tip of the Amiens salient. Holding on desperately, despite furious counterattacks, they lost more than sixteen hundred men, but maintained the position. On 6 June, the 2nd Division counterattacked. "C'mon, you sonsabitches, do you want to live forever?" shouted Sergeant Daniel Daly, as he led his marines into Belleau Wood—and into the annals of Marine Corps history.[31]

The fighting was fierce in Belleau Wood, Boursches, and Vaux, but the Americans moved forward. The German offensive was stopped all along the line. Total casualties for the American debut were 11,384. While the United States' contribution resulted in only modest gains, they provided bloody affirmations of American combat capability both to skeptical Allies and the scornful enemy.[32] Although it was not known at the time, the German offensive had been virtually terminated. Many credit the infusion of the large American divisions with "tipping the balance," as the author John Toland has stated. He added, "The great spirit of our soldiers and marines was an inspiration to the tired French, and struck terror in the Germans. We attacked so recklessly."[33] The author Don Lawson agrees with Toland. "The entry of the Americans into the fighting was simply the straw that broke the German camel's back. Had the Americans not entered precisely when they did, the war might very well continued in a stalemate situation . . . followed by a forced political settlement."[34] Colonel William Griffiths, a devoted student and analyst of The Great War, adds: "The very size of the U.S. square division, reaching 28,000, compared to the 9,000 of the understrength European divisions infused great strength to the Allies. The U.S. would play their trump—inexperienced but willing man-power. . . . They would succeed by manpower and enthusiasm."[35]

On 9 June 1918, Ludendorff tried to regain his momentum. Attacking westward from Soissons and southward from the Amiens salient, his armies attempted to merge the Amiens and Marne salients into one. But the French were ready, and the Germans were tired. By the fifth day, the attack had run its course, having gained only nine miles. A lull settled over the front. In June, Pershing created three corps. I Corps, under Major General Hunter Liggett, took over responsibility for the American divisions in the vicinity of Chateau-Thierry. II Corps, under Major General George W. Read, took responsibility for the 27th and 30th Divisions moving to fight with the British forces. III Corps, under Major General Robert L. Bullard, awaited assignment. On 4 July it was announced that one million Americans were in France; three hundred thousand were to arrive each month thereafter. Nine divisions had experienced some com-bat; two others were completing training, and eight had just arrived—totalling nineteen divisions in country.[36]

Back at the War Department Headquarters, manpower deployment agreements made in Europe and changes thereto, arrived in fragmentary fashion. Often, departmental headquarters gained crucial information from the press before hearing of decisions from Pershing's own headquarters. Frequently, they also received more complete details of agreements, and even of changes in the fighting situation, from General Bliss at the Su-preme War Council than they did from their counterparts in the AEF. This was the result of a very strict interpretation on the part of Pershing's headquarters of the need for and adherence to strict censorship, a series of restrictions to which the Army's Chief of Staff, General March, in par-ticular, did not fully agree.[37]

A strict secrecy of plans, and particularly of schedules for troop ship-ment, was necessary because of the German submarine threat, and to prevent the enemy from knowing the full value and timetable of American reinforcements. However, censorship was an unpopular measure and newsmen used all sources, professional and personal, to gain and publish information of a sensitive nature. While many were restrained by their own sense of ethics and patriotism, much sensitive information was, in fact, published in the press, and as well much nonsensitive news was classified and withheld by staff officers overly concerned with secrecy.

These communications problems often made the discussion of routine disagreements blossom into major confrontations between the commands, which frustrated Pershing even though he normally won every contest over conflicting aims and objectives. In the meantime, the AEF formed its own staff coordination section, modeled on that of the War Department, and a veritable blizzard of paperwork began descending from these headquarters to all their agencies, providing guidance and directing action.[38]

All American problems were now increasing rapidly in scope. But the problem of shipping more and more men, as the historian Edward Coffman put it, became a nightmare of schedules and revisions, commitments and overcommitments for the War Department. The shipping program reached its peak during the summer of 1918. In the months of June, July, and August, a daily average of almost ninety-five hundred soldiers made the Atlantic crossing. Pershing, encouraged by the Allies, urged an even greater program.[39] On 1 June 1918, the three prime ministers, Lloyd George of Britain, Clemenceau of France, and Orlando of Italy met as the Supreme War Council at Versailles. This meeting was primarily to determine the requirements for American reinforcement, as a follow-up to the conference held at Abbeville the month before. It was held at a time when remarkable German successes at the Marne had provoked great uncertainty as to the future of the Alliance. The following message was approved and sent to the president of the United States:

> We desire to express our warmest thanks to President Wilson for the remarkable promptness with which American aid was provided. . . . The crisis, however, still continues. General Foch has presented to us a statement of the utmost gravity which points out that the numerical superiority of the enemy in France (162 Allied divisions now oppose 200 German divisions) is very heavy, and, there is no possibility of the British and French increasing the number of their divisions . . . He, therefore, urges the utmost insistence that the maximum possible number of infantry and machine gunners . . . be shipped from America in the months of June and July. . . . He places the total American force required at no less than 100 divisions, and urges the continual raising of fresh American levies which, in his opinion, should be not less than 300,000 a month.
> Signed Clemenceau, Lloyd George, Orlando.[40]

After much animated discussion, Pershing agreed to the Allied proposal that had been sent to the President, provided that shipping would be allocated also for support troops to build up the AEF structure, as had been done for the previous month. His agreement, cabled to the War Department 10 June, read:

> The following agreement has been concluded between General Foch, Lord Milner, and myself in reference to the transportation of American troops in the months of June and July. The recommendations are made on the assumption that at least 250,000 men can be transported in each of the months of June and July by the employment of combined British and American tonnage. We recommend: (a) For the month of June: First, absolute priority be given to the transportation of 170,000 combatant troops (viz. six divisions without artillery, ammunition trains, or supply trains, amounting to 126,000 men and 44,000 replacements for combat troops). Second, 25,400 men for the services of the railways, of which 13,400 have been asked for by the French Minister of Transportation. Third, the balance of the troops in categories to be determined by the Commander in Chief American Expeditionary Forces. (b) For the month of July: First, absolute priority for the shipment of 140,000 combatant troops of the nature defined above (four divisions minus artillery etc., amounting to 84,000 men, plus 56,000 replacements). Second, the balance of the 250,000 to consist of troops designated by the Commander in Chief American Expeditionary Forces. . . . (d) We recognize that the combat troops to be dispatched in July may have to include those which have had insufficient training, but consider this a temporary emergency such as to justify an exceptional departure of the United States from sound principles of training, especially as a similar course is being followed by France and Great Britain. Signed: Foch, Milner, Pershing.[41]

The upshot of the conference was that Pershing got another commitment from the Allies to help build up the AEF.

With respect to planning the American build-up, however, many problems had been created: Pershing had called for a sixty-six-division AEF in May 1918; now, on 10 June, he upped this figure to the round number of one hundred divisions. His cable reflected confidence that the War Department would be able to provide both troops and supplies with the help of Allied shipping and resources. One hundred American divisions would be equivalent to two hundred European divisions—a figure that would match the strength of the entire German force. The War Department general staff worked mightily to determine the feasibility of a hundred-division commitment. Finally, they set a figure between Pershing's first and his second request, a total of eighty divisions, to be the maximum that could be handled even by the straining of all resources. The eighty-division project would, the War Department estimated, require 3,335,000 Americans in France; to ship and sustain these would incur a cargo deficit of over 4,850,000 tons, utilizing American and projected Allied transport resources. The "eighty-division program," however, was the one upon which the War Department generally worked and around which they planned. Even this figure would require the reduction of all resources not absolutely necessary for operations in the field. Automatic resupply of food, ammunition, and other expendables for the theater was cut from fifty pounds per man per day to thirty pounds, in hopes of effecting this eighty-division program.[42]

Still another problem plagued planners at AEF and War Department Headquarters. By agreeing to an "eighty-division program," Pershing thought he had agreed to a total of eighty combat divisions, plus twenty divisions for training and replacement duties. The War Department considered that it had agreed to a grand total of eighty divisions. Thus, the numbers of men required for various categories of troops were always in disagreement.

These rapid changes in plans and programs were not fully coordinated with the military supply agencies and throughput facilities. Not only were there considerable problems within the continental United States (problems that saw the shipment to Europe of troops in a relatively untrained state, lacking items of uniform, weapons, and equipment), but there were also tremendous backlogs of supplies at the ports in Southern France and at the various support installations within the Services of Supply. The War Department considered one of the major problems to be the failure to evacuate material from the ports and docks, and the failure to turn around shipping for return to the United States. Accordingly, General March and Secretary Baker developed a plan for better management of the Services of Supply by separating them from Pershing's control. Under this plan, the Services of Supply would be a co-equal command in France under the command of Major General George W. Goethels, then quartermaster for the War Department. This plan, which had apparently been approved in concept by President Wilson, was sent to Pershing for comment—it received his violent rejection! Pershing noted that it was a principle of war that all forces in a theater should be under one commander.

While Goethels was preparing for deployment overseas, Pershing appointed the former AEF chief of staff, Major General James G. Harbord, as the new commander of the Services of Supply, replacing General Kernan. Pershing then made a whirlwind tour of the Services of Supply, together with Harbord, and he reported that his inspection, and his new appointment, had assured him that the services of supply were now capable of handling their difficult tasks without further action being needed on the part of the War Department.[43] This skirmish ended attempts on the part of the War Department to limit the scope of Pershing's responsibilities.

The confrontations between AEF Headquarters and the War Department Headquarters came to a head in August 1918. Pershing had complained forcefully in letters to the secretary of war that the Chief of Staff,

General March, was assuming a curt and commanding tone in his cables. In the middle of August, Pershing wrote again to Baker telling him that the War Department general staff was poorly organized and functioning in a faulty manner. He also had the temerity to suggest that a change in the chief of staff of the army might be in order. (General March, with a date of rank of 20 May 1918, was junior to Pershing as a four-star general.) Baker stood by General March during this assault, and, to establish clearly March's authority over both the AEF and the War Department bureaus, Baker issued General Order No. 80 in late August, which stated that "the Chief of Staff is the immediate adviser of the Secretary of War . . . charged by the Secretary with the planning, development and execution of the Army program." The order provided that this officer would take rank and precedence over all officers of the army. This appeared to settle, at least in terms of ultimate responsibility, the problems between the War Department staff and the AEF.[44]

On the western front, the German forces, although physically close to Paris, were fading rapidly in strength as June turned into July. Foch still reported that Germans outnumbered the Allies in divisions, but the weight of numbers was fast swinging to the Allies. Foch himself was enthusiastically preparing a counteroffensive when the Germans launched their final offensive of the war.[45]

Ludendorff called it the *Friedensturm* (Peace Offensive). Its results did, indeed, hasten the coming of peace, but not as Ludendorff had intended. Massing a total of fifty-two divisions in two armies, the Germans drove one army southeast from the Marne salient, the other attacking south from the vicinity of Reims. The two forces were to meet on the Marne; but the French had recovered their Gallic "esprit," and no "heart" remained in the German forces. East of Reims, the French commander, apprised of the pending attack by aerial observation, withdrew his troops (including the American 42nd Division) from forward positions prior to the attack. During the German advance, their supporting fire beat down on empty trenches, while the French counterbattery fire decimated the advancing German ranks. Then the French and Americans repeated their withdrawal from their second (intermediate) zone; on the third line, they held.

To the west, a French division had been outflanked and folded rearward, leaving the American 3rd Division beset on three sides. Their steadfast defense (especially by the 38th Infantry Regiment) earned the division the title "The Rock of the Marne"! Going around the Americans, the driving Germans "forced" the Marne, and established a sizable bridgehead Southwest of Reims; two Italian divisions were driven back. British divisions moved in and stopped that advance. French resistance around the Marne bridgehead anchored on the American 3rd Division. As early as 17 July, it was apparent to Ludendorff that the offensive had run its course. He terminated this operation and turned his attention to Flanders, moving his headquarters there. Although Ludendorff planned to make another great offensive (against the British in Flanders), the attacks in the Champagne-Marne in July were the last westward movement of the German Army until 1940.[46]

It is to the credit of the spirit of General Foch that he was confidently planning an Allied counteroffensive before the German attacks ceased. Even as the Germans (and Austrians) were attacking in the Champagne-Marne area, Foch launched a limited counterattack on 18 July 1918 in the Soissons region to cut the highway from Soissons to Chateau-Thierry—the German supply route to the Marne Salient.

The 1st and 2nd United States Divisions led this attack, under the French Tenth and Sixth Armies, respectively. Some American units reached their attack positions on the run at "H hour" (the time for beginning the attack). Preceded by a short, heavy bombardment of artillery, in a rainstorm, the units jumped off at 0430 in the morning. The attack struck the "trench" (second-rate) German divisions as a complete surprise. Assisted by French tanks, American and French divisions made gains of up to five miles the first day. This success caused the offensive to be extended to the east. When notified of the Allied gains, Ludendorff shifted reserves to Soissons, cancelled the attack on Reims, and, later, abandoned the planning for an offensive in Flanders.

The American 3rd, 4th, 26th, and 28th Divisions took part in the Allied drive east and northeast; the American I and III Corps began actively directing the advance in their sectors, joined by the American 32nd, 42nd, and 77th Divisions. On 19 July, the German resistance stiffened; then Ludendorff directed a phased withdrawal from the Marne salient to the line of the Aisne and Vesle Rivers, covered by "stay-behind" machine gun teams and artillery barrages. The Allied counteroffensive halted at the new German positions on 6 August 1918.[47]

Eight American divisions had performed creditably in the offensive. In his postwar report to the secretary of war, Pershing described the tactical direction of the American troops in this operation as "excellent."[48] Major General Liggett, who commanded I Corps, and Major General Bullard, commander of the III Corps, also cited their troops for creditable performance.[49] It is, however, too early in this narrative for me to make a definite evaluation of the performance of American forces in combat. There is no question that they had advanced aggressively; their casualties (fifty thousand) attest to that. But the Aisne-Marne counteroffensive was launched against second-rate troops. It was planned, directed, and supported by Allied commanders, and its advance was against a force engaged in deliberate withdrawal. Although it was not recognized at the time, this counteroffensive did signal the turning point in the war. American combat strength (the equivalent of sixteen or seventeen Allied or German divisions) had tipped the balance. On the German side, Graf von Hindenburg (the titular commander of the forces of the Central Powers) was beginning to note signs of lack of discipline and the breakdown of unit integrity in his withdrawing armies. The initiative had passed to the Allies; the German countermarch had begun.[50]

5

THE FIRST AMERICAN OFFENSIVE— ST. MIHIEL

In mid-July, Marshal Foch turned exuberant and impatient; he ventured to predict the end of the war in 1919. Meeting with Field Marshal Haig, General Pétain, and General Pershing at his headquarters in Bombon on 24 July 1918, he proposed a general plan of attack designed to prevent an orderly German withdrawal, a withdrawal that might allow the Central Powers to continue fighting indefinitely. Foch outlined his immediate objectives as the clearing of railway lines, indispensible for later offensive operations: the freeing of the Paris-Amiens railway line by action of the British and French armies, and the freeing of the Paris-Avricourt rail line by eliminating the St. Mihiel salient—the latter operation "to be executed by the American Army, as soon as it has the necessary means."[1] Haig claimed that the British Army was "far from being reestablished"; Pétain pled that the French Army was "worn out, bled white, anemic." Pershing asserted that the "American Army asks nothing better than to fight; but it has not yet been formed!" Foch demurred; he offered to pace the offensive to the conditions of the armies. The Allies all agreed, then, to Foch's offensive plan. Pétain later advised that he thought an attack on the St. Mihiel salient—in conjunction with clearing the Armentieres Pocket— should be the main offensive for the remainder of summer and autumn.[2]

In consequence of Foch's instructions to attack, and notwithstanding their reservations, the French and British undertook an offensive on 8 August 1918 to reduce the Amiens salient. The attack of British and French infantry with 300 tanks, supported by artillery and 1700 Allied aircraft, surprised the enemy. The defenders fell back in great confusion; 13,000 prisoners were taken; 300 cannon and much material were abandoned. Up to six miles were gained by the attackers on a twelve-mile front in a single day. Subsequent days saw equal or greater advances. Ludendorff later called 8 August the "Black Day" for the German Army.[3] Jubilant, Foch pressed Haig for a British advance north of the Somme. He also urged the French to extend their offensive east of the Oise. Despite stiffening German resistance on the 13 August, Foch insisted on the resumption of the offensive beginning on the 16 August. Haig, however, refused—he felt that it was necessary for the BEF to reorganize and resupply. The French needed, and took, the same brief rest.[4]

Finally responsive to Foch's entreaties, the British Third and French Third Armies attacked on the left and right flanks (respectively) of their previous combined advance. Advances were slow and methodical. Aircraft strafed German positions that lay ahead of the advancing infantry, while accompanying tanks knocked out machine gun emplacements. The British Fourth Army extended the attack in the center; then the British First Army attacked east from Arras. In the face of these attacks, Ludendorff abandoned his salients on 26 August. A strong Canadian attack in the Arras region on 2 September forced a further German withdrawal, to the Siegfried-Hindenburg Line. German losses for this defense and withdrawal were high; the count of prisoners of war captured by the Allies was significant—over one hundred thousand! But the Allies had again outrun their logistics; none of their forces had the remaining capability for an exploitive dash. The front stabilized as both forces reorganized.[5]

At the late July conferences at Foch's headquarters, Pershing had gained approval to activate two American armies: The First Army would take the sector of the French Sixth Army, commanding the two American corps operating against the Marne salient; the Second Army would be formed in the quiet sector of the Woevre Plain, taking over the sector of the French Third Army. With the denouement of fighting along the Aisne-Vesle Line, Pershing requested, on 9 August, that the American forces be concentrated instead in one army in the Woevre, with the St. Mihiel attack their sole responsibility. Foch, who had been appointed Marshal of France on 6 August, approved. Accordingly, with the cooperation of General Pétain, the commander of the French Forces, Pershing activated the American First Army in Lorraine on 10 August 1918. This American force was placed under the "operational control of General Henri Pétain, Commander of the French Armies of the North and Northeast."[6] On that date, there were 1,275,000 Americans in France, including thirty-five divisions.[7] Most didn't have their authorized complement of artillery, the result of the expedited shipment of infantry units. Corps artillery was nonexistent. Initially, Pershing had assigned fourteen divisions to the First Army. He requested a tremendous level of support for these forces for the upcoming St. Mihiel offensive:

100 batteries of 75 millimeter cannon
50 batteries of 155 millimeter howitzers
86 heavy batteries for counterbattery and interdictory fire.

He also brashly requested:

300 light tanks
150 heavy tanks

and a sizable aviation augmentation:

7 observation squadrons
9 pursuit squadrons
5 day bombardment squadrons
10 balloons
plus the support of the British Independent Royal Air Force, for night
    bombardment.

Nearly all of this requested support (or its equivalent) was provided by the French.[8]

The St. Mihiel salient had existed as a threatening bulge into the French lines (fifteen to twenty-six miles south of Verdun) since its seizure by the Germans on 24 September 1914. In 1915, the French had conducted repeated unsuccessful assaults to eliminate this salient. In 1916, the Germans assaulted Verdun from this prominence. After the Verdun bloodletting, both sides had manned the area lightly and used it as a rest and training area.[9] The geography was a giant inverted triangle with the apex at the town of St. Mihiel; the base leg was the front line, running east twenty-six miles to Pont-a-Mousson; from St. Mihiel, the vertical leg of the front ran north seventeen miles to Haudiomont. (See Map 2.) The area is low, rolling terrain, marshy north to south in the center of the salient, lightly wooded, with a line of low hills running north-northeast from the town of St. Mihiel. The towns were small and they were clustered along the few roads. Roads were narrow and unpaved.[10]

German forces in the area were largely "trench" troops, those too old or infirm for offensive combat. They were part of German Composite Army C (General Fuchs in Command); the German Nineteenth Army (General Bothmer) tied in with Army C and held the eastern five miles of the salient. Around the salient from north (Haudiomont) to south (St. Mihiel), the Germans were disposed along wooded high grounds in well-prepared positions, protected by multiple strands of barbed wire. The position was strongly manned in only one sector—the vicinity east of Les

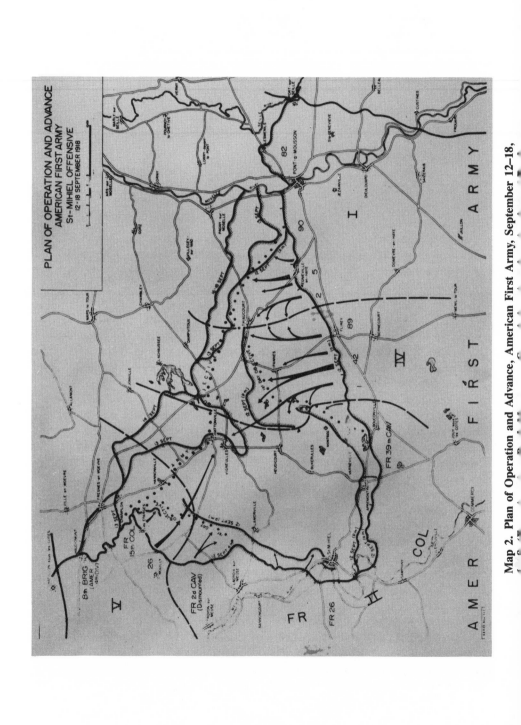

Map 2. Plan of Operation and Advance, American First Army, September 12–18,

Eparges, where one division was arrayed in two-and-a-half miles of multiple defensive works: south of Les Eparges around the salient to Apremont three divisions occupied six miles of front each. For the nineteen miles from Apremont east to the Moselle River, three more divisions were similarly arrayed, generally on low, wooded ground, with lakes and marshy obstacles to their front. One or two divisions were identified in army reserve, with two more within two-day reinforcing capability. Total defensive strength in the St. Mihiel salient and in local reserves was estimated at twenty-three thousand. Across the northern base of the salient were strong defensive emplacements called the "Michel Stellung."[11]

The St. Mihiel region had been selected as the operation for christening the American First Army because it appeared to present a relatively easy task for the strong force. It was also likely to provide an early success, more symbolic than important to the Allied cause. It would give the American forces, and their people at home, a long-awaited victory for American arms. From a logistical standpoint, it was the focal point of most of the American lines of supply and communication from their ports in the south and southwest of France.[12]

Strategically, the salient was important, as it posed a constant threat to Verdun and to the flank of any Allied offensive to the north. Beyond the "Michel Stellung" to the north lay the old, formidable fortress complex of Metz-Thionville. If the Metz defenses were overcome, the Metz-Lille railroad could be disrupted, cutting off supplies to the southern wing of the German armies to the west. Such an offensive would also threaten the Briey iron ore region and the coal mining area of the Saar.

The AEF staff (primarily Lieutenant Colonel George C. Marshall) had been studying the area and planning an offensive there since midsummer.[13] The first concept or "preliminary" study called for a force of four American divisions in the assault, with three in reserve for exploitation or "mopping up." This was prepared on 6 August 1918. An important note in this study was that the offensive should begin no later than 15 September, the onset of the rainy season, because the ground was subject to flooding.[14]

With new guidance, the plan was changed on 9 August to a ten-division drive with French support; by 13 August fourteen divisions were included in the attack. By 16 August, under pressure to use more of the thirty-five American divisions in France, Marshall drew up a plan of attack utilizing seventeen divisions—a grand total of 476,000 men—to attack about 23,000 German troops in an area of approximately three hundred square miles.[15] Were even half of these men to move into the contested area, the troop density would equal approximately eight hundred men per square mile. Such a density makes for uncomfortable urban living; it certainly becomes a crowd difficult to manage on a battlefield![16] The proposed attack would launch nine divisions against the southern face of the salient through Thiaucourt; six divisions would attack the northern face through Fresnes; while two divisions would conduct a supporting attack on the heights east of the Moselle. (The problem of troop density in attack will be taken up later in reviewing the Meuse-Argonne campaign.) By the end of August, the AEF plan contemplated a drive beyond the salient, to pierce the "Michel Stellung" and open the way for a drive on Metz.[17]

Another problem arose in gaining adequate fire support to assist the infantry attack. Pershing's request to Pétain for one hundred fifty heavy tanks had been passed to the British Marshal Haig, who had reported that none were available. According to some planners in the AEF Operations Section, the absence of heavy tanks required the substitution of a long, heavy artillery preparation (fourteen hours) to break gaps in the barbed wire. Others favored an attack without an artillery preparation, to maximize surprise. Pershing seemed attracted to this option; his operations staff finally convinced him to authorize a five-hour preparatory artillery bombardment.[18]

In establishing the forces for the American First Army's attack on the salient, a tremendous reshuffling was necessary to gather American divisions that had been spread from Flanders to Marseilles. With respect to divisions that were serving with the Allies (in a training status), General Pétain was agreeable to releasing those requested by Pershing; the AEF was taking over a portion of his area of responsibility. As Pershing had feared, Marshal Haig was distressed at having to honor the agreement he had made when the "Six Division Plan" was executed (the agreement to release these divisions on call from Pershing). The British were planning, and hoping for an American Army in their zone, based on Dunkerque. Lloyd George was pushing for this plan. The British also appeared to be anxious about the growing association of the Americans with the French. Pershing agreed to British retention of the American II Corps (with the 27th and 30th United States Divisions) for the upcoming fall campaign.[19]

This experience with the British highlighted the continuing pressure being exerted by all the Allies to use American troops to spare their own and to forward their plans. The Italians were pressing for an American front in Italy. Foch also recommended the greater integration of American and French logistical support. The great blow to the independence of the American military effort came on 30 August 1918, the same day General Pershing assumed command of the United States First Army (while retaining command of the AEF). General Foch visited Pershing's headquarters at Ligny-en-Barrois. After the usual pleasantries, Foch presented an entirely new plan for the employment of the American forces. Pointing out the great successes of the ongoing Allied offensives, especially in the north, and the relative disarray of the German forces, Foch then presented his concept for exploiting that continuing success and preventing German reorganization: The British, supported by the left of the French armies, would continue to attack in the general direction of Cambrai-St. Quentin. The center of the French armies would continue their "energetic" actions to throw the enemy behind the Aisne. A combined American-French army on the right of the French center, acting on the Meuse and to the west, would attack in the general direction of Mezieres. Marshal Foch then went on at greater length on his proposal for the employment of American troops: The St. Mihiel operation should begin September 10; the attack should be limited to reaching the Vignuelles-Regneville line (eliminating the salient only). Four to six American divisions should be turned over to the French Second Army for attack between the Meuse and the Argonne Forest; an American army (eight to ten American divisions) should be employed immediately west of the Argonne on both sides of the Aisne River to attack in conjunction with the French Fourth Army. The attacks on either side of the Argonne were to be made between 15 and 20 September. To assist Pershing in planning and in directing the offensive west of the Argonne, two French generals, "with sufficient authority to expedite the solution to all questions," should be assigned to the commander in chief of the American Army.[20]

Pershing immediately objected to this late change in plans, and especially to dismembering the American Army. He offered to take over the sector from the Meuse west to the Argonne from the French Second Army, rather than split his command. Foch then queried: "Do you wish to take part in the battle?" Pershing replied, "Most assuredly, but as an American Army and in no other way." Foch referred to the lack of artillery organic to the American Army. Pershing reminded him of his earlier promises to make up for this deficiency, caused by the shipping of American infantry without support that had taken place at Foch's request. Pershing then suggested that the American First Army take over a sector east of the Meuse River; or alternatively, for it to form two armies east and west of the Argonne Forest. He noted that Foch rejected both these proposals. Foch does not record such proposals in his memoirs.[21] (The matter of the location of an American sector is important to the later discussion of the Meuse-Argonne campaign.) Rising from their conference table, Foch stated, "I must insist upon the arrangements." Pershing replied: "You may insist all you please, but I decline absolutely to agree to your plan. While our army will fight wherever you may decide, it will not fight except as an independent American Army!"[22] Foch left, leaving with Pershing a memorandum of his plan. Pershing responded the next day, reiterating his objections and principles, stressing the necessity of eliminating the St. Mihiel salient and the desirability of reserving the decision as to exploiting any success achieved there, even within the limited objectives proposed. He also stated the impossibility of conducting the St. Mihiel operation and of assembling the necessary divisions for the Mezieres operation by the date desired by the marshal. He then proposed to carry out the St. Mihiel operation, then to continue the offensive in the region of Belfort or Luneville, taking over the entire area from St. Mihiel to the Swiss border. His response concluded:

> Finally, however, there is one thing that must not be done and that is to disperse the American forces among the Allied armies. . . . If you decide to utilize American forces in attacking in the direction of Mezieres, I accept that decision even though it complicates my supply system and the care of my sick and wounded. I do insist that the American Army be employed as a whole either east of the Argonne or west of the Argonne and not four or five divisions here or six or seven there.[23]

Pershing also took the occasion to demand the return of his corps and divisions serving with the British and the French.

Upon receipt of Pershing's response, Marshal Foch called a conference to meet at his headquarters on 2 September 1918 to resolve the matter. After considerable discussion and disagreement, it was concluded:

> To limit the attack on the St. Mihiel Salient to the objectives of attaining the line Vigneulles-Regneville; the attack to be launched on the 10th of September, with eight to ten divisions. The American Army will attack to the west of the Meuse, covered on its right by the Meuse River, and supported on its left by the attack of the French Fourth Army along the west flank of the Argonne Forest. The American attack will be prepared without delay, to be launched between the 20th and 25th of September. The American Army will attack with all forces which it has available (12 to 14 divisions), and will bring to this attack such of the divisions from the St. Mihiel Region as may become available. Organization of the communications in this sector requires bringing under the same command all the troops operating on the right and left banks of the Meuse. General Pershing will also take under his command for the attack west of the Meuse the front of the II French Army as far as the Argonne. The French divisions holding the passive front to the east of the Meuse will be provisionally retained there and placed under the American command. Operation will be carried out by direction of the Commanding General of the Armies of North and Northeast.[24]

British Marshal Haig was the agent who caused this sudden change in Foch's grand design. British successes in Flanders, and the apparent disarray in the German resistance efforts, convinced Haig that the war might be won in 1918. He inspired Foch to abandon the French and American offensives aimed at freeing the railroad complexes; the weight of the American attack should, he argued, be turned from the axis toward

Metz to that of convergence with the British drive. The southern wing of the "pincers" should advance on and seize the Mezieres-Sedan complex. Considering the difficulties Foch had just experienced getting Haig to attack, he was most happy to accept this new offensive projection for early victory proposed by Haig.[25] To what extent Haig's proposal and Foch's subsequent decisions were based upon a desire to reduce the significance of the American role in the climactic campaign can only be surmised. However, the attitude and actions of both the Allies toward the formation of an American Army is consistent with such a supposition. The knowledgeable persons including European authors with whom I discussed this issue were nearly unanimous in their disagreement with Allied plans for the piecemeal employment of American forces. As to the political-military motives of the Allies, the following comment by James Stokesbury of Acadia University, author of the text, *A Short History of World War I,* is typical of the responses I received:

> One of the few things Lloyd George and Haig and to a lesser extent, Clemenceau and Foch, agreed upon was that they didn't want too intrusive an American participation in the war. . . . if the Americans fought . . . only as fresh blood for the British and French, that was going to give the Americans a lot less clout when it came to making peace terms.[26]

Some of the authors consulted in preparing this work excused or at least explained this Allied attitude by noting that the Allies had borne the brunt of a long war and that the Americans were new in this war.[27]

The major changes that had been made in the AEF mission tended to overshadow the upcoming attack on the St. Mihiel salient. Downgraded to a limited offensive by a total of fourteen divisions (only six of which would make the inital assault), the preparations for the attack continued amid a veritable whirlwind of planning and movement for the Meuse-Argonne offensive to follow.

As railway and motor transport became available, the necessary divisions and their supporting forces were shifted into position. Artillery pieces (numbering a total of 3000, half of them manned by Americans) had to be moved into support positions. Ammunition totalling 40,000 tons was moved into forward dumps. Telephone, telegraph, wireless (radio), and pigeon communications systems were installed. Railheads were established in nineteen locations to break out daily supplies to the combat units. As many as 2,000 French trucks assisted in moving the men and material, 2,000 hospital beds were provided. Engineers stocked material for 300 miles of railway reconstruction. Rock crushed for roadways was over 100,000 tons. Water plants were established at 120 locations able to disperse 1,200,000 gallons per day.[28]

The revised and final order for the St. Mihiel offensive directed an attack by I Corps (82nd, 90th, 5th, 2nd, and 78th Divisions) and IV Corps (89th, 42nd, 1st, and 3rd Divisions) against the south flank of the salient, with the objective of sealing off the salient from Vigneulles to Regneville. The attack was to proceed in four phases during a two-day period. The V Corps (26th, French 15th, and 4th Divisions) was to attack from the west face of the salient to link up with the southern attack along the line of Les Eparges–Vigneulles. The attack was to be conducted in two phases, linking up on the second day. The French II Colonial Corps (with three divisions around the southwest ring of the salient) was to advance after the American attacks had cleared the areas on the flanks. In First Army Reserve for the attack were the 35th and 91st Divisions.[29] (Overlaid on Map 2 is the American attack plan.)

The long period of preparation for this attack, the frequent moves and countermoves, and the apparent need for most staff officers at all echelons to see the area and coordinate their parts of the offensive tipped off the Germans well in advance. After considering a number of offensive and defensive alternatives, Ludendorff ordered withdrawal from the salient to the "Michel Stellung" defenses at the northern base of the salient—choosing that option in view of the Allied advances in Flanders and the tremendous American build-up.[30] Execution of the withdrawal began on 11 September; the American attack jumped off at 5 A.M. on 12 September. Preceded by an intensive four-hour barrage by 3000 artillery pieces and accompanied by 267 light tanks (under the command of Lieutenant Colonel George Patton), the infantry slogged forward in the rain. They struck and quickly overran the German rear guards. The attack came, according to General von Ledebur, chief of staff of Composite Army C, at "the most unfavorable moment imaginable." Detailed German plans for a phased withdrawal were scrapped, and their units were told to move quickly through the nearest escape routes.[31] A "combined aviation element" (American, French, British, Italian, and Portuguese) of fifteen hundred planes (six hundred under United States Colonel William "Billy" Mitchell) gained and maintained air superiority and supported the attack. Air and artillery interdicted enemy columns attempting to move north out of the pocket.[32] The advance was rapid and coordination was good. Most of the tanks fell victim to mechanical failure or ran out of fuel, but the infantry moved rapidly. Both American and Allied leaders had worried about the U.S. infantry crossing the barbed wire, because artillery had failed to cut gaps and "bangalore torpedos" (to blow the wire) and wire cutters were limited. Some of the troops used chicken wire to breach the obstacles. Others stepped on the wire and just walked over it. The French were amazed and claimed it was possible only because the Americans had big feet. Norman Roberts, of the 168th Infantry Regiment, recorded in his dairy:

> Day had not broke and you could hardly tell where to go. Bullets, millions of them, flying like raindrops. Rockets and flares in all directions. Shrapnel bursting and sending down its deadly iron. High explosives bursting on the ground and sending bricks, mud and iron. . . . A mad dash of 50 feet, then look for cover. A stop for a minute . . . Then another mad dash![32]

By nightfall of the first day, the converging southern and western divisions were only ten miles from juncture.[34]

The American secretary of war (Baker) visited the front on 13 September. That "pacifist" reported that he was "delighted" with the success of the attack. Pétain and Pershing visited the town of St. Mihiel. Pershing reported that the troops had behaved "splendidly." The action was a good present for him; it was his birthday—Pershing was fifty-eight.[35] During the first night, it was reported that German columns were streaming north through Vigneulles and Thiaucourt. Pershing directed the advance to continue all night. The 26th Division drove east, entering Vigneulles at 2 A.M. on the 13th. Soon after dawn, elements of the 1st Division linked up with the 26th from the south.[36] The salient was closed.

Field Order No. 10 from the First Army directed a continuation of the attack. On the morning of 13 September the attacking divisions moved northward, bringing all units on the line of the army objective that day.[37] During the night of 13–14 September, several counterattacks were repulsed; by the 16th, strong reconnaissance patrols were probing the Michel Stellung—a position that had been reinforced by four divisions. But reports of continuing withdrawals led Pershing to the conclusion that he could have broken through this portion of the Hindenburg Line. Major General Joseph Dickman, commander of the IV Corps during the operation and Brigadier General Douglas MacArthur of the 42nd Division argued that the Americans should have been allowed to go for Metz and could have taken it. However, Major General Hunter Liggett, one of the more astute military thinkers in the operation (commanding I Corps), later said, "the possibility of taking Metz . . . existed only on the supposition that our Army was a well coordinated machine, which it was not, as yet!"[38]

The operation ended. Congratulations came from all Allied offices and headquarters and from the president of the United States. Critics, however, point out that the enemy had presented no challenge. "The Americans," some said, "merely relieved the Germans."[39] Whatever the case, it is unarguable that two hundred square miles of territory had been returned to France, and a dangerous salient had been removed. Prisoners of war were taken, totalling 15,000; also captured were 450 artillery pieces. American casualties were about 7,000.[40] Major General Robert Bullard, commander of III Corps in the operation, admits that the gap was not closed quickly enough. Of the Germans in the salient, perhaps four-fifths escaped capture. Pershing apparently blamed V Corps for not having reacted swiftly enough to his orders to seal off the escape routes. Bullard adds:

> St. Mihiel was given an importance which posterity will not concede it. Germany had begun to withdraw. She had her weaker divisions, young men and old and Austro-Hungarians. The operation fell short of expectations.[41]

However, the engagement had been a good "shakedown" for part of the American forces. Unfortunately, the units that participated in the St. Mihiel offensive, the most experienced American divisions, would not be available for the start of the greatest effort to come—the attack in the Meuse-Argonne on 26 September 1918.

6

THE AEF ACCEPTS THE CHALLENGE: THE MEUSE-ARGONNE

The geography of the Meuse-Argonne sector (about eighteen miles east-west) is ideal for defense, deadly for the attacker. The area and the German defenses are depicted on Map 3. Facing the region (looking north from friendly lines running east to west from Regneville to Binarville), it is apparent that the area is divided by three dominating features: the heights of the Meuse along the east bank of the unfordable Meuse River, the hills of Montfaucon in the center, with approaches from east and west, and the rising terrain of the heavily wooded Argonne Forest, a plateau in the west of the zone. Moving back east from the Argonne Forest, the valley between the Argonne and Montfaucon is drained by the Aire River (fordable in a few places). The valley is narrow, dominated by the buttes of Vauquois and Montfaucon, and dissected farther north into a maze of ridges and valleys connecting with the Barrois Plateau. The valley east of Montfaucon is intersected by east-west parallel ridges and ravines running east to the river. The heights east of the Meuse River, running north-northwest along the east flank of the zone provide observation over the eastern half of the sector. The wooded hills offer a multitude of concealed locations for machine guns to lay flanking fire on any advance on a south-north axis. The low-lying areas are covered with thick brush varied with open spaces. During the fall rains, the low areas flood and the soil has poor trafficability. Montfaucon (Falcon Mountain) dominates the center of the zone.[1] Three hundred forty-two meters high, it constituted a visible obstacle against which French attacks failed in 1914 and 1915. It was a promontory from which the German crown prince directed the sanguinary assaults on Verdun in 1916. The watershed is the great hogback, the Barrois Plateau, which runs north-northwest from Montfaucon to Romagne, Cunel, and Stonne. This divides the sector in two, allowing crossfire into both valleys.

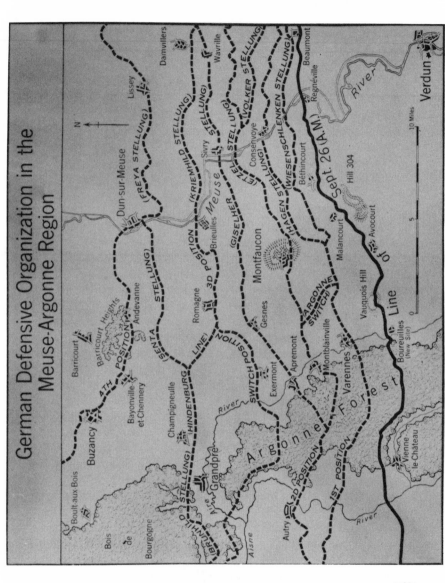

Map 3. German Defensive Organization in the Meuse-Argonne Region. (*From American Battle Monuments Commission, American Armies and Battlefields in Eu-*

The Germans had been building an interlocking network of defenses in this area for three years. They had constructed a defensive zone from the line of contact. Three east-west belts of fortifications, named after the witches of Wagnerian lore, crossed the zone: a lightly manned defensive position ran from the line of contact at Regneville on the Meuse west to Bethincourt, to Boureuilles and to Vienne-le-Chateau. Buttressed by pillboxes containing machine guns, it was crossed by cleared lanes, providing successive interlocking bands of fire across the front. Barbed wire entanglements ran along these fire lanes to impede attackers in the killing zones of machine gun crossfire. An intermediate defensive position (Hagen Stellung) ran from Bethancourt to Varennes.

Etzel-Giselher Stellungen. The first major belt of fortifications lay five kilometers behind the first battle positions. This defense line ran from just south of Sivry on the Meuse, west across Montfaucon, to Apremont, to Autry on the Aisne River. The Giselher line was on the high ground north of Montfaucon. Along these lines the defenses were stronger and more continuous. Pillboxes (some made of concrete) were connected by trenches; machine gun fire lanes covered a dense array of multiple barbed-wire fences laid along the "final protective lines" of these guns. Artillery and mortar barrages were registered in defiladed areas, and trench mortar positions were emplaced well forward. The stone houses in the towns contained defensive implacements.

Kriemhilde Stellung. The second belt was the main defensive position, six kilometers north of Montfaucon. The Kriemhilde line was the strongest series of concrete and bunkered emplacements, running from Brieulles on the Meuse west along the east-west rocky ridges of Romagne Heights, through Grandpre, and west through a break in the Argonne Forest. A switch position ran forward from Romagne to Exermont.

Freya Stellung. The last line of German defenses, lightly manned at the time of the offensive, was about eight kilometers north of Kriemhilde; this defensive array extended from just south of Dun-sur-Meuse west through the Barricourt-Buzancy Heights to north of Boult-aux-Bois in the Argonne.

These German defensive lines were continued east and west beyond the American sector. The defensive lines were closer in the Meuse-Argonne than elsewhere, on the front to provide maximum protection for the vital railroad line from Sedan to Metz—the rupture of which was one objective of the right wing of Foch's grand attack plan.[2] The defenses were considered impregnable by the Allies. Pershing allowed that "no Allied troops had the morale or aggressive spirit to overcome the difficulties to be met in that sector." Pétain thought the Americans would do well to take Mountfaucon before winter halted the fighting. Pershing expected to take Montfaucon the first day.[3]

Before the offensive could begin, a great deal of planning and a gargan-
tuan movement of men and material had to take place—moves and countermoves had to be made over inadequate road and rail nets in a very short
period of time. George Marshall described in terse and unemotional terms
the terrible task given him—to move and reorganize the bulk of the First
Army for a major offensive campaign in a mere two weeks. The campaign
was to be conducted in an area sixty miles north of the northern flank of
the same army that was just commencing its first independent offensive at
St. Mihiel. Marshall was apprised of this task on 8 September 1918 at a
meeting called by the Chief of Staff of First Army, Brigadier General Hugh
Drum. Drum announced that the army would launch an attack from the
Meuse to the Argonne Forest on 25 September; operations section was
preparing the attack order. Marshall would be responsible for the move of
all units from St. Mihiel to the Meuse-Argonne Front; Marshall's associate, Colonel Walter Grant, would plan and supervise the relief of the
French Second Army in the new position, and Colonel Monroe Kerth
would arrange for the billeting of the units and coordinate all the actions.
Drum then listed the divisions that would be in the first attacking echelon
for the Meuse-Argonne offensive, those to be in corps and army reserve,
and their supporting artillery. Running over the order quickly and check-
ing locations on a map, Marshall made the hasty judgment that some of
these units would have to begin redeploying from the St. Mihiel battle
zone on the same day that attack "jumped off." "This appalling proposition rather disturbed my equilibrium," he later wrote. The next few hours
he remembered as "the most trying mental ordeal" he experienced in the
war.[4]

Marshall's alert order for the movement of organizations from St. Mihiel
was considered by him to be the best piece of work he accomplished
during the war. Though simple and lacking in detail, it established a good
framework for conduct of an extremely complex and delicate redisposi-
tioning. Because of its importance to the success of the Meuse-Argonne
operation, it is reproduced, in part, below:

Subject: Release and readjustment of units following reduction of St.
Mihiel Salient.

1. The following information will serve as a guide to Army Corps
Commanders during the course of the pending operation. . . .

2. Plan of Readjustment
As soon as the advance has terminated, and assuming that a threat of a
heavy hostile counterattack does not exist, Corps Commanders will com-
mence the reduction of the number of divisions in line and regrouping of
the divisions so released. . . .

3. Units to be relieved

Organizations	Estimate Date for Relief		Relieving Organizations
	To Start	To be completed	
	(NIGHTS)		
58th F.A. Brig.	D plus 2/3	D plus 3/4 (a)	None
55th F.A. Brig.	D plus 2/3	D plus 3/4 (a)	None
82d Div.	D plus 2/3	D plus 3/4 (b)	French Div.
1st Corps. Hq. and Troops.	D plus 3/4	D plus 4/5 (b)	4th Corps Hq and Troops

Note: (a) To move by marching.
       (b) To move by bus and marching.[5]

Marshall and his assistants then worked out a similar plan for the nondivisional artillery, mostly French—three artillery brigades and sixty-eight separate artillery regiments—to be relieved of fire-support missions during St. Mihiel, moved, and then given new support tasks and locations. Both these movement schedules would have to be integrated with those of American logistical support and administrative units, and with French and Italian units moving out of the Meuse-Argonne area after relief by the American units. Three corps headquarters, fifteen divisions, and corps support and army troops had to displace forward. The totals involved were approximately 600,000 men moving in; 220,000 moving out. Also moving into the sector were 3,980 artillery guns and 90,000 horses; these moved in a steady stream, forwarding personnel, equipment, or a portion of the required 900,000 tons of ammunition and supplies.[6]

For secrecy, this huge agglomeration of men and materiel had to be moved only at night over three feeder railroads and three roads described as "farm roads." Considering that a division required 900 trucks to move its personnel and its towed light artillery (seventy-two guns) required fifteen kilometers of road space, some appreciation of the extent of the planning and coordinating effort can be gained. To obviate the problem of the different rates of speed of motor, animal, and foot transportation, Marshall programmed all motor vehicles on the best road, the southernmost, until the convoys turned north at Bar-le-Duc. To carry out the movement in the time allotted required that the road be filled with traffic all night.

Marshall's intelligence and decisiveness in planning this move have been praised by many. However, even Marshall knew that writing such an order is infinitely easier than executing it. The implementing movement orders were insufficiently detailed and poorly executed. Their execution immediately revealed their inadequacy. Marshall admits that the night of 15 September was a bedlam of traffic jams, breakdowns, misunderstandings, and changes in movement orders. Since transport had been routed on separate roads according to their rate of movement, unit integrity was destroyed, and control could not be exercised by the normal chain of command. High- and middle-ranking officers often demanded road priority, while the mixing of French and American columns brought language problems to the routing and sorting process.

Toward the end of the movement, tempers of all transport personnel grew "testy"; animals were worn out, and many of the moving troops were ill with the "flu." Motor breakdowns were numerous and traffic jams continued. With the considerable help of experienced French transport officers, Marshall and his associates were able to program and reprogram the movements so that all units reached their new assembly areas on schedule—according to Marshall's recollection.[7] Marshall's biographer, Forrest Pogue, states that Marshall has left a vivid record of the way in which he had to depend on overworked trucks and drivers, and, in some cases, horse-drawn vehicles.[8]

The assemblage of logistical and administrative elements for the Meuse-Argonne campaign, mostly part of the services of supply (SOS), was itself a complex linking of hundreds of agencies tied together by a fragile network of roads and rails. Ammunition depots were established at twenty-four locations to store and send forward 40,000 tons of ammunition per day (twelve trainloads of over 3,000 tons each). Railheads at nineteen points provided automatic resupply to the army; twelve ordnance depots issued and retrofitted weapons and equipment; nine gas and oil depots provided fuel; nine furnished quartermaster supplies (food and forage); twelve engineer supplies (bridging, road building materials, lumber); eight, water supplies; six, chemical warfare supplies; as well as smaller depots for signal and motor and tank supplies. Thirty-four evacuation hospitals were set up; 164 miles of light railway lines were constructed or rebuilt. Personnel replacement camps were built and freight regulating stations were expanded. Aviation gathered at forward fields. Of the 668,000 personnel assigned to the services of supply, 291,000 were engaged in direct logistical support of the First Army, including personnel of the three divisions used as laborers in the rear.[9]

On 22 September, Marshal Foch fixed the dates and confirmed the objectives of the general offensive for the Allied forces on the western front:

—26 September: A Franco-American attack between the Suippe and Meuse Rivers.

—27 September: An attack by the British First and Third Armies in the direction of Cambrai.

—28 September: An attack by the Flanders group of armies between the sea and the Lys River, under command of the Belgian King.

—29 September: An attack in the center of the Allied line by the British Fourth Army, supported by the French First Army, in the direction of Busigny.

Foch further explained his mission for the Franco-American attack as follows:

(1) The American First Army's attack was to be carried out between the Meuse River and the Argonne Forest in the general direction of Buzancy-Stonne.

(2) The French Fourth Army was to attack between the Aisne and the Suippe Rivers with their axis the Chalons-Mezieres road.

(3) A mixed Franco-American detachment was to maneuver on the right bank of the Aisne to ensure liaison between the French and American operations.

Close reading of Foch's directives indicates that the American attack, which commitment Foch had accepted only reluctantly, was in the nature of a supporting attack to that of the French Fourth Army, which had the mission of seizing Mezieres and clearing the line of the Aisne River. The mission of the American Army, which Foch had earlier given as seizing Mezieres, became the lesser strategic task of advancing on Buzancy-Stonne. This change of axis may have been an attempt to keep the American Army away from Sedan, a prize desired by the French to expiate their defeat there in the Franco-Prussian War. Pershing recognized this supporting role, for he later stated that the mission was to "draw the best German divisions to our own front and consume them."[10] The Meuse-Argonne offensive would, of course, assist the attack of the French Fourth Army on the Aisne by drawing German reserves east.

The American First Army Headquarters displaced to Souilly on 21 September 1918. At midnight 22 September, Pershing assumed responsibility for the area formerly held by the French Second Army, giving his command the entire sector from the Moselle River west to the juncture with the French Fourth Army on the west of the Argonne Forest. The First Army also assumed operational command of the French II Colonial Corps and XVII Corps, both corps, along with elements of the American III Corps, defending territory from the east bank of the Meuse to the Moselle. In planning the Meuse-Argonne offensive, the AEF staff assumed the ability to concentrate sixteen divisions with ten organic artillery brigades for the initial attack in the Meuse-Argonne area. The additional artillery would be provided by the French from elements relieved in the St. Mihiel area. Pershing approved the plan for a three-corps attack on the front between the Meuse River and including the Argonne Forest, with nine divisions in the initial assault. (The plan for the attack and the first phase of the attack are depicted on Map 4.)

The maneuver plan was for the I Corps (Liggett) to drive north along the Aire valley, clearing also the eastern portion of the Argonne Forest; the V Corps (George Cameron) was to advance on Montfaucon and seize that commanding terrain after bypassing it on both flanks. The III Corps (Bullard) on the right was to advance in sector. A major mission of the two flank corps was to assist the advance of V Corps by outflanking Montfaucon. Maneuver lines were drawn by the First Army as intermediate objective and control measures. The corps were to come abreast at the corps objective line running east-west north of Montfaucon, then to guide the advance of V Corps (along the high ground) to seize objectives on the army first phase line—from Brieulles (neary Ivoiry) west-northwest to and including Cunel and Romagne, then southwest to Apremont and to the boundary with the French Fourth Army near Binarville. Pershing desired the corps to reach the corps objective line in one day; the army first phase line the second day, a projected advance of ten miles. Further advances to link up with the French Fourth Army (at Grandpre) were to be directed as the battle progressed. Pershing was aware of the restrictive terrain and the extensive defenses which he planned to overcome in such a short time. However, he counted upon surprise to overwhelm the outnumbered defenders before reserve forces could be moved into the Meuse-Argonne to strengthen their positions. Apparently, Pershing also believed the reports of his staff that German morale and fighting capabilities were low. Although the American troops were relatively unskilled and inexperienced, General Pershing counted on their vigor and aggressiveness to compensate for these deficiencies.[11] His assessment was wrong in all respects.

Last minute visual reconnaissance of attack routes and objectives was made by Americans wearing French uniforms to ensure that the American presence would not be tipped to the enemy by this reconnoitering. Units were moved laterally and repositioned during the night of 25–26 September, causing much confusion in their approach to the line of contact. As the assault divisions moved into their attack positions, the remaining detachments of the French Second Army withdrew from the front. The American order of battle for the initial attack, from east to west, was:

> III Corps: 33rd, 80th, and 4th Divisions in line; 3rd Division in reserve.
>
> V Corps: 79th, 37th, and 91st Divisions in line; 32nd Division in reserve.

Plan of Attack of First Army, September 26, 1918

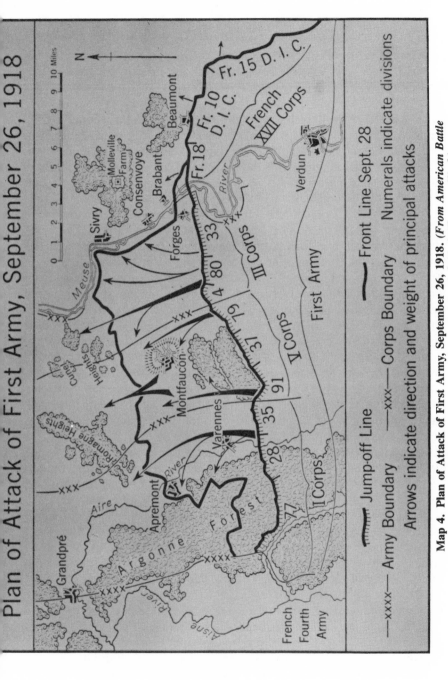

Map 4. Plan of Attack of First Army, September 26, 1918. *(From American Battle Monuments Commission, American Armies and Battlefields in Europe. Washington: GPO, 1938.)*

I Corps: 35th, 28th, and 77th Divisions in line; 92nd Division in reserve.

Army Reserve: 1st, 29th, and 82nd Divisions, placed in rear of the III, V, and I Corps respectively; French 5th Cavalry Division vicinity of Souilly.

A total of 2,775 artillery pieces (more than half of them manned by the French) were registered to support the attack. The density of artillery was one gun for eight meters of front. The French had supplied 189 light tanks to attack in coordination with the advance of the infantry; 142 of these tanks were manned by Americans. Fuel had been stockpiled in the forward area by the commander of the tankers, Lieutenant Colonel George Patton. Poised at support airfields were 821 aircraft, 604 of which were piloted by Americans.[12] The attacking infantry were armed, primarily, with the British Lee-Enfield rifle, which was believed to be a better weapon than the German Mauser rifle. But the Americans had little or no experience in active combat; only four of the divisions had had any front line duty. Over half of the troops were recent draftees; some had only received individual training; a few said they had never had the chance to fire their rifles.[13] As "H Hour" (the hour for the assault) approached, all of the one hundred thousand men in the first wave felt tension, as they crouched in the night, waiting for the order to move out. George Marshall recorded that the troops were tired from the exertions of the move forward; sickness (the flu) had spread through the ranks. Marshall expressed his empathy with Pershing, "as yet untried in the role of commander of a great combat army, accepting battle under most unfavorable circumstances—his reputation was decidedly in jeopardy."[14]

Arrayed in attack and support positions facing the Meuse-Argonne defenses was the greatest military force which America had ever sent into battle. The "yanks" had overwhelming superiority in fighting strength—on the order of eight to one, depending upon who and what is counted. They were far stronger in artillery, in aircraft, and in tanks—the Germans had no tanks in this campaign. The enemy, however, were in strong fortifications; the Argonne Forest was a maze of camouflaged, mutually supporting strong points. The front from Verdun to the Argonne Forest was the responsibility of German Army Group "von Gallwitz." Along this front were eighteen divisions, with twelve more in reserve, most of the reserve clustered around Metz. Five divisions were in defense between the Meuse and the Argonne under command of the German Fifth Army. It was estimated by AEF G-2 that the Germans could reinforce the front with four divisions the first day, two the second, and nine the third day.

The enemy troops were of poor quality; a large number were Saxons and Austro-Hungarians, who were of doubtful dedication to the German

cause. The enemy divisions were at one-third authorized strength. However, the command structure was effective, and the German high command had stressed the need for stubborn defense in Lorraine. The entire
German Army was at risk, the high command stated, if their southern
flank were turned. The intelligence estimate of von Gallwitz' headquarters
on 16 September 1918 concluded that a large-scale French and American
attack was due in the direction of Conflans (on the Woevre Plain). Other
estimates cited Metz as the purported ultimate objective.[15] Donald
Smythe, author of two texts on the life of General Pershing, has found
evidence that despite the secrecy of the movement of the AEF at night
into attack positions facing the Meuse-Argonne, the Germans divined U.S.
intentions, pulled some of their outposts back, and started reinforcements
toward the Meuse-Argonne area before the Americans launched their
attack. The British historian, Hubert Essame, in his text *The Battle for
Europe, 1918* (New York: Scribners, 1973), noted that the Germans were
prewarned, adding that the Germans learned of the planned American
attack in the Meuse-Argonne from French deserters. The German Commander, von Gallwitz, also told of the capture of a soldier from the U.S.
4th Division west of the Meuse, which gave him some indication that the
American attack was to be in that area.[16]

Pershing had, again, opted for a short artillery preparation—to achieve
surprise. Bullard described this preparation, observed from the infantry
attack positions:

At 2:30 A.M. September 26, silent blackness gave way to what one vivid
imagination described as the sound of the collision of a million express
trains. Besides the noise there was the feel of concussion, quivering
ground, livid skies—and that inevitable wait, while officers scanned
luminous watch faces, and engineers and sergeants gazed at compasses
with which, by dead-reckoning, they were to lead through a No Man's
Land where past shell fire and present fog obliterated landmarks.

On the other side of the line, von Gallwitz recorded that his windows
rattled at Montmedy, 25 miles away.[17]

At 5:30 A.M. the assault troops moved forward behind a rolling barrage
one hundred meters to their front. In a heavy fog mixed with cordite
smoke, accompanied by the incessant roar of artillery, the doughboys
climbed in and out of great shell holes, "bunching up" at the barbed wire;
someone cut some of the wire, some worked their way over and through it;
whistles sounded in the mist, and shouting. Then the enemy machine guns
opened up, and their artillery and trench mortars joined in firing heavy
defensive barrages. Crouched in their positions in the Argonne from La
Harazee east to Vauquois was the 1st Prussian Guards Division. Behind
them on the Kriemhilde Stellung were the 5th Prussian Guards, both good

units, but low in strength. The 117th and 7th Reserve Divisions east of
Montfaucon were reinforced by the 5th Bavarian Reserve, all rated as
"poor" units. But they were fighting tenaciously. Among the Americans,
cries went up for aidmen and litters. Some men in the assaulting units
became lost; others drifted into the low ground, where they gathered in
groups. But their spirit was up, and the pressure of those advancing from
behind pushed the line of contact forward. The initial German defenses
were quickly overrun—the enemy had manned these lightly and would
make his stand on the Etzel-Giseler Stellungen. The tanks supporting the
American attack came forward slowly, many breaking down a few hundred
meters into the attack. Control of the supporting artillery was poor because it was difficult to ascertain the exact locations of the attackers. The
artillery continued firing blindly their prearranged barrages. Some of the
infantry insisted their own artillery was firing into them.[18]

At 9:30 A.M., the sun broke through the mist—at the same time, some of
the American "mystique" evaporated too! Whenever the doughboys burst
into a patch of open terrain, they were hit by frontal and flanking fire from
hidden machine guns. The "green" troops moved fast until they hit the first
effective enemy fire; then, according to friendly and enemy observers,
they tended to "mill about," remaining in the killing zone, taking no action
to silence the fire.[19] This was, clearly, a failure in small unit leadership, and
in training. Another early observation: The Americans were not using
their grenades! Many had none; either they had failed to draw any or they
had dropped the ones they were issued. In the close-in fighting, they could
not see targets for direct rifle fire. They did not think either to lob grenades
at hidden machine gun nests or to call for supporting fire from their trench
mortars. Many had also neglected to don gas masks when gas shells
struck. Obviously, the lack of training, appropriate training, was paying off
the wrong way—in casualties.[20]

The initial situation reports from the attacking corps, received at 9:00
A.M. by First Army Headquarters, stated that all units were advancing
with light contact. Later reports—vague and uncertain as to locations of
forward elements—showed III Corps moving well on the right of the
advance; V Corps was held up in front of Montfaucon; I Corps, on the left,
was tangled in the heavy brush of the Argonne interlaced with concrete
bunkers and machine gun fire lanes.[21] By 12:30, First Army reported four
hundred prisoners had been taken. Allied planes had established air
superiority throughout the zone; they were strafing enemy positions and
directing artillery on deep targets. Tallies of twenty enemy planes and
three balloons were reported "shot down." The 2:30 P.M. AEF press
reports confirmed the air action, adding that enemy planes had been swept
from the skies.[22] On the ground, from east to west, the 33rd Division
(George Bell, Jr.), on the right of the III Corps, had swept through the Bois

de Forges against heavy enemy machine gun fire, and had turned half right to occupy a flanking position along the Meuse by 4:00 P.M.[23] The right flank brigade of the 80th Division (Adelbird Cronkhite) fought its way through strong machine gun defenses in the Bois Jure, clearing that woods by noon; the left of the division succeeded in capturing Hill 262 after an all-day fight.[24] The 4th Division (John Hines) took Septsarges early; its left advanced one mile beyond Montfaucon, on the low ground to the east, but, because of its exposed position, it was withdrawn to the forward limits of the rest of the division between Nantillois and Septsarges. III Corps had advanced about five miles the first day. The 4th Division repulsed three counterattacks during the afternoon.[25]

V Corps in the center was meeting the most resistance. The 79th Division (Joseph Kuhn) on the corps' right took Melancourt, but encountered heavy machine gun and artillery fire in the open ground before Montfaucon. They assaulted the mountain during the late afternoon and evening, but they were driven back by a hail of machine gun and artillery fire.[26] The 37th Division (Charles Farnsworth), in the center of the corps, drove through strong defenses in the Bois de Montfaucon, moving abreast of the mountain on the low ground to the west. The division established positions just south of Ivoiry.[27] The 91st Division (William Johnson) advanced rapidly against strong initial resistance and took Epinonville in the late morning; it was driven out by immediate counterattack and fire, turned left, and occupied Very.[28]

I Corps (on the left of the army) made good progress, except on their left. The 35th Division (Peter Traub) captured Vauquois and Cheppy against strong resistance. Some elements got to the corps objective line (east of Charpentry) but were withdrawn to divisional positions west of Very. The left brigade of the 35th Division was held up between Varennes and Cheppy. A further attack carried it to the high ground south of Charpentry.[29] The 28th Division (Charles Muir) took the western half of Varennes and moved a mile north. The left brigade of the division was unable to overcome intense machine-gun fire down the eastern spurs of the Argonne from the vicinity of Champ Mahaut.[30] The 77th Division (Robert Alexander), on the left of the corps and army, made small progress (about one mile) against strong, well-sited positions in the Argonne Forest during the first day.[31]

A detailed review of the battle for Montfaucon is instructive.[32] This was the most critical attack along the entire line for the First Army. It involved the highest, most defended peak, which provided observation over most of the First Army's zone. Nevertheless, it was assumed by First Army planners that Montfaucon would fall more easily than would the associated woods on its flanks. First Army assigned the mission for this critical assault to the V Corps. The First Army order directed: V Corps will attack

Bois de Montfaucon

Bois de Cuisy

Cuisy-Montfaucon Road

German defenders' view of the sector of the U.S. 80th Division, looking west-southwest from the heights of the Meuse vicinity of Harremont. (*American Battle Monuments Commission, Terrain Studies, Meuse-Argonne. Washington: Battle Monuments Commission, n.d. Reproduced with permission of U.S. Army Military* on the front, Melancourt including Vauquois. This included Montfaucon, but not by direct statement. III Corps, on the right of the Army line, was to drive through its sector outflanking Montfaucon from the east by its advance. To the left of the 79th Division was the 37th Infantry Division, which was to make small advances on the west of Montfaucon. Both the 79th and the 37th were totally "green" divisions, never having been in significant combat before.

The 79th Division was an unfortunate choice for this critical mission. Composed of draftees from Maryland and the District of Columbia, it was one of the National Army divisions that had been depleted by two personnel levies to fill other divisions going overseas. Fifty percent of its personnel had been assigned since 25 May 1918, the date when the unit was alerted for overseas shipment. A War Department inspector had visited the division in its training camp at Camp Meade and had recommended that its personnel receive more training before going overseas. Before the publication of the inspector's report, the unit was on its way overseas. Arriving in France in July 1918, the division had moved into a training site that had insufficient water. They were moved to another area, began training, then nearly all their senior officers were transferred; they were assigned new officers late in their training. The 79th was placed in a quiet defensive sector behind the front in Lorraine. There they conducted some individual and small-unit training. AEF headquarters judged them to be well trained.

While the fighting was going on at St. Mihiel, they were among the divisions that were moved quickly into position on the Meuse-Argonne front. Their artillery remained in their training area in Lorraine; they were given the artillery of another division, which joined them in their attack position. Their frontage was changed twice, as the organizations were poised for the Meuse-Argonne attack; it was not until nearly midnight some five hours before the attack, that they were finally able to halt, dig in, and reorganize in the mud. Some of the troops had never fired their individual weapons. Former Private Robert Hoffman, who served in Company E, 315th Infantry Regiment, 79th Division during this campaign, said his training before being sent into combat was poor; it involved primitive tactics and poor equipment.[33] Most of the soldiers did not know their commanders, above the immediate leaders in their squads or platoons. This "green" and ill-organized unit had been given the major task of the attack—capturing the notorious Butte des Montfaucon, with its twin strong points heavily fortified and protected. Also, the town of Montfaucon on the immediate left of the highest peak, from which the crown prince had directed the attack on Verdun two years before, and the Bois de Tuilerie on the right of the second peak, high against the skyline, were

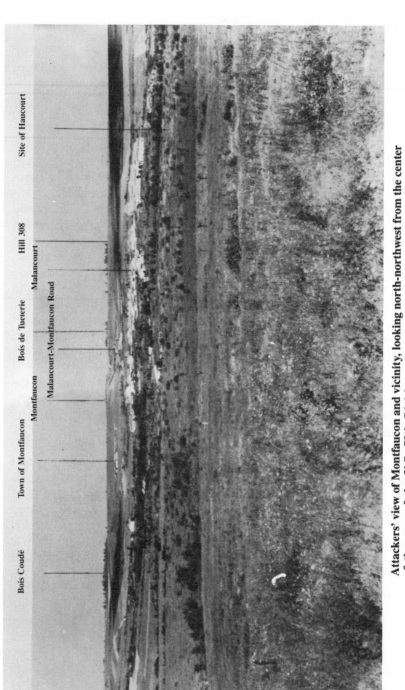

Bois Coudé   Town of Montfaucon   Bois de Tueterie   Hill 308   Site of Haucourt

Montfaucon   Malancourt

Malancourt-Montfaucon Road

Attackers' view of Montfaucon and vicinity, looking north-northwest from the center of the area of the U.S. 79th Division. (*American Battle Monuments Commission, Terrain Studies, Meuse-Argonne. Washington: Battle Monuments Commission, n.d. Reproduced with permission of U.S. Army Military History Institute, Carlisle Barracks, Pennsylvania.*)

both fortified and defended. There were open fields in front of all these promontories, "zeroed in" by machine gun, artillery, and mortar fire.

Major General Joseph Kuhn, commander of the 79th, was a regular army officer well respected in the AEF. His plan was to attack with his 157th Brigade leading the assault, followed by the 158th moving in support and acting as reserve. The 157th moved out on the attack at 5:30 A.M. on 26 September, with the 313th Infantry Regiment on the left and the 314th Infantry Regiment on the right.

At seven in the morning, the telephone line between the 79th Division Headquarters and the 157th Brigade went out; all communication with the brigade was lost until about noon. Immediately, the 157th Brigade lost contact with its 314th Infantry Regiment and was only able to maintain contact with the 313th by moving the brigade's command post forward behind that unit. Twenty thousand men were moving in an area approximately one-and-a-half miles wide in heavy fog and smoke through barbed wire and shell holes, over ground pockmarked and shattered by former years of fighting. On the left, the 313th moved initially without significant resistance. Colonel Sweezey, the regimental commander, reported to brigade headquarters at 8:30 A.M. that everything was progressing well, with no fire from the enemy. The smoke that was being fired in support of the movement caused some of the troopers to shout "gas," and there was some delay while gas masks were adjusted; then the "all clear" order was given. The line moved forward again. The 313th overran the first enemy position with comparative ease and entered the Bois de Melancourt within their sector without serious fighting. By eight o'clock in the morning they had come out in the open in the Golfe de Montfaucon, with the menacing slopes of Hill 282 looking down upon the attackers. From these heights, the Germans opened up with heavy machine gun fire. The artillery loaned to the 79th had been scheduled to provide a rolling barrage ahead of the infantry; now, it moved fast and fired far ahead of the attackers. Communications could not be established with the artillery to slow its rolling barrage. Without artillery support, struggling through mud, barbed wire, shell holes, deep trenches, around fallen trees, pools of water, the boys from Baltimore climbed the slopes of Hill 282 and seized the position; but it took five hours, and their losses were heavy.[34]

Enemy artillery had by now become very accurate; machine gun fire from the heights and the Bois de Cuisy was taking its toll. The 158th Brigade, following the assault, was pressing forward into the ranks of the 313th Infantry Regiment and there was a mix of troops, commanders, equipment, wounded, and supply parties. The supporting light artillery was ordered forward by division headquarters, but it became mired in the mud off of the north-south road and was unable to continue moving to support the advance. Unsupported, the 313th, leading the entire attack, fought its way into the Bois de Cuisy and was able to drive the enemy almost entirely from the position. Counterattacked, they were forced to dig in and reorganize as they attempted to "mop up" the enemy in the woods. Higher headquarters informed the 79th that a German counter-attack from Ivoiry was driving back the 37th Division on the left of the 313th, and that they should be prepared for heavy counterattacks. Colonel Sweezey determined to hold the Bois de Cuisy at all costs.

On the right of the divisions sector, the 314th Infantry Regiment, out of touch with higher headquarters had continued to move forward almost without opposition, taking Haucourt and Melancourt by ten o'clock in the morning. As they moved up the slopes toward the high ground of Montfaucon north of Melancourt, they came under heavy automatic weapons fire and were pinned down in a hollow between two noses of land approximately one half mile north of Melancourt. The regiment dug in and called for artillery support. None came. Receiving neither support nor direction from the rear, the 314th dug in. Colonel Oury, their commander, decided to hold in position on the high ground north of Melancourt.[35]

The "chain of command" from the 79th Division to V Corps headquarters to First Army headquarters was not operating. There was very little information being sent back from the fighting positions and little direction or support from "on high." As is so often the case in such circumstances, the higher echelons tended to believe that all was going well. At 10:40 A.M., V Corps reported to First Army headquarters that the line of contact was "at the north edge of the Bois de Montfaucon, running from there in a northeasterly direction."[36] Such a line as drawn put the 79th Division far ahead of where it really was; in fact, it showed that they had taken Montfaucon. This location was easily believed, however, because the 4th Division on the right of the 79th had already moved beyond Cuisy and was moving on Septsarges, generally east of the Montfaucon heights. V Corps headquarters, in a surge of optimism, called the chief of staff of the 79th Division, advising him to be sure to report when the division reached the corps objective, which was many kilometers beyond Montfaucon. At 4:30 P.M., the army liaison officer at V Corps headquarters reported "Aviator reports our patrols entering Montfaucon." At 7:30 P.M., the V Corps Operations Report sent to First Army headquarters the information that the 79th Division was a kilometer north of Montfaucon; a later report from the corps stated, "The report of the capture of Montfaucon has been verified by aviation reports, balloon reports, and by statements of prisoners captured within a hundred yards of Montfaucon."[37] The daily communiqué from AEF Headquarters announced to the world that Montfaucon had been seized on 26 September 1918. But it wasn't so![38]

The only report that the 79th could have given on 26 September 1918 was that the division's men were dying on the slopes leading to the heights of Montfaucon. Colonel Sweezey of the 313th Infantry Regiment had been calling for artillery and tank support all afternoon. Colonel Oury of the 314th Infantry had been calling for artillery support all day. Both regiments were stalled by heavy enemy fire. The 314th finally overcame machine gun nests on the hill south of Cuisy by maneuvering the infantry without artillery support, without even the fires of the division's machine gun battalion or the one-pounder guns both designated for direct support of the 314th. By afternoon of the first day, the 4th Division on the right of the 79th had moved past Septsarges and was approaching the Bois de Septsarges, receiving only intermittent fire from the woods. On the left, of the 79th the 37th Division had moved swiftly through the woods of Melancourt and Montfaucon (the First Army attack plan had assumed a slow advance through those woods). The 37th under fire, was approaching the town of Cierges by nightfall. Directly south of Montfaucon, the enemy fire was thickest. With the help of some remnants of the 314th Infantry Regiment, the 313th, late in the day, had taken the right portion of the Bois de Cuisy.[39]

At about the same time, the word went out from First Army through V Corps to the 79th Division: You must take Montfaucon tonight. The 79th Division is holding up the whole army! Guidance such as this is of little help to hard-pressed commanders. Runners from division headquarters stumbled through shellfire and over obstacles to find the command post of the 157th Infantry Brigade and that of the 313th Infantry Regiment in front of Montfaucon. Under pressure of the army's orders, Colonel Sweezey of the 313th Infantry, in spite of previous failures, made preparations to advance out of the woods of the Bois de Cuisy against the slopes of Montfaucon after dark. He was advised that V Corps would support the advance with artillery fire upon the heights of Montfaucon. Supporting tanks were also moving up the valley to assist in the attack. It was nearly 8:00 P.M. before the tanks arrived. Artillery support could not be obtained, because communications were again interrupted. Nevertheless, despite all the confusion and lack of support, the 313th broke out of the Bois de Cuisy at 9:00 P.M., heading across the fire-swept draw toward the ruins of Montfaucon two kilometers to the north. Although they were concealed by the darkness, the leading troops were immediately engaged by heavy machine gun fire from the southern slopes of Montfaucon. These fires were joined by flanking fires on the advancing elements and by artillery raining down on them, adjusted by observers on the mountain. Under heavy fire, the tanks deserted the infantry and moved to the rear. Every "field grade" officer except the colonel himself was wounded. Casualties mounted quickly, as the fire appeared to come from all directions. The regiment, what was left of it, fell back and dug in again in the Bois de Cuisy. Montfaucon had not been taken. It had been a fight against pillboxes and machine gun nests; fighting had been at close range with grenades, rifles, and bayonets.[40]

On the right and left, the divisions flanking the 79th had moved considerably forward, at least abreast of the heights of Montfaucon. The 4th Division had gained a position east of Nantillois, well north of Montfaucon. They were halted and driven back by a storm of fire three kilometers ahead of the 79th. One of their elements had become lost and had actually moved up a ridge of Montfaucon, temporarily occupying a position in the Bois de Tuileries. Later commentators have stated that this action, if it had been reinforced, could have caused the fall of the heights the first day. Perhaps so, but the amount of fire received by the forward elements of the 4th Division ultimately forced it back to Septsarges.[41]

During the night of 26 September 1918, III Corps, on the right of the 79th, ordered the 8th Brigade of the 4th Division to move by night march through the position of its 7th Brigade (which was south of Nantillois) to attack north against the Cunel heights, seizing a position on the army first phase line. This was a bold move, which, if it had been properly executed, certainly would have turned the defenders out of their defenses on Montfaucon. The 79th Division, attempting to reorganize under fire from the major defenses of Montfaucon, received word that the 4th Division was going to send a brigade across its front that night to seize the high ground behind Montfaucon. This action would require delicate coordination to ensure that the supporting fires of the 79th Division did not engage the attacking troops of the 4th Division moving across their front. However, no such problem was actually to occur, for the 8th Brigade of the 4th Division got only as far as Cuisy, still far in the rear of the fighting organizations of the 79th and the 4th Division's own 7th Brigade—and, for some inexplicable reason, halted there until daylight, 27 September. Whether the anticipation of the movement by the 8th Brigade caused the 79th to remain in position for the remainder of the night can only be a matter of conjecture. Survivors, veterans of the 79th, say that anticipation of the movement of the 8th Brigade was the reason they did not take Montfaucon the first night. Postwar studies show that the enemy on Montfaucon, part of the 11th Grenadier Regiment, were actually planning to withdraw, but the absence of continued pressure during the first night of the American attack caused them to dig in and reinforce.[42]

Just before midnight on 26 September, V Corps sent word to the commander of the 79th Division: "Commander in Chief expects the 79th to advance to positions abreast the 4th Division in the vicinity of Nantillois." This would mean that the remnants of the 313th Infantry Regiment would have to gather their forces and take Montfaucon as soon as possible. The 314th, in intermittent communication with their brigade headquarters, was to be moved left to join the attack of the 313th. The division commander had only uncertain contact with the 158th Brigade in the rear of the moving units and was, for the most part, out of contact with the 157th Brigade in the lead. The commander of the 157th, Brigadier General William Nicholson, was maintaining his command post with the lead battalion of the 313th and had no knowledge where his other regiment, the 314th, actually was. Runners were scattering across the dark, battle-scarred landscape, attempting to establish contact and to relay orders. Nevertheless, a calm prevailed back at First Army headquarters that was exemplified by the following situation report:

> The enemy has been driven back on the whole front of attack. American First Army will continue its advance to the Army Objective; the V Corps will continue its advance at 5:30 o'clock this morning. Divisions will advance independent of each other to the Army First Phase Line, troops will be organized to resist counterattack and will be sent forward in exploitation.[43]

At approximately midnight on the 26 September, the commander of the 79th Division, Major General Kuhn, got in touch with the commander of the 158th Brigade, Brigadier General Evan Johnson. The 158th was ordered to move forward at once, to advance through and to the right of the 157th Brigade, and to establish contact with the 4th Division in the vicinity of Nantillois. The 158th Brigadier commander had the same problem as the others; his units were scattered throughout the dark battle area. The 316th Infantry of his brigade had swept to the west into the low ground between the hills west of Melancourt and had wound up in the rear of the 313th Infantry of the 157th Brigade. The 79th Division commander seemed to realize the disorganization of his troops, for he amended his orders to the 158th Brigade; they were now to move forward on the right of the division sector with the 315th Infantry Regiment (the only regiment which the brigade commander could contact), take command of the 314th Regiment of the 157th Brigade as the brigade advanced, then attack and take a position on the left flank of the 4th Division in the vicinity of Nantillois. Brigadier General Johnson made a valiant attempt to organize and move his forces, but by 6:00 A.M. of 27 September, they had not moved. He was relieved of his command![44]

The division commander then reorganized his two brigades; the two regiments on the left of his sector became part of the 157th Brigade, those on the right became part of the 158th Brigade. The division attack was executed that morning with two brigades abreast. The 313th on the left went up through the ridges and captured the town of Montfaucon and the ridge on the left of the mountain by 11:45 A.M., under heavy fire and with severe losses. They used their one-pound supporting gun to knock out enemy machine guns; they overcame nests of hard-fighting enemy troops with grenades and with bayonets. On their right, the 314th, somewhat in the rear of them, pushed along a ridge in the face of heavy fire and finally broke through the Bois de Tuilerie, coming abreast of the 313th about noon. German resistance weakened. Montfaucon was declared in the hands of the 79th by noon on 27 September 1918.[45]

Studies made of this attack by the inspector general of the AEF, and by the AEF operations staff, indicated that the 79th Division had achieved all that could have been expected of it under the unique pressures of enemy resistance, terrain, and weather. The division's attached light artillery had been too far to the rear to continue in support of the advancing forces during their surprisingly easy advance from their assembly positions. Once that artillery started to shift forward, it became stuck on the roads and trails and was, in effect, lost to the division for several days. The heavy artillery had been scheduled to fire a rolling barrage in support of the advancing infantry; but this schedule of movement was much too optimistic, and the artillery outran its infantry, who were moving slowly forward against heavy opposition. Communications between the infantry and artillery were, as we have seen, sporadic to nonexistent. The roads in the rear of the 79th Division, indeed, in the rear of the entire First Army, were so badly blocked by vehicles and by the collapse of the roadbed that it took twenty-four hours for anyone to move approximately ten kilometers. Pioneer engineer troops and other units in the vicinity of the roads were directed to assist in hauling rocks from the fields to attempt to establish a roadbed. The entire division special staff, including the two judge advocates (lawyers), the maintenance officer, and the division's ammunition officer, were pressed into service directing traffic; they did a miraculous job untangling the terrible traffic jams. The AEF inspector general's report concludes:

> Considering the fact that this was the first time under fire for some divisions, and that none had received prior training considered necessary, these operations were very creditable to all concerned.[46]

The fact remains that a green division was given the main offensive mission on the entire Army front; it was given inadequate support by an artillery organization that was unfamiliar with its operations; it was out of contact with headquarters and relatively unsupported during its operation; it was given little aid by V Corps and the First Army; and it was literally driven forward by "guts" and determination. The employment of the 79th may be a grand story for military history, but it does no credit to the commander of First Army in the Meuse-Argonne campaign.

Along the First Army front during the first night of the attack, divisions and corps reported a total of approximately 950 prisoners of war (POWs) taken. However, the army report for the same period lists five thousand POWs and fifty guns captured. Heavy casualties were reported by the 35th, 79th, 4th, and 80th Divisions. Others reported light casualties or gave no casualty reports. Situation reports from the divisions were poor in content throughout. All corps reported increasing resistance as the Kriemhilde Stellung was approached. All reported supply and evacuation problems and increasing traffic congestion in their rear. Unit locations were reported and corrected frequently during the night of 26 September.[47]

In his book, *My Experiences in the World War,* Pershing stated that the initial advance had been relatively rapid. The First Army had outgained the French Fourth Army on their left. The forward defenses had been lightly manned; the Germans were obviously not fully prepared for an attack in the Meuse-Argonne sector. The German commanders agreed with Pershing's judgment. They were strong on the Aisne, expecting the attack there because of the long French artillery preparation.[48] Enemy fire from the Argonne Forest had delayed the American advance in the west of the army sector, and from Montfaucon in the center. German artillery fire directed from the heights of the Meuse (on the east of the river) was effective, but it had not developed the volume and accuracy it later attained. General Bullard, commander of III Corps (speaking also for Liggett of I Corps), later said the flanks corps should not have been required to wait on the corps objective line for the V Corps to come abreast. Pershing and his corps commanders have also been criticized for not having committed a reserve division to take Montfaucon from a flank when the center corps was held up.[49] Both criticisms have some validity. But allowing the flank corps to get too far forward of a strong defensive position such as Montfaucon might subject the forward elements to the risk of isolation and defeat, especially as German reserves were reinforcing defenses along the ridges running toward Montfaucon.

As to the propriety of committing a reserve, Pershing already had approximately 140,000 men struggling in an area of about seventy square miles. The few roads and trails into "no man's land" were jammed with human, animal, and vehicular traffic. Communications with moving units was almost nil. Situation reports were few and highly inaccurate.

In the quiet of my library almost sixty-eight years after the battle, with faded maps spread all over the room, I, acting as Pershing at Souilly, would remove the limits on advance, and would direct the corps commanders to reinforce their forward elements to outflank resistance. But, reading Liggett's description of his lack of information and control: "100,000 men were trying to kill each other within clear vision of a normal eye, and yet, as came often to be the case in this war, we couldn't see a single living person." And Bullard's: "At headquarters, all dumb, blind, deaf. Even I, a corps commander, was told nothing." Reviewing this stage of the fighting, Essame said, "The fog of war had come down like a blanket."[50] If I were in command on that confused battlefield that September day, I probably would have taken no action—waiting until the situation cleared.

It rained the night of 26 September 1918, and it was raining hard when the troops moved forward again the next morning. The doughboys ran into immediate fire from the German main defenses along the Kriemhilde Stellung. The Germans were reinforcing their lines, although heavy U.S. and Allied artillery fire was interdicting the forward movement of some of their reserves. When the attack commenced, General von Owen, commanding Group Meuse West, ordered the 5th Bavarian Division apportioned behind the 117th Division near Melancourt, and the bulk of the 7th Reserve Division to the Nantillois area. On the 26 September, von Gallwitz ordered the 115th Division to move west, while the German supreme command, directed the 236th Division toward Dun and ordered their 28th Division to march northwestward from the Moselle Region. These units were supposed to close into the Meuse-Argonne area before nightfall on the 26th; they arrived, however, on 27 September. On the same day, elements of the 37th German Division moved west across the Meuse and counterattacked at Ivoiry.[51]

After the American 79th Division, as hard-pressed by the chain of command as by the enemy, captured Montfaucon on the 27th, the 4th Division captured Nantillois, but was driven out by counterattacks. That town was retaken by the 4th Division on 28 September with the assistance of the 79th Division. The 4th moved on to seize the Bois de Brieulles; it fought in and lost the Bois des Ogons.[52] The American 37th Division advanced west of Montfaucon on 27 September but was driven back by heavy artillery fire. On 28 September, it crossed the Cierges-Nantillois road and attacked Cierges, but was again driven back.[53] The 91st Division fought through Epinonville to Eclisfontaine, but it could not hold those towns. On 28 September Epinonville fell and the Bois de Cierges was taken in hard fighting. Two attacks from the Bois de Cierges on the 28 and 29 September were forced back, but on 30 September, the 91st Division took Gesnes, with heavy losses. The American 37th Division was unable to advance and form on the right of the 91st, and the 91st had to withdraw to the forward positions of the rest of V Corps.[54]

In the I Corps zone, the 35th Division on the corp's right, took Charpentry on 27 September, suffering heavy casualties. The next day, it took Montrebeau Woods and reached Exermont on 29 September; but a strong counterattack drove the division south of Montrebeau Woods.[55] The American 28th Division made headway in the east of the Argonne Forest, capturing Montbainville on 27 September and Apremont on 28 September, against strong defenses and counterattacks.[56] The 77th Division in the

Argonne crawled forward another mile by 29 September, against strong, hidden defenses. Casualties were high, especially in the 35th and 79th Divisions. The Germans later reported that they had trapped both of these divisions in the open. Firing artillery directly into the ranks of Americans and raking them with machine gun crossfire, the Germans reported that their "enemy" streamed to the rear out of control. Smythe stated that the 35th Division's organization had dissolved into chaos by 29 September.[57] By this time the Germans had moved six additional divisions into First Army's area, and had placed five more in local reserve. The defenses stiffened all along the line and counterattacks were strong. Front line and rear areas of First Army were saturated with gas. The Germans were ordered to hold their Argonne positions at all costs. Casualties were high in all U.S. divisions: the American offensive had run out of steam.[58] Reluctantly, on 29 September, Pershing accepted the need to go over to the defensive temporarily—to reorganize and to bring his experienced divisions from St. Mihiel into the line.[59] The location of the First Army's line on 30 September was approximately along the corps objective line, shown as front line 28 September on Map 4.

Rain continued to fall, and the roads and trails through no man's land turned into quagmires. Craters and shellholes from earlier fighting had limited the capacity of these routes at the beginning of the offensive; by this time they were virtually impassable. Long lines of traffic were stalled for days. Wounded could not be evacuated; food and ammunition could not get forward. Smythe stated that by 29 September, First Army "was dead in its tracks." He cited Sir Frederick Maurice's conclusion that the Americans had created the worst traffic jam of the war.[60]

Overworked engineers struggled to shore up the roadbeds with any solid material they could find. Reserve units, headquarters personnel, and even malingerers drifting to the rear were pressed into service to move the traffic and shore up the roadway. By the evening of 28 September, all artillery had been shifted forward. Divisions continued to report communication and supply problems through the end of the month. Many units were without food for days. Tank strength had been reduced to one third by breakdowns and by accurate enemy artillery fire. Front-line units conducted local attacks, repulsed counter-attacks on 29 and 30 September, and improved their defensive positions. Relief of the most depleted divisions by "veteran divisions" began on 30 September. The 1st Division (Charles Summerall) relieved the 35th Division in I Corps. The 32nd Division (William Haan) relieved the 37th Division; the 3rd Division (Beaumont Buck) relieved the 79th Division on 1 October 1918, and the 91st Division was withdrawn to corps reserve—a complete change of front-line units in V Corps.[61] Despite the continuing bad weather, and resulting from herculean efforts by engineers and logistic units, supplies were stockpiled forward, and personnel replacements were moved to understrength divisions. Positions were improved, units reorganized, patrols sent forward—and the men gained some badly needed rest. The AEF had undergone its "baptism of fire." It had met the challenge of the Meuse-Argonne and advanced. Badly mauled and mired in the mud in front of the main German defenses, the Kriemhilde Stellung, it was hardly a victorious army.[62]

7

THE TEST OF BATTLE:
FIGHTING THROUGH TO VICTORY

When the offensive was halted, units began refitting and reorganizing. General Pershing and his staff analyzed the deficiencies of First Army, as these had been revealed in the offensive thus far, and they set about correcting them. It was apparent that the infantry unit leaders were inadequately trained and not sufficiently motivated to continue to press an attack against strong defenses. Fred Ross, who served as a sergeant in Company I, 317th Infantry Regiment, 80th Division, stated that his company's officers were former sergeants who knew nothing but drill; German fire cut the unit to pieces, while the officers did nothing. Sergeant Stephen Murphy, Company B, 307th Infantry Regiment, 77th Division, noted that his company officers were learning the hard way, by making mistakes and getting men killed.[1] "The gaining of objectives, for the present, does not seem possible without undue casualties," stated an AEF report on 29 September 1918. The AEF Headquarters was, it seemed, beginning to appreciate the effectiveness of well-directed defensive fire, especially from the machine gun. Hubert Essame called the Kriemhilde line the most difficult sector on the whole front, excepting Ypres.[2]

Communications between major organizations and with the French had been poor, as had fire-support coordination at all levels. Units were not digging in immediately after taking their objectives, leaving them vulnerable to counterattacks. The Americans had taken heavy casualties from enemy gas, but they had not used gas intensively. The deteriorating health of the troops was of growing concern; the number of influenza cases grew each week (sixteen thousand new cases during the week ending 5 October 1918).[3]

The personnel replacement picture was bad. The War Department had included in its breakout of the "Eighty-Division Program" divisions to be used as replacement and depot units, while the AEF was working on an eighty-division combat force—therefore, the personnel requirement schedules of the two headquarters were different. The War Department also used a lower figure than the AEF for the number of support personnel required in relation to combat personnel. In any case, the War Department was unable to fill its own personnel shipping quotas, even though these were lower than those requested by the AEF. Furthermore, losses through combat and disease were higher than projected. The AEF had to break up two newly arrived divisions in September 1918 to supply replacements. The authorized strength of the rifle company was reduced from 250 to 175 men; some divisions needing rest and refitting were retained in the line.[4]

Meanwhile, Pershing and his staff conducted a furious schedule of visits and inspections and published correctional directives.[5] Pershing continued to relieve commanders who were not able to tolerate the physical and emotional strains of combat. Allied criticisms of the conduct of the offensive thus far hit Pershing at the same time as the German fire slackened. Mood of the senior Allied commanders reflected an "I told you so" attitude. Premier Clemenceau visited Pershing on 29 September and insisted on visiting Montfaucon. Moving forward despite Pershing's admonitions, he became enmeshed in a gigantic traffic jam on the road to Montfaucon (the 1st Division was relieving the 35th). Returning to Paris without completing his visit, Clemenceau told Foch that the American attack had stalled and the AEF was in "complete chaos." He demanded that Foch relieve Pershing. Foch stated, "The Americans have got to learn sometime. They are learning now, rapidly."[6] Despite repeated demands from Clemenceau over the next few weeks, Foch did not relieve Pershing; however, he did take action to goad Pershing forward. On 30 September, he sent Major General Weygand (his chief of staff) to Pershing to announce his intention to "allocate" the American I Corps to the French Second Army, which would be injected between the American First Army and the French Fourth Army to operate through the Argonne. Pershing would command the remainder of the American Army to the west and east of the Meuse. Pershing reacted with hostility to this change, and he convinced Weygand to withdraw the proposal. Foch got his point across, however, in a letter to Pershing on 2 October 1918, in which he stated:

> Amending what I wrote you September 30, I agree to maintaining the present organization of command, as you propose, under the condition that your attacks start without delay and that, once begun, they be continued without any interruptions such as those which have just arisen.

Foch's reasoning behind this proposition may have been more devious than it appears to be on the surface. Marshal Haig, whose troops had broken through the Hindenburg Line in the north, criticized the slowness of the American advance and that of the French on the Aisne. The British and the French had long been suspicious, each that the other was trying to hold down its own casualties, at the other's expense. In attempting to assign I Corps to the French Second Army, Foch was likely trying again to infuse American strength into the French drive to increase their advance by adding American reinforcements. During this period, Lloyd George had also importuned Secretary of War Baker to let him retain the American troops that had been sent to the BEF for training. The historian Cyril Falls, in his text, *The Great War, 1914–1918* (New York: G. P. Putnam's Sons, 1959) added to his review of problems of the AEF at the end of September the offsetting note that Anglo-Belgian forces in Flanders had halted at the same time for the same reasons.[8]

Criticism of the AEF's rear-area services was also coming from the fighting divisions. Sergeant Major Harold Craig of the G-2 office of the 79th Division admitted he had better living conditions than the men in the attacking echelons. Still, he complained of the food: "Beans and slum [stew] for the 119th time." He also stated that the traffic jams on the roads were unimaginable; it took five hours to move five miles along the roads, he estimated.[9]

Criticism of the logistical tangles in the services of supply and all the way forward along the line of communications had reached Washington. Pershing blamed the War Department for having failed to provide horses and trucks in the amounts programmed. The War Department criticized Pershing's management and began, again, to propose the reorganization of the services of supply. The French were demanding the return of their truck trains, on which the AEF depended for survival. To ensure that Secretary of War Baker understood the AEF's perspective on the problem, Pershing sent Major General Harbord (the commander of the services of supply) to talk to Baker, who was then in Paris. Baker promised to expedite the shipment of transport. Meanwhile, roads and trails had been made "passable" for the twenty-five thousand tons of supplies which had to be moved daily across "no man's land" in the Meuse-Argonne.[10]

The German strength facing the Americans from the Moselle to the Argonne (as estimated by AEF G–2 on 4 October 1918) increased to twenty-three divisions in line and in local reserve. In the next week, this strength increased to twenty-seven divisions, with eleven between the Meuse and the Argonne. Many of these divisions were very low in strength. Orders from their supreme command were to defend "until the last man."[11]

The Order of Battle for the Resumption of First Army's attack was, from east to west:

—III Corps (Bullard) on the right: 33rd Division (Bell), 4th Division

(Hines), and 80th Division (Cronkhite) in assault, with no reserve designated.

—V Corps (Cameron) in the center: 3rd Division (Buck) and the 32nd (Haan) in assault; the 42nd (Menoher) and the 91st (Johnson) Divisions in reserve.

—I Corps (Liggett) on the left: 1st Division (Summerall), the 28th Division (Muir), and the 77th Division (Alexander) in assault; the 82nd (George Duncan) and the French 5th Cavalry Divisions in reserve.

—Army Reserve: 29th Division (Charles Morton), 35th Division (Traub), and the 92nd Division (Charles Ballou).[12]

The relative strengths of the units in contact between the Meuse and the Argonne totaled about nine Americans to one German, according to some accounts. The Germans, however, were less vulnerable in hidden, strong defenses; they were making maximum use of preregistered machine gun and artillery fire, including heavy use of poison gas. The Americans, with about two hundred thousand men pressing forward in an area of restricted terrain a mere twelve miles wide, were counting on manpower to overcome the German defenses. The author David Kennedy, who wrote *Over Here,* a text on the attitudes of U.S. and Allied personages, says:

> The AEF had an immense numerical superiority over the Germans in the Meuse-Argonne, and made most of its advances simply by smothering the enemy with flesh. One American commander estimated that ten of his men perished for every dead German.[13]

Such a trade-off—bodies for bullets—was certainly not intended, but the restrictiveness of the terrain, the quality of the defenses, and the poor training of the massed attacking forces brought about that result.

On 4 October, the First Army resumed its offensive—with rested troops, and wiser, somewhat more experienced leaders. These attacks were being made against the main German defenses of the Kriemhilde Stellung. Key positions in this defensive complex were the heights of Cunel in III Corps' zone, Romagne (including the Cote Dame Marie) in V Corps' sector, and Hill 272, St. Juvin, and the Argonne Ridges in I Corps' zone. (See Map 5.) These defenses were supported by interlocking direct fires and observed artillery fire from flanking promontories and from the heights east of the Meuse. Pershing instructed his corps commanders to keep smoke on the high "observation points," and to maneuver so as to avoid flanking fire. III Corps and V Corps, acting in concert, were to seize both the Cunel heights and those on the east of Romagne. Pershing specified that their main effort should be concentrated on the western approaches to Cunel to avoid the galling fire from the heights of the Meuse. Elements of V Corps and I Corps were to take the Romagne

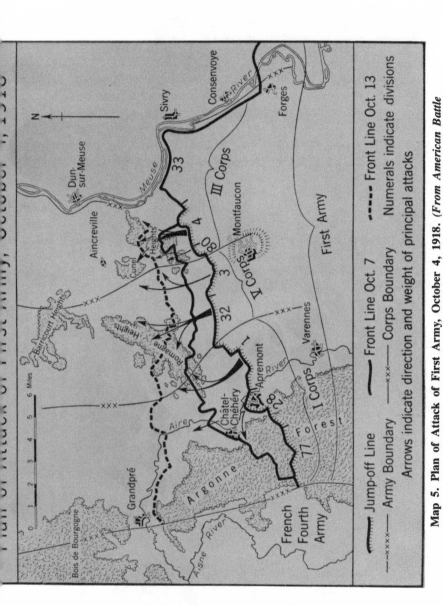

Map 5. **Plan of Attack of First Army, October 4, 1918.** *(From American Battle Monuments Commission. American Armies and Battlefields in Europe. Washington: GPO, 1938.)*

Bois de Chaume	Route Natl. 64	Meuse River	Bois de Consenvoye	Consenvoye

The Heights of the Meuse, looking over the river northeast from positions of U.S. 33d Division north of Consenvoye. (*American Battle Monuments Commission, Terrain Studies, Meuse-Argonne. Washington: Battle Monuments Commission, n.d. Reproduced with permission of U.S. Army Military History Institute, Carlisle Barracks, Pennsylvania.*)

heights. I Corps was also directed to neutralize the artillery fire coming from the eastern flanks of the Argonne Forest by means of smoke and heavy counterbattery fire. Strong supporting fires were planned throughout the First Army's zone, using high explosives and gas shells.[14]

The infantry attack moved out at 5:30 A.M., 4 October 1918, and immediately made heavy contact with the enemy all along the front. In the center of the III Corps area, the 4th Division fought its way into the Bois du Fays southeast of Cunel, but only after three days of bitter fighting. Heavy and accurate artillery fire was delivered from the heights of the Meuse, American counterbattery fire was neither masking nor suppressing that enemy fire. The 4th Division's attempts to seize the Bois de Peut de Faux were unsuccessful; sharp counterattacks drove the division back to positions in the Bois du Fays, about one mile from their original line of departure.[15] The 80th Division on the left of the 4th gained and held a foothold in the Bois des Ogons south of Cunel against unusually heavy machine gun fire.[16] Both divisions reported that the enemy was entrenched in strong positions along the Cunel heights and that they could make no further headway.[17] In the V Corps' attack, the 3rd Division (Preston Brown), on the corps' right, made repeated sallies into the Bois de Cunel but was driven back, with little gain and heavy casualties.[18] The 32nd Division, on the left of the 3rd, advanced against Gesnes (south of center of Romagne Heights), with tanks clearing enemy from the low ground south of the town. Although they encountered strong resistance in the town and fire directed from Hill 265 and from the Romagne heights, the 32nd seized Gesnes on 5 October and held it.[19]

I Corps, attacking down the Aire Valley behind a rolling artillery barrage, made the greatest gains. Led by tanks, the 1st Division (on the corps' right) attacked Hill 240 (on the west of Romagne Heights) moving against frontal and flanking machine gun fire from the Argonne, from the hill, and from farms in the valley. Their attack was slowed by the enemy's accurate adjustment of artillery, including gas shells, on their moving elements. In two days, the 1st Division gained three miles and seized Hill 240 and Arietal Farm. The 28th Division, on the left of the 1st, captured Chatel Chehery. Their western brigade, however, could make no progress in the Argonne Forest.[20]

The 77th Division, on the corps' left, continued its grinding assault, day after day, in the gloomy Argonne Forest—the fighting characterized by small-unit attacks against well-dug-in machine gun emplacements.[21] Recruited from Yiddish, Polish, Italian, and Latin laborers from the East Side of New York City, the soldiers of the 77th were learning woodsmanship and soldiering the hard way. One man, caught malingering, complained, "I can't make the bullets go into this thing." Only 10 percent of the men knew how to use hand grenades. The morale of the division was low, casualties high.[22] On 2 October, several units of the 77th reached Charlevaux Creek, (approximately on the 7 October line in the forest) then fell back. The 1st Battalion, 308th Infantry Regiment, remained forward of the others and was surrounded by the Germans. (This became the "Lost Battalion" of later legend.) For several days, attempts by the 77th Division to link up with the battalion were thwarted, while the battalion fought off repeated enemy attacks. German guns "zeroed-in" on the battalion's perimeter, and American casualties quickly reduced the fighting strength of the unit to half of the 550 men in the unit. Runners sent to request support were captured. Ammunition and food ran out, and the water point was under fire.[23] Still, the commander, Major Whittlesey, refused the repeated demands of the Germans to surrender. Walking among his men, the major saw a soldier eating a chunk of black bread. "Where did you get that?" he asked. "Off one of the dead Boches; want some?" the soldier rejoined. "No," said Whittlesey, "you deserve it all." By messenger, he sent a plea: Men are suffering from hunger and exposure and the wounded are in very bad condition. Cannot support be sent at once? There was no reply. With his last pigeon, the major informed his headquarters: "Our artillery is dropping a barrage directly on us. For heaven's sake, stop it." Finally, the artillery ceased. After six days of fighting off the German attacks, the 77th broke through to the beleaguered battalion, their advance assisted by a flank attack by the 82d and 28th Divisions. Only 194 men of the "Lost Battalion" were able to walk to the rear, but they walked with pride.[24]

On 5 October, the Germans threw fresh troops into counterattacks all along the front. Front-line divisions reported close-in fighting, with many hand-to-hand engagements. Enemy planes were active over the front during the early hours every morning. Casualties were reported as "heavy" in all corps. The roads, however, had improved, as had the supply situation. Even the weather had improved; but in the valleys, the mud, which is the soldier's constant companion, clung to everything. New enemy units were identified, especially opposing the I Corps' advance. There were reports of German tanks with the counter-attacking forces in the Aire Valley; however, I have found no evidence that the Germans used tanks in the Meuse-Argonne. The tank was one new weapon whose effectiveness the Germans were late to recognize.

Remembering the fighting in the Meuse-Argonne, Brigadier General Edwin Randle said, "Junior officers, mostly, were courageous, and motivated by patriotism, but their training was poor for that kind of war. Some of the senior officers were poor. . . . Attack plans were mostly forward movements. Platoon and company commanders had little chance to maneuver their units."[25]

By the evening of 7 October 1918, the United States First Army held a

Binarville-Apremont Road   Terrain of Lost Battalion   Bois de la Buironne

Terrain of the Argonne Forest, looking north-northeast at the area where the "lost battalion" was surrounded. (*American Battle Monuments Commission, Terrain Studies, Meuse-Argonne. Washington: Battle Monuments Commission, n.d. Reproduced with permission of U.S. Army Military History Institute, Carlisle Barracks, Pennsylvania.*)

line shown on Map 6 from Bois de la Cote Lemont west through Bois du Fays, Gesnes, Hill 240, Fleville, southwest to Chatel Chehery, and through the Argonne.

It was time, past time, for Pershing, the large AEF staff, and the small First Army staff to examine, in detail, how they were meeting the German challenge. Despite Pershing's emphasis on "open field warfare," the attack plan had, thus far, been nothing more than a frontal assault on a fortified position. Was this operation an American Battle of the Somme? It's true that the casualties (approximately seventy-five thousand up to 6 October) were not as great as they had been on the Somme, but the uninspired tactics were the same as had prevailed during that earlier Allied debacle.[26] Fortunately, below army level, some lessons had been learned and some innovations developed. The "trooper" had learned not to pass a German machine gun nest whose personnel "appeared" to be dead. Too many of these dead men had "opened up" on our troops after they had passed. Private Wiley Goudy of Battery F, 314th Field Artillery Regiment, 8th Division, remembers running into booby traps placed in houses and on dead bodies.[27] The Americans were also becoming accustomed to using grenades on machine gun nests. More fire-and-movement was being used in the ravines and defiles to knock out barricaded emplacements. It became apparent also that much of the German direct and indirect fire was "unobserved." Machine guns and artillery were firing their "final protective fires," on order, as the Americans approached, without exposing their gunners and observers—the Americans were advancing into "blind fire." It was also concluded that many machine gun emplacements forward of the main positions were manned by well-trained, fatalistic veterans. Engaging these by fire and bypassing them was the best technique.[28] Corporal William Sibley, Company B, 109th Infantry Regiment, 28th Division, reported that his unit was told some of the German "sacrifice" gunners were chained to their machine guns.[29] The Americans were also learning that most of the enemy's defensive positions were mutually supported by the fires of other positions throughout the depth of the defenses.

Ludendorff was reinforcing in the Meuse-Argonne, even at the expense of his defenses in Flanders, where the Allied offensive had gained much more ground. It was apparent to the German high command that they must hold the line from Verdun to the Aisne in order to withdraw the bulk of their armies from positions to the north and the west. It was also apparent to Ludendorff that the end was fast approaching. American troops were landing in France at the rate of three hundred thousand per month, and he had no reserves of manpower to oppose these reinforcements. By the end of September, Ludendorff and Hindenburg both urged Germany's political leaders to request an armistice. On 6 October 1918, Prince Max von

Baden, the new German chancellor, cabled President Wilson requesting an armistice based on Wilson's "Fourteen Points."[30]

On the battlefield, artillery support was improving; but the artillery had failed in one major mission: to silence the galling fire from the ridges of the Argonne Forest and from the Meuse heights flanking the line of advance on both sides.[31] There are four ways to attenuate hostile fire from a promontory: mask it (with smoke); knock it out by counterbattery fire; bypass the area beyond the range of effective observation and fire; or attack the promontory itself. In the First Army's attack thus far, the first alternative to silence the enemy artillery had failed—as any private lying in the "beaten zone" of the German artillery fire, working, methodically, up and down the Aire Valley, could have told Pershing. To bypass the German observation points meant, for all practical purposes, to attack outside the Meuse-Argonne, for it would have been necessary to advance beyond the limits of visual observation from the two hill masses. Observation from the eastern heights of the Argonne only covered the Aire Valley; from the heights of the Meuse only the approaches to the Cunel heights were visible. The only bypass alternative for the AEF was sufficiently east of the heights of the Meuse to prevent both effective enemy observation and fire. Unfortunately, this alternative had not yet been considered. Pershing, in *My Experiences,* said that there was a contingency to attack the Heights of the Meuse as part of the initial attack plan. Apparently, this was not approved for execution; First Army attack orders through 4 October 1918 only required the divisions on the right of the army to protect the army's flank along the Meuse.[32] By 6 October 1918 it was apparent that in order to seize the Cunel-Romagne heights (the key positions of the Kriemhilde Stellung west of the Meuse), the defenses on heights east of the Meuse would have to be neutralized.

Pershing's directive for continuing the attack tasked the French XVII Corps along the Meuse River to assault and seize the heights of the Meuse, while the American corps of First Army drove forward from their line of contact in the Meuse-Argonne.[33] The XVII Corps, reinforced by the American 29th and 33rd Divisions (which attacked across the Meuse) stormed the heights on 8 October. They took Consenvoye and fought up the slopes of Richene Hill, but they were stopped just short of the high ground.[34] This attack was fiercely resisted, because the area was the hinge of the German defenses of their entire westward extension into France (the so-called Loan Bulge). I contend that this should have been Pershing's main attack—on the Meuse Heights, or farther to the east to flank the heights. It is possible that Pershing, in *My Experiences,* was reacting to postwar criticism of his concentration of force between the Meuse and the Argonne, for he went into some detail to explain the narrowness of the

Bois de Chenois   Canal   Meuse River   Bois de Bussy   Route Natl. 64   Hill 260

Heights of the Meuse

The Heights of the Meuse flanking the route of the attack of the U.S. 5th Division, looking over the Meuse east-northeast from Clery le Petit. *(American Battle Monuments Commission, Terrain Studies, Meuse-Argonne. Washington: Battle Monuments Commission, n.d. Reproduced with permission of U.S. Army Military History Institute,*

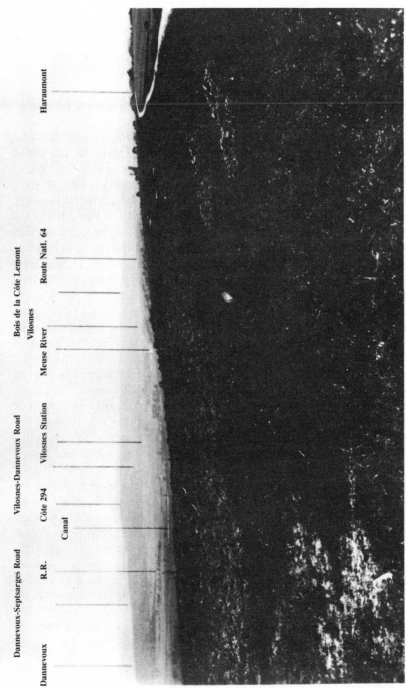

Dannevoux-Septsarges Road   Vilosnes-Dannevoux Road   Bois de la Côte Lemont

Dannevoux   R.R.   Côte 294   Vilosnes Station   Meuse River   Vilosnes   Route Natl. 64   Haraumont

Canal

German defenders' view of the center of the AEF's Sector, looking south from Montfaucon. (*American Battle Monuments Commission*, Terrain Studies, Meuse-Argonne, Washington: *Battle Monuments Commission, n.d. Reproduced with permission of U.S. Army Military History Institute, Carlisle Barracks, Pennsylvania.*)

ridges and the difficulty of access to the Heights of the Meuse. True, the heights were nearly ideal for observation and defense, but so was the Cote Dame Marie against which III and V Corps were committed. Although the attack of XVII Corps against the Heights of the Meuse was stalled, it did so press the defenders of the heights that flanking fire upon III and V Corps was considerably attenuated.[35]

I Corps, whose left was entangled in the Argonne Forest, was ordered to take the eastern ridges of the forest without delay. This time, the corps delivered a fifteen-hour preparatory artillery bombardment on the ridges; on 7 October the infantry moved against the wooded hills, supported by a well-controlled rolling barrage. The Corps Commander, Major General Liggett, then demonstrated an innovativeness unique among AEF commanders: pulling the 82nd Division up from Corps Reserve, he flung this division, together with elements of the 28th, in a westward drive across the Argonne Hills, cut off the forest, and sent the Germans tumbling back into Grandpre.[36] This oblique attack enabled the 77th to move forward rapidly, relieving the "Lost Battalion."[11] This attack also cleared the way for the French Fourth Army to advance on the west of the Argonne.

The V Corps, relieved of the observed fire from its right, launched an all-out assault on the Bois de Romagne on 9 October. By nightfall, they had seized Fleville and were fighting up the slopes of Hill 255. III Corps advanced on the right on 10 October, and the whole army line moved forward against stubborn resistance. The Bois de Romagne fell on 10 October, but strong enemy fire stopped the right of V Corps and the left of III Corps short of Romagne and Cunel. By the night of 10 October, the advance had slowed. The First Army went into a temporary defense on 11 October.[37] The halt was necessary in order again to reorganize and resupply. The brutal fighting had rendered some of the divisions ineffective for further attack. The 91st Division, bled of its strength from repeated assaults against Hill 255 (which it had seized) and against the Cote Dame Marie (from which it had been driven back), was relieved on 11 October. The 1st Division, which had wrested Hill 272 from the enemy, was pulled out the same night; it had lost 9,387 officers and men, the highest casualty figure of the campaign. The 1st's position was taken over by the 42nd Division. The 80th Division came out of the line also, replaced by the 5th Division (John McMahon). On 13 October, the front line (shown on Map 6 by a dashed line) ran from south of Brieulles on the Meuse directly west through the lower Cunel Heights south of the Cote Dame Marie, through the Bois de Romagne to the break in the Argonne Forest south of Grandpre.[38]

Casualties had risen to over one hundred thousand, according to later estimates. Adding to the army's other woes, the weather had turned cold; rain slashed the troops dug in along the line of contact. Sickness was

Argonne Forest   Pleinchamp Fme. Croix de Bayle   Cornay   R.R.   Aire River
Côte 180

The sector through which the U.S. 82d Division operated in its flank attack, looking west along the route of the 82d on the north of the forest. (*American Battle Monuments Commission. Washington: Battle Monuments Commission, n.d. Reproduced with permission of U.S. Army Military History Institute, Carlisle Barracks, Pennsylvania.*)

U.S. Cemetery   Bois des Rappes   Bois de la Pultière   Cunel   Romagne-Clierges Road   Romagne-Charpentry Road   Bois de Cunel

Hills around Cunel and Romagne in the center of the sector of the U:S. 32d Division, looking northeast from Gesnes. *(American Battle Monuments Commission. Terrain Studies, Meuse-Argonne. Washington: Battle Monuments Commission, n.d. Reproduced with permission of U.S. Army Military History Institute, Carlisle Barracks,* increasing in the war theater.[39] Bugler Herbert Summers of Company I, 314th Infantry Regiment, 79th Division, remembers the cold, the rain, and the mud. Everyone had diarrhea; eating cheese from the ration helped.[40] The replacement situation was bad—not more than forty-five thousand replacements were available for all the combat divisions; the divisions were short a total of eighty thousand personnel. The "flu" was so bad at home that President Wilson had considered stopping the replacement flow altogether. Pershing's request for the return of the American divisions with the British and French resulted in requests from these allies for more American units.[41]

It finally became obvious to Pershing that he would have to expand his zone of attack to the east—a conclusion his staff and he should have reached much earlier. Pershing created the Second Army, effective on 12 October 1918, to take responsibility for operations on the east of the Meuse River, from Fresnes-en-Woevre to the Moselle River. Major General Bullard of III Corps took over this command. Pershing turned over the First Army to Major General Liggett, formerly commanding I Corps, effective on 16 October. Pershing replaced the two vacant corps commands, with Major General Joseph Dickman taking I Corps and Major General Hines to command III Corps. Major General Muir replaced Dickman as commander of IV Corps. At his own request, Major General Cameron stepped down from command of V Corps, to retake his old command, the 4th. Division; Major General Summerall replaced Cameron as commander of V Corps.[42]

It was well Pershing made these changes, including removing himself from field command. He had driven his corps and division commanders unmercifully. Goaded on by Allied criticisms and by his own driving ambition to succeed in breaking the strong German defenses, fighting the War Department for men and supplies, beset by wet and cold weather, tired and ill himself from the flu that was affecting his army, Pershing appeared to be losing his sense of judgment and perspective.[43] Our French ally chose this moment to again attempt to reduce the American force, and with it U. S. influence on the war and on the coming peace settlement. According to Frank Vandiver, a Pershing biographer, Marshal Foch sent General Weygand to Pershing on 12 October with a curt message relieving him of command of the U.S. First Army, (to be replaced by the French General Hirschauer) and assigning him to command a southern region from Pont-à-Mousson, on the Moselle, south to the Selle. Pershing rejected the order. "It would forever obliterate the part America has taken in the war," he (allegedly) said to his French aide.[44] If effected, this action would have been in line with Foch's earlier attempt to shift Pershing eastward and to employ American forces on both sides of the Meuse. Now, however, Pershing would be relegated to a sector well to the east of the Meuse only. Vandiver, citing a memorandum concerning this incident, believed Foch was, in fact, attempting to relieve Pershing. Neither Pershing nor Foch mentioned this attempt in their memoirs. The historian Donald Smythe, whose second volume of his biography of Pershing (*Pershing: General of the Armies*) covers this period, was skeptical that Foch would have attempted a direct relief, as am I. However, Paris was full of rumors that the French were trying to have Pershing relieved. Hearing these, Secretary of War Baker said, "It would be a long time before any American commander would be removed by any European premier." This statement reflected the prevailing opinion that Clemenceau was behind the attempt to remove Pershing.[45]

The records show that, on 13 October, Pershing had a conference with Foch at Bombon. Foch, disarmingly, queried Pershing about Wilson's position on an armistice, hoping, ever tactfully, that "Wilson would not presume to speak for the Allies!" Pershing's icy manner forced Foch to the main issue: The Americans were not advancing as rapidly as the other Allies, he stated. "I judge only by the results. . . . If an attack is well planned and executed, it succeeds with small losses. If not, the losses are heavy and there is no advance," said the tiny Marshal—apparently forgetting the stalemates and Allied defeats of the past three years. He then brought up the fact that Pershing had "selected" the area for the American Army and was therefore responsible for the results. To break the impasse, Weygand mentioned Pershing's plan for creating two American armies. Commenting again on "results," Foch approved the plan. He insisted, however, that Pershing operate near the front.[46] The new First Army Commander, Major General Hunter Liggett, was thus saddled with Pershing's presence until nearly the end of the war. According to Charles Dawes, Pershing's chief of procurement, Paris was buzzing with rumors that the French were going to relieve Pershing—to reduce American influence in the coming peace settlements.[47]

The weary American Army was tasked again with producing immediate results against an enemy reinforcing his strongest, most strategically important defenses. The result was more bloodshed and only minor gains. But the reasoning behind the American drive, and the Allied criticisms, was obviously political—the AEF had to fight to gain for the United States a position of influence at the peace conferences soon to come. Bliss warned the War Department that France and Britain would "attempt to minimize the American effort as much as possible. They think they have got the Germans on the run and they do not need as much help as they were crying for a little while ago."[48]

As is often the case, a political problem had to be solved on the battlefield. Pershing had "selected" the area; now he had to get an offensive going there. The new American Second Army east of the Meuse was, relatively, ignored by Pershing. Given fewer forces than the First Army, it was tasked to lean forward from its defenses, while Pershing kept his attention on the heights of Romagne.

There was no relaxation of the pressures applied by Pershing on his commanders; nor was there slackening in the German defensive efforts. The First Army was fighting its way directly through a series of defiles to break the "crown" of the German defenses. It was a hard, costly, uphill battle, not rendered easier by rotten weather and increasing sickness among the troops. Criticism of the sterile tactics of the AEF came now even from the troops themselves.[49] Pershing ranged over the battle area, lectured commanders, and even sent his aviators into the trenches so that they could learn how better to support the infantry. The organization of captured terrain for immediate defense, maximizing fire support of moving elements, coordination, command presence at the point of contest—these lessons were stressed by Pershing in his visits to commanders.[50]

The First Army plan for continuing the attack is on Map 6. The offensive was resumed on 14 October 1918. After advancing around Romagne, the 5th Division of III Corps became disorganized on the 15th under a hail of enemy fire in the Bois de Rappes and withdrew in confusion. The division commander, Major General John E. McMahon (a West Point classmate of Pershing) excused the performance to Pershing by saying that the men were "tired." Pershing thought that the commander was tired—McMahon was relieved, replaced by Major General Hanson E. Ely, who had won fame at Cantigny. Earlier the same day, Pershing had relieved Major General Beaumont B. Buck from command of the 3rd Division; Pershing was distressed to note that the 3rd, a "regular army" division, was low in morale. He replaced Buck with the hard-driving Brigadier General Preston Brown. Buck was notified that his reassignment was in accordance with a policy of rotating commanders home to provide experienced commanders for stateside units. The most controversial relief was that of Major General Clarence R. Edwards from command of the 26th Division, the National Guard division from New England. It was well known that Pershing had been dissatisfied with Edwards and with the 26th. Though among the organizations longest in theater, it was poor in discipline and low in morale. Its commander, Edwards, seemed to be unable to organize and direct the division; it had done poorly in training, movement, and battle. Edwards and his subordinates were convinced that Pershing was "down on them" because they were National Guard—and this may have been true: Pershing and his "regular" elite considered the National Guard to be commanded by poorly qualified "political generals." Edwards, however, was a "West Pointer"; Pershing had a low opinion of him even at the academy, however. Edwards had a strong political base in New England and was revered by his men. The relief caused a political storm at

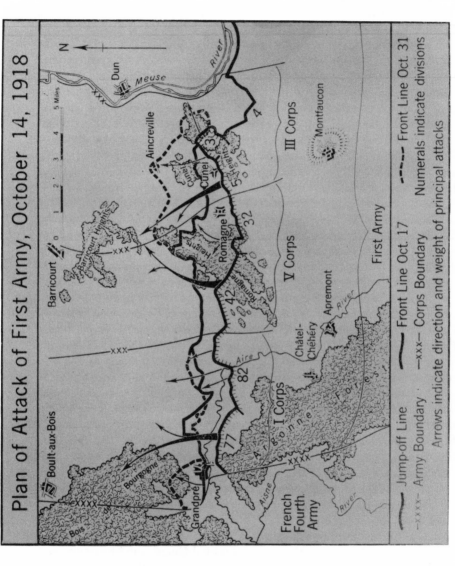

Map 6. **Plan of Attack of First Army, October 14, 1918.** (*From American Battle Monuments Commission. American Armies and Battlefields in Europe. Washington:*

home, despite Pershing's note to Edwards that, like Buck, he was merely being rotated to gain experienced leadership in the stateside training base.[51]

While III Corps was driving against the fortified defenses of Cunel, the French XVII Corps, with the American 29th and 33rd Divisions in the lead, attacked and were stalled on the ridges leading to the Heights of the Meuse, the 29th taking the wooded heights north of Molleville Farm (see Map 4 for location of Molleville Farm).

The V Corps, under its energetic commander, Major General Charles P. Summerall, drove the enemy from the top of the Cote Dame Marie on 14 October. Then, led by the 32nd Division, they took Romagne. That assault broke the crown of the Kriemhilde defenses and allowed a movement by the corps forward of the Romagne Heights to the southern edge of the Bois de Bantheville.[52] On the corps' left, the 84th Brigade of the 42nd Division (Douglas MacArthur in command) took the western half of the Bois de Romagne; that division continued to advance on 15 October to line up with the 32nd Division.[53] The advance of I Corps was less rapid. The 77th crossed the Aire River under heavy fire and attacked Grandpré. This was the western anchor of the German defenses in the area, and the town was strongly defended. Former Private Lawrence Meyers, Battery A, 303rd Field Artillery of the 77th Division, related that he manned a single artillery piece called forward to fire directly at machine gun nests. Artillery so used were called "Pirate Guns," he said. This was a very effective way to knock out machine guns that were in strong emplacements.[54] After two days of close combat in Grandpré, some of it being hand-to-hand combat with bayonets, the 77th was relieved by the 78th Division. Meanwhile, the 3rd Division and the 5th Division of III Corps penetrated the woods and heights from Cunel to Romagne.

The Kriemhilde defenses finally had been penetrated, and the Americans now occupied part of the dominant heights. The Metz-Sedan-Mezieres railroad lay within heavy artillery range. But the attack had been another costly frontal assault, and the First Army had to go into a defensive posture, again. Later, local attacks by I Corps cleared the woods north and east, and finally captured Grandpré on 27 October after heavy fighting. The Bois de Bantheville was cleared by V Corps, while III Corps fought through the Bois de Rappes and held it against counterattacks.[55]

The 5th Division (III Corps) took Aincreville on 30 October. Thus the last strongholds of the Kriemhilde Stellung were taken, and the First Army was on good terrain for the renewal of the offensive. (The line of contact for the First Army at the end of October and the plan for continuing the attack are shown on Map 7.) Pershing turned his attention to proposals for an armistice, and Liggett refitted and trained his army.[56] Ludendorff admitted that the defense of the "Kriemhilde Stellung" had been costly:

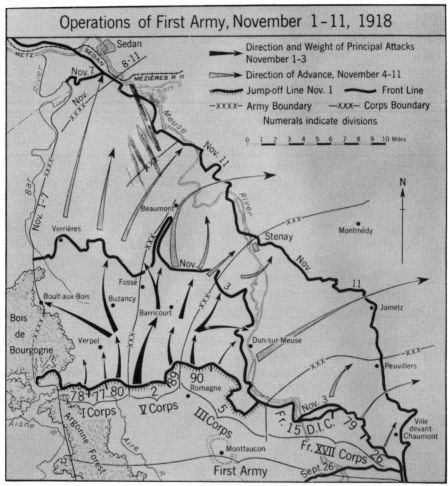

Map 7. Operations of First Army, November 1–11, 1918. *(From American Battle Monuments Commission.* **American Armies and Battlefields in Europe.** *Washington: GPO, 1938.)*

"Our best men lay on the bloody battlefield." A general withdrawal plan was adopted, and Ludendorff pinned his hopes on the tenuous defenses of the "Freya Stellung." No major reserves remained available to the defenders.[57]

Although Pershing remained too close to First Army headquarters and repeatedly urged Liggett to continue the offensive, the new army commander showed a surprising firmness with his boss: he refused to attack before the army was "tightened up." And much tightening was needed. Divisions, such as the 4th and 33rd, had been in the line since the beginning of the offensive. The 33rd had taken over 2,000 gas casualties. The 32nd Division was probably lowest in strength, with less than 2,000 combat-effective soldiers. These divisions needed to go into reserve, to reorganize and refit. The combatants of all divisions needed to rest, to be better trained in fire and maneuver, in the techniques for attacking fortified positions; unit commanders needed to learn to maximize the use of supporting fires. The artillery had bogged down; the chief problem was the acute shortage of draft horses. The 6th Division, which never saw active combat, labored along the roads, manually hauling artillery and supplies forward. Ammunition had to be stocked forward to support a new offensive. Most of the commanders were still deficient in the use of smoke to screen their locations and movements. And, despite the terrible effects of the poison gases, with which the Germans literally drenched the Americans, Corps and lower commanders were still reluctant to employ this weapon to disable enemy units. A further major problem, truly a disgrace to the AEF, was the large number of stragglers and malingerers, lounging around kitchens and aid stations, hiding in dugouts, stealing and drifting about in the rear. Liggett thought there were as many as 100,000 "stragglers," who needed to be rounded up. In the 3rd and 5th Divisions, badly mauled and disorganized, only about one-fourth of the combat infantry were present for duty. While many were casualties and many more were evacuated because of influenza, a great many—too many—had fled to the rear. Military police set up straggler lines and routed out hidden groups. Still, Pershing had to break up two more newly arrived divisions to provide replacements to units in the field. The authorized strength of divisions was reduced by 4,000 men each. Pershing again requested that the Allies return the American divisions with their forces, in order to build the strength of his Second Army.[58] The high rate of "straggling" is a clear indication of poor morale in First Army at this time.

By agreement with the French Fourth Army (on the west), the continuation of the attack of the First and Second American Armies was set for 1 November 1918. Foch had attempted (on 28 October) to turn the American First Army west against the Bois du Bourgogne, but Pershing considered these instructions to be beyond Foch's charter and he directed a general attack to the north, with his main objective being the seizure of the Barricourt heights in the center of the First Army's zone. He did order the Bois du Bourgogne to be cleared after the Barricourt operation. The Second American Army, well to the south, east of Meuse, was directed to conduct only local attacks and to improve their positions. For this attack, Pershing set no limits on the advance; he prescribed only an all-out and continuing attack to uncover the line of the Meuse and the defenses of Sedan.[59] Liggett's First Army was rested; it had been retrained, really "remodeled," for attack against fortified positions. Artillery supporting plans had been developed to isolate the hills under attack by interdictory fires on rear slopes and rear approaches, while heavy counterbattery fires were planned on likely German artillery and infantry reserve positions. Heavy use of gas, including mustard gas, was planned. Special training had been given to infantry squads grouped into heavily armed "assault teams." These teams were trained to eliminate machine gun bunkers by fire and movement, crawling up to lob grenades or explosives into the bunkers. While these teams engaged the men in the bunkers, the rest of the infantry were trained to bypass these strong points.

The other Allied ground armies were also attacking: the British and Belgians were driving on Brussels; the British right and the French center were flattening the "Laon Bulge" slowly, while the French right and the American First Army were closing the gap from the south.[60]

—The First Army was deployed to attack, from east to west, as shown below:

—III Corps (Hines), with the 5th (Ely) and 90th (Henry Allen) Divisions in line east to west and the 3rd Division (Brown) in reserve.

—V Corps (Summerall), with the 89th (Wright) and 2nd (John Lejeune) Divisions in line and the 1st (Frank Parker) and 42nd (Menoher) Divisions in reserve.

—I Corps (Dickman), with the 80th (Cronkhite), 77th (Alexander), and 78th (McRae) Divisions in attack, and the 82nd (Duncan) in reserve.

—The 32nd (Haan) was in Army reserve.

This time, Liggett was not going to have First Army attack all along the front. V Corps was to conduct the main attack, seizing the ridges from Barricourt west to Fosse. The 1st and 42nd Divisions were located in the rear of V Corps to exploit the V Corps's attack. The other corps were to support the V Corps, with III Corps seizing the high ground east of Barricourt and I Corps striking northwest to seize Boult-aux-bois.[61] All divisions in the attack were veteran. All were ready.

The Army's artillery was well prepared to support the attack. Heavy artillery had been moved well forward, including railcar-mounted fourteen-inch naval guns, which guns began hurling fourteen-hundred-pound shells deep into the enemy's rear late in October. Two days prior to the infantry attack, the Army's artillery began to place heavy fires, including all types of gas, on known and suspected enemy artillery and reserve-troops locations. For the first time, the artillery was saturating the defensive area. All of the artillery was supporting this attack, including those guns that would normally support divisions now in reserve. "Cannon enough to conquer hell," said the writer Fairfax Downey.[62]

At 3:30 A.M. on 1 November, the black of night burst bright as day as the last great barrage of the war struck the enemy positions "like a million hammers."[63] Gun barrels glowed as the artillery rained fire on enemy battery locations, reserve positions, crossroads, headquarters, bridges, and areas suspected of being occupied by reserve units.[64]

The infantry assault jumped off at 5:30 A.M., the doughboys following the customary rolling barrage. This time, however, smoke and gas were adjusted along the flanks of the advancing forces. The artillery preparation had devastated the enemy's defenses. The attackers closed quickly on their objectives; active strong points were invested by direct-fire weapons, while the bulk of the troops swung around these and surged forward. The German defenses broke, the defenders fleeing northward, followed by the fast-moving yanks. III Corps quickly took Andevaune (west of Dun-sur-Meuse), protecting V Corps's flank. V Corps stormed and seized the heights of Barricourt. After supporting V Corps's movement by fire, I Corps drove the Germans out of Buzancy on 2 November, and the entire Army line moved north. By the end of 3 November, V Corps had seized the town of Barricourt and had advanced to the southern edge of Beauclair. In a daring night advance, the 2nd Division moved through the Bois de la Folie, their columns slipping between enemy defenses, and took the high ground east and north of Fosse on the morning of 3 November. That same night, they again moved through a gap in the Germans' positions and captured some headquarters men in their billets. By midnight, they had taken La Tuilerie farm just south of Beaumont. These advances compelled the withdrawal of the German forces facing I Corps and the French Fourth Army.[65] The 77th now advanced beyond Champigneulles to Harricourt. The 78th attacked again on 3 November 1918 and captured Germont and Verrieres.[66] III Corps, on 1 November, captured Clery-le-Grand, turned northeast, and drew up along the Meuse south of Stenay. By 4 November, the First Army had advanced twenty kilometers. At First Army headquarters, staff officers could hardly keep up posting locations on the maps.[67]

On the night of 4 November 1918, German forces on the western front began a phased, general withdrawal, designated the *Kriegsmarsch;* it was designed to break contact with the Allied advance, then to reestablish the German defenses along the northeast bank of the Meuse River. The American First Army, having reached open ground, was preparing for

Bois de la Folie   Buzancy-Nouart Road   Buzancy-Barricourt Road

The area through which the U.S. 2d Division conducted its night attack, looking north-northeast along their route of march from Bois de la Folie. (*American Battle Monuments Commission. Terrain Studies, Meuse-Argonne. Washington: Battle Monuments Commission, n.d. Reproduced with permission of U.S. Army Military History Institute, Carlisle Barracks, Pennsylvania.*)

pursuit.[68] German bodies littered the roads and fields. Von Gallwitz knew that the situation was hopeless. On 2 November, he had reported:

All of the front line commanders report that the Americans as [sic] attacking in mass formations in the general direction of Stenay, that the German troops are fighting courageously but just cannot do anything. Therefore, it has become imperative that the Army be withdrawn in the rear of the Meuse and that said withdrawal be effected immediately.[69]

On 5 November, Pershing ordered the continuation of the pursuit: The First Army was to cross the Meuse and advance in sector to clear the region between the Chiers and Bar Rivers. The Second Army finally was ordered to advance between the Moselle and Etang Rivers toward Gorze and Chambley and to prepare plans for a broad offensive in the direction of Briey. All forces were to advance in zones, without regard to terrain objectives or the advance of forces on their flanks.[70]

On 8 November 1918, the soldiers' newspaper, *The Stars and Stripes,* reported:

The thick walls of German resistance in the Argonne, against which the First American Army has been hammering since the last week in September, gave way with a crash on November 1. . . . The very earth and sky seemed in alliance with the doughboys. For a week, the weather has been kindlier. . . .[71]

The First Army was already on the move. By 5 November, 5th Division of III Corps had crossed the Meuse under fire and established bridgeheads south of Dun-sur-Meuse. The Division then captured Milly and extended its line south to the Bois de Chatillon. The 79th Division fought against strong defenses on the heights of the Meuse, turning south against the Borne de Cornouiller., The enemy forces were fighting to keep their pivot anchored there until forces to the north could withdraw. The Borne de Cornouiller fell on 7 November. The following day, the 79th, part of the French II Colonial Corps, took Wavrille on the east flank of the heights of the Meuse. (These locations are north of Ville devant Chaumont on Map 7.) On 8 November the 79th Division drove southeast and seized Ville-devant-Chaumont. The 81st, on the night of 7 November, captured Mantieulles and Moranville, southeast of Ville-devant-Chaumont.[72]

In V Corps' zone, the 89th captured Beaufort on the 4th and reached the Meuse north of Stenay. The 2nd Division took heavy casualties in its attack along the Barricourt Heights, but it reached the Meuse south of Villemontry (where the Meuse turns again north seven miles north of Stenay, Map 7).[73] In I Corps, the 80th Division fought through a German unit committed to a "last-man battle" and captured Vaux-en-Dieulet and Sommauthe. The enemy then withdrew, and the 80th pursued them to a

Bois de Remoiville

Brandeville-Bréheville Road

Looking over the plain of the Woevre, north-northeast from the 5th Division's forward positions. (*American Battle Monuments Commission. Terrain Studies, Meuse-Argonne. Washington: Battle Monuments Commission, n.d. Reproduced with permission of U.S. Army Military History Institute, Carlisle Barracks, Pennsylvania.*)

line north and west of Beaumont by the night of 5 November. The 80th was relieved the next morning.[74] The 77th was still meeting stubborn resistance. On 5 November, however, it pushed its forward elements north of Stonne and La Besace. By the evening of 6 November, it had driven to the Meuse, sending patrols northward into Villers and Remilly (five miles southeast of Sedan). The 78th Division captured Les Petites Armoises (northwest of Verrières) on 4 November. The 42nd Division took over from them, and by 6 November had established its line north of Bulson (six miles south of Sedan).[75] The 1st Division entered the attack on the left of V Corps on 6 November (taking over from the 80th Division) and immediately attacked and secured Villemontry on the Meuse.[76] Von Gallwitz remembers that it was about this time (6 November) that he was out of reserves and could only hold on as long as possible, while the German armies fought back to a line along the trace Meuse-Antwerp.[77]

Meanwhile, Pershing had been playing politics during early November, pronouncing himself to be for the continuation of the war until the "unconditional" surrender of the Germans, in contravention, even in defiance, of the known stand of President Wilson, who favored an armistice. For a brief period, it again seemed that Pershing might be relieved, this time by his own national authorities. The president's advisor, Colonel Edward House, talked the matter over with Pershing and advised President Wilson that nothing further should be done.[78] On 6 November 1918, Pershing caused another furor by announcing that it was his desire that American forces take Sedan. At Pershing's request, First Army directed I Corps, assisted by V Corps, to bend all its energies to capturing Sedan. Although Pershing says he had the approval of the commander of the combined French Fourth and American First Armies (General Maistre), he reckoned without the sense of pride of the French. Sedan was the site of the great French defeat in the Franco–Prussian War! Understandably, the French were determined to have the honor of liberating Sedan—but the "doughboys" were on the way, while the French fumed. Pershing halted his more aggressive commanders just before the 42nd Division and the 1st Division became hopelessly entangled, partly in the zone of the French Fourth Army, on the heights overlooking Sedan. The American Second Army moved east in the Woevre Plain on 9 November, reaching a line Marcheville-Lachausee. Both armies of the AEF continued their attacks on the 11th of November and took casualties. The armies were planning further pursuits north and east when the Armistice instructions were received. At the eleventh hour on the eleventh day of the eleventh month of 1918, all fighting ceased![79]

Units fought until the last minute, and some Allied artillery, it was later charged, "shot" past the deadline. For most of the soldiers, the Armistice came as a gradual realization—of silence! Then the question: Is it really

Balan

Sedan   Hill   252

Gd. Torcy

Looking north at Sedan from positions at which U.S. 1st Division was halted on the heights south of the city. (*American Battle Monuments Commission. Terrain Studies, Meuse-Argonne. Washington: Battle Monuments Commission, n.d. Reproduced with permission of U.S. Army Military History Institute, Carlisle Barracks, Pennsylvania.*)

over, asked of buddies for reassurance, half in disbelief? It is over! I'm alive, I made it. Some of the bolder soldiers on both sides of the front advanced, haltingly, toward each other. Almost shyly, they waved, came closer, then shook hands. Corporal William Sibley, Company B, 109th Infantry Regiment, 28th Division, recalls the happy sensation: "One of our platoons was over a hill. . . . A few Germans came to them to shake hands; they gave our men coins, and even pulled buttons off their clothes to give them."[80] The wounded George Patton wrote in his diary, "Got rid of my bandage. Wrote a poem on peace."[81] And peace it was for the tired, victorious soldiers from America. The AEF had fought through the Argonne, uncovered the Meuse. The Americans passed the terrible test of battle in the Meuse-Argonne. They had punched through strong defenses by frontal assault—with heavy casualties. Their leadership had revealed that it was insufficiently trained and experienced to meet this trial by fire.

8

IN RETROSPECT

As the American Armies "stacked their arms" along the heights overlooking Sedan, messages of congratulations poured in from American political leaders and from the leaders of the Allied nations.[1] Certainly there was every reason for the AEF, and for the American people, to be proud: of the 2,084,000 American soldiers who had reached France before the Armistice, 1,390,000 saw active service at the front. Of the forty-two United States divisions that had reached France, twenty-nine took part in active combat service. Seven of these were Regular Army divisions, eleven were from the National Guard, and eleven were organized as part of the National Army. Draftees made up the bulk of the soldiers in all of these divisions. The American Army had a total of two hundred days in battle and engaged in thirteen major operations. From the middle of August until the end of the war, the American divisions actually held a bigger part of the front than that held by the British during the same period. During October and November, American divisions occupied 134 kilometers of the southern portion of the Allied line (21 percent of the western front). On 1 April 1918, the Central Powers possessed a superiority on the western front of 324,000 riflemen. As a result of the arrival of American reinforcements, Allied strength exceeded that of the Germans in June and was more than 600,000 over the enemy strength by the time of the Armistice. American battle losses in this war were 50,280 killed and 205,690 wounded. These were heavy losses, considering the short period of intensive fighting for the Americans; they are small, however, when compared with the 7,485,000 lost by the Allies during the four years at which they were at war. The European belligerents had killed nearly a whole generation of their young men.

The Meuse-Argonne campaign lasted forty-seven days. A total of 1,200,000 Americans were engaged in the campaign, of which 850,000 were combat troops. Twenty-two American divisions were engaged in the battle; 2,417 artillery pieces supported this fighting, firing a total of more than four million shells (a greater tonnage of ammunition than was used by Union forces during the entire five years of the American Civil War). The American ground battle was supported by 840 airplanes, most of these manufactured by the Allies. In addition, 324 tanks also supported the American campaign in the Meuse-Argonne; all of these tanks were of Allied manufacture, and many were manned by Allied troops. The AEF claimed to have drawn to the Meuse-Argonne a total of 44 enemy divisions; this figure was disputed by the Allies and could hardly be proven. The First Army reported the capture of 26,000 prisoners of war in this campaign, though other statisticians cite only 16,000. They also listed the capture of 874 artillery pieces and over 3,000 machine guns.[2] The First Army claimed to have inflicted 100,000 enemy casualties, at a cost of 117,000 American casualties.[3]

With regard to costs of the war, the total expenditure of the United States came to thirty-three billion dollars, of which ten billion were lent to the Allied nations. The United States spent about two million dollars per hour during its period of war. This cost was about equal to that of Great Britain and Germany, and one third greater than the cost to France in dollar equivalents. However, the cost to the United States was only 14 percent of its estimated prewar wealth, while the cost to Great Britain, for example, was 44 percent of its prewar wealth.[4]

Following the celebrations and parades came Allied criticisms and deprecations of the importance of the American effort on the western front and of performance of the AEF in battle. The Allies definitely wanted to "play down" the significance of the American military contribution to the victory of the alliance. The writer David Kennedy makes the point that Wilson himself recognized "Pershing's modest military successes against Germany had given him little diplomatic leverage on the Allies."[5] To demonstrate by statistics the importance of the effort by the United States, AEF Headquarters, in its postway report, concluded that the presence of "fresh" American divisions on the western front was the main factor leading the Germans to accept a settlement.[6] In Appendix 3 a tabular representation of the report of the status of divisions on the western front on 11 November can be found. It makes the point that of the thirty fully equipped American divisions in France, seven were considered to be in good condition, their strength equalling fourteen divisions of the other contestants. The other Allies had fifty-seven divisions considered to be "fresh," while the Germans were estimated to have a total of only forty-nine divisions considered to be in good condition. The table also shows that the Allies, on 11 November, had 127 divisions in reserve, while the Germans/Austrians on the same date had a total of only 41.[7]

In considering the relative manpower strength of the Allies, augmented by the tremendous American presence, compared to the Germans, one must take into account the fact that the Germans had succeeded in withdrawing their forces, in good order, along their line of communications to a front that was 150 kilometers shorter than that which existed during the height of the 1918 German advance. If they had had to continue the war, they would have been able to stand on the defensive anchored on the difficult terrain of the Ardennes; they should have been able to put up a creditable defense against Allied attacks from there.[8]

How effective were the Americans in combat, as compared to the Allies and to their enemies? The Allies were critical of the Americans' performance, partly for reasons that would serve their own military and political ends. However, in their secret official reports to their headquarters, Allied observers were equally critical of the Americans from a professional standpoint. A French military report in October of 1918 stated that American troops under Allied command "have done splendidly," but, "owing to inexperience, particularly in the higher ranks, American divisions . . . under their own command, suffer wastage out of all proportion to results achieved." The blame for this state of affairs was laid to Pershing's "insistence on the premature formation of large American armies."[9] A British official report of 21 October 1918 declared that:

> the American Army is disorganized, ill-equipped and ill-trained with very few non-commissioned officers and officers of experience. It has suffered severely through ignorance of modern war and it must take at least a year before it becomes a serious fighting force.[10]

Marshall Haig made a similar judgment, but withdrew the statement when challenged by Pershing.[11] It is difficult to refute such professional condemnations of American leadership—unless one rejects all criticism as biased, which I do not. In responding to my questions concerning the American battlefield performance, about half of my correspondents tended to give the Americans credit for greater combat effectiveness than did the Allied leaders at the time of the appearance of the AEF in battle. Inexperience was the deficiency most often cited.

The British author of military histories, Correlli Barnett, made the point to me that the Americans were probably equally as good in 1918 as were the Allied troops in 1915.[12] Barnett's comment was echoed by Peter Simkins, historian of the Imperial War Museum, with the proviso that such a comparison can be faulted by dozens of exceptions. The similarities between the Kitchener Divisions on the western front in 1915 (about which Simkins has made a four-year study) and the AEF in 1918 is worth noting. Both had been given poor and inappropriate training and most performed poorly in early combat, he stated. However, a few of the Kitchener Divisions did very well on The Somme, in 1916. What many of the Kitchener Divisions possessed was a "social cohesion"—units such as the "Pals Battalions," which came from small neighborhoods or specific industries. Simkins posited that such social commonality gave esprit, competitiveness, and moral support to these men, enabling these units to hold up in combat better than others, despite their poor training. The dominion divisions had similar spirit and seemed eager to prove their worth and their superiority over the English organizations. It may be postulated that the dominions units were better in combat than English units because of their pride in their uniqueness. Simkins made the point, however, that a study of social cohesion and its contribution to morale and combat effectiveness remains to be made.[13]

Some who observed the AEF in early combat gave similar evaluations to U.S. National Guard Divisions, for similar reasons. Some guard divisions, notably the 28th and the 42nd, did indeed do as well as any division called "regular"; others were rated poor in leadership and discipline. Captain Frank W. Showman, who commanded Company H, 110th Infantry of the 28th Division during the campaign, stated, "The National Guard proved that they could fight as well as the Regular Army. We are proud of the 28th."[14] Any rating in this regard is subject to the questioning of the rater's prejudice; such prejudice is, unfortunately, easier to document than to discount in any rating.

Returning to the rating of the AEF, the military author and analyst Trevor Dupuy maintains that the Americans were the best soldiers on the western front in 1918, all the others being spent.[15] George Marshall reflected his and Pershing's opinions in a postwar article in *Infantry Journal*: "The Americans who fought only at St. Mihiel and the Meuse-Argonne will probably never realize the vast difference between the enemy then and the German of April or May."[16] Marshall's point can be translated to a general postulate: excessive personnel losses in combat units can more than offset capabilities gained by the combat experience. This statement can be applied to Allied armies as well as to those of the Germans. In commenting on problems of the AEF, the historian Allan Millett noted that all armies had and still have problems displacing artillery and moving supplies; however, veteran organizations perform better than "green" units.[17] I agree substantially with both of the above comments. Fighting capability may decline as the number and quality of replacements diminish, but administrative and logistical infrastructure generally improves with experience.

Combat performance results from the interaction of a great many factors; among these are leadership, training, experience, physical condition, and unit spirit (or esprit). Using statistics supplied by the AEF, it is interesting to attempt an evaluation of the "veteran" divisions as against the relatively inexperienced ones.[18] Statistics on the number of days spent by each division of the AEF in quiet sectors of the line and in active military operations are shown in Appendix 4. This chart confirms the very natural assumption that those American divisions that had arrived in France the earliest had the most time in combat, the 1st Division, the first to arrive in Europe, having had the most combat time. However, some divisions, notably the 3rd, 27th, and 30th, had all of their front line time in active combat, extending over periods of about two months; the 36th and 80th Divisions were in active combat for their entire experience, which totaled one month each.

The distance advanced against enemy forces by each division is graphically indicated in Appendix 5. A relatively good match can be made between the lengths of the bar graphs for each division in Appendixes 4 and 5, which generally indicates that those divisions with the longest period in active combat advanced the farthest. The distance advanced, however, has a great deal to do with the nature of the ground being traversed, the strength and effectiveness of the opposing enemy forces, and the mission (offensive or defensive) given to each division. The graph shows that the 77th National Army Division, whose ranks were filled largely by draftees from New York City and vicinity, made the longest advance; it also did some of the toughest fighting. Dividing miles advanced by the number of days in active combat shows the 42nd Division slightly higher than the 77th in miles advanced per active day (.87 to .67 miles per day). In this comparison, both the 42nd and 77th rank well ahead of the 1st and 2nd Divisions. I do not believe one can rate the combat capabilities of an organization from these statistics alone.[19]

One reasonable criterion of combat success is the number of awards for valor in action given to combat units. Individuals are generally so rated. The chart at Appendix 6 shows this breakout for the Congressional Medal of Honor (the highest decoration given by the United States government for military action) and for the Distinguished Service Cross (the second highest award given for combat action). While it may be argued that the award of decorations is very much a consequence of location, timing, and luck, as well as command policy, I believe awards are, in general, fairly representative of combat effectiveness, and by their number reflect a degree of unit performance as well. In this criterion the 2nd Division is highest, followed by the 1st and 3rd. Appendix 7 lists casualties by division. Again, it may be argued that the number of casualties is as indicative of enemy proficiency as it is of friendly, and that it may even indicate poor unit performance, leading to excessive casualties. However, my study and experience lead me to sense a positive relationship between casualties and unit combat effectiveness. Those units that perform well are given, unfortunately, the harder tasks, and they are given these more frequently than other units. This was true for the Meuse-Argonne Campaign. Thus, over time, the higher standards of these units led to higher casualties.

The chart at Appendix 8 shows the number of prisoners of war (POWs) captured by each division in the AEF. With the aforementioned reservations, I would affirm a relatively direct relationship between numbers of POWs captured and combat proficiency.

For the purposes of determining the degree of relationship among these factors, I have juxtaposed the figures for each division in each category except time in combat upon a graph in Appendix 9. Although there are many exceptions in specific categories, the chart shows a positive relationship of each of these categories to the total. The eighteen highest scoring divisions are shown on the chart. The totals chart, unfactored, yields a ranking of: 2nd Division, 1st, 3rd, 26th, 42nd, 32nd in that order. Factoring by days in active combat yields this ranking: 2, 42nd, 26th, 28th, 1st and 77th. It is readily admitted that these gross figures give far greater numerical import to casualties and prisoners of war than to other categories. However, factoring and weighting each category does not change the ranking order significantly. These ratings appear to be in line with the subjective judgments of those observers of the AEF in combat and those historians who have made qualitative comment, including me. Pershing and his associates would likely reject the high rating of the 26th National Guard Division from New England, and that of the 77th National Army Division from New York, and so do I.[20]

One may conclude from these few rankings that the Regular Army divisions and those of the National Guard performed generally better than those of the National Army. Since all divisions were filled with draftees at the lower levels of rank, the discriminator in combat performance may be in leadership. Experienced leaders at all levels were assigned to the units deploying early; the numbers of experienced leaders available for assignment thinned out considerably as the pace of deployment accelerated in the spring of 1918. Thus, one may also make the unsurprising conclusion that units performed well, in part, according to the degree of military experience possessed by their leaders. Not a great deal of difference can be found in the performance indicators for National Guard organizations and those of the Regular Army using this gross method. An extension of this examination might provide an argument for the American "mililtia system" versus a large regular military establishment.

Using these criteria, the British Expeditionary Forces (BEF) would far outstrip the AEF in time in combat and ground gained for the same period. They and the French gave fewer awards, however; thus they would show up less well in that category. In terms of casualties, one can judge that for the personnel involved in the war during this period, the American figures were the highest. Also, as Smythe noted, the British captured twice as many guns and nearly four times the number of POW's as the Americans. The AEF staff did not make a national statistical comparison—and it is just as well they didn't.

Attempts at finite measurements of relative combat proficiency suffer from a plethora of unquantifiables, as noted by General Theodore Conway and the historians, Edward Coffman and Theodore Ropp, in responding to some of my questions. John Keegan, in his recent book, *Six Armies in Normandy,* found a distinct cultural bias in national armies that predisposes the way they fight; in his comments to me, Keegan reflected on the complex nature of any qualitative judgments. Pershing himself rejected the AEF comparisons as invalid.[22]

The efficiency of the AEF Headquarters may be more readily evaluated, as it was the subject of debate ever since the headquarters began operations. Marshall took pride in the output of the overworked staff of which he was a key director. However, even he commented upon the inflexibility and the inexperience of the hundreds of staff officers placed in responsible positions.[23] Allied observers were early in criticizing the AEF staff for poor management of human and material resources, particularly citing the logistical tangles that occurred early in the Meuse-Argonne campaign. This criticism was also reflected in reports of visitors from the War Department.[24] Pershing blamed the War Department Headquarters for having failed to coordinate with and to respond to his requests and guidance.[25] The War Department blamed Pershing for trying to manage too large and complex an organization.[26] Each was justified in criticizing the other! John Toland, author of *No Man's Land,* sympathizes with the overworked AEF staff, the adverse weather conditions, and restrictive terrain that affected planning; but he did judge the AEF staff's planning and staff actions as "second rate."[27] The British author Correlli Barnett blamed the clumsiness of AEF staff work on their inexperience, "a condition facing all hastily expanded forces."[28] James Rainey agreed with Barnett's judgment.[29] Gordon Brook-Shepherd, author of *November 1918: The Last Act of the Great War,* commenting on AEF staffwork, concluded that the great problem of the AEF was certainly logistical.[30] Donald Smythe declared that there were at least two occasions when the AEF and its First Army were in a state of virtual paralysis (the last days of September and mid-October 1918).[31] AEF staff were at least partly to blame for that condition. Commenting specifically upon First Army staff, Edward Coffman noted that "First Army planners were gambling that the sheer weight of numbers they committed in the Meuse-Argonne would achieve the breakthrough.[32] The fact that the army's headquarters was a new organization when it directed the Meuse-Argonne campaign could explain their failings; however, most officers assigned to First Army's staff had had staff experience in the theater. Allan Millett made a key observation: "If the First Army staff can be faulted, it is for underestimating the limitations of its troops."[33] Timothy Nenninger, whose text, *The Leavenworth Schools and the Old Army,* dealt with command and staff training and experience, added another key point: "The remoteness of general staff officers from the combat troops . . . led to operations orders based on incomplete information, especially on the conditions and capability of the troops to carry out the assigned missions. Consequently, operational demands were made that could not be fulfilled."[34] These are key points. While noting these problems, Russell Weigley stated, "American staff work was remarkably good considering our newness to large-scale war."[35] The historians Theodore Ropp and Irving Holley, Jr. echoed Weigley's judgment.[36]

I conclude that the comments made about the AEF staff are all correct. The staffs produced adequate orders, directives, instructions, and other guidance—perhaps too much paper guidance to be of value to commanders in intensive combat. They did not give enough thought to problems that might occur in executing these plans and orders. Probably, there was not enough time for "wargaming" each major plan, but the staff should have done a better job in anticipating operational constraints, communications failures, logistical chokepoints, and enemy reactions. They should have asked themselves and each other, "What if. . . .?" The AEF staffs did not master the techniques of forward positioning of support and supplies, automatic resupply and evacuation, alternate transport, task organization and reorganization, and the full employment of the massive combat power available to them. They operated in an *ad hoc* experimental fashion throughout the campaign. Chronically short of transportation, forced to buy or borrow aircraft, tanks, supporting weapons, and equipment, saddled with management problems that would have strained even the most experienced of Allied headquarters, the staffs met and overcame most of their challenges by hard work, sheer willpower, and improvisation upon encountering obstacles. They improved daily; however, General Harbord said after the war that had the Armistice not occurred when it did, the AEF would have had to cease fighting until its logistical problems could be solved.[37]

The initial strategic plan for employment of the AEF from the St. Mihiel area, driving east in the direction of Metz, was a good strategic concept. Probably, the fortified zone around Metz was too tough a bastion for the fledgling First Army to have seized, as Liggett judged; an early assault that far east in isolation from the Allied main thrust may have provoked a disasterous defeat, as Rainey theorized.[38] However, the AEF could have broken out of the St. Mihiel area to the northeast, on the axis Etain-Longuyon, created a second army to tie in with the First Army while the

Second echeloned east of the Meuse, and advanced on a broad, new front against the very vitals of the Laon Bulge held by the Germans. Ludendorff stated after the war that had the Americans launched such an attack, he would have been compelled to make a general withdrawal of all forces in the bulge.[39] Pershing stated after the war that this was just what he wanted to do.[40] I believe the AEF could have launched, expanded, and supported a broad offensive on this axis. If this American offensive had been even partially successful, it would have cut off the prospect of retreat for the southern armies of the Central Powers; in any case, it would have required the Germans to reinforce quickly and to make a major defensive effort on their southern shank, thus easing the situation for Allied advances elsewhere on the front.

Assuming, however, that Haig and Foch were correct in August 1918, in changing direction of the American offensive in order to make it converge with those of the British and French in the Mezieres area, why did Pershing not opt to launch his main attack east of the Meuse in the more negotiable terrain of the Woevre Valley? It is likely that when Foch first discussed with Pershing abandoning the St. Mihiel campaign, he was mainly interested in securing American divisions for the French operation along the Aisne. The right pincer of Foch's grand envelopment was drawn along the west of the Meuse. Foch also dismissed Pershing's offer to operate the American Army entirely east of the Meuse, saying there were "no communications." I have reconnoitered the area east of the Meuse flanking the area in which First Army attacked. True, the hills are higher, but the valleys are wider and the trafficability is fair. At the time of the American offensive, the roadways on the east of the Meuse were more extensive and in better condition than on the west. Foch may have been concerned that the Meuse was, at that time, unfordable; Pershing may have also considered the unfordable river an obstacle to operations on both sides of the river. But there were many bridges, and the AEF was strong enough to support operations east and west of the river. Reviewing the Allied demands and Pershing's counterproposals of late August–early September 1918, I gain the impression that Pershing, under terrible pressure to accept one of a number of undesirable alternatives, opted to take the Meuse-Argonne area because it appeared to be the only choice open to him for employment of an American army, from the tenor of Foch's discussion.[41] Having accepted that area, Pershing was, possibly, reluctant to suggest modification or expansion of the zone, since such a proposal might result in a reopening of the issue of splitting American forces. The mission accepted, Pershing focused his attention straight ahead. Once surprise was lost, attrition of the defenders was the only means of advancing. As noted earlier, Pershing even described the First Army's mission: "to draw enemy forces to our sector and consume them."[42] A commander does not consume more enemy forces than his own by direct assault on strong defenses; the German General von Falkenhayn discovered this fallacy at Verdun in 1916.

An offensive strategy based on the attrition of an enemy in strong defenses is really no strategy at all. In the First World War, industrialization had given a primacy to the forces in defense. It is understandable that there was a nadir in strategic innovation, confronted, as the belligerents were, with a deadlock in France with no land flanks to turn. I could criticize the Allies, who controlled the sea, for not using it to envelop the northern flank of the German front with an invasion behind their lines.[43] But transport was slow, communications limited, and the Germans could have reinforced within their perimeter faster than the Allies could from without.

I do criticize the American military leadership for not bringing their power to bear over a broader front in France. One could say that this was a tactical rather than a strategic failing.

I will now criticize AEF tactics in the Meuse-Argonne campaign. In the main, there weren't any tactics employed. Committing hundreds of thousands of infantrymen in a narrow zone directly against heavily fortified and defended positions guaranteed high casualties and small gains. The zone should have been adjusted and expanded, allowing for more flexibility in advance and maneuver. The left boundary of First Army was mainly within the tortuous fortified maze of the Argonne Forest. French Fourth Army was supposed to operate along the left and provide a "liaison detachment" to maintain contact with the Americans. This was a bad arrangement and it did not work: First Army's left flank was often open. It is generally bad attack tactics to divide a major defensive position between two forces that are not under the same battlefield commander. Pershing should have arranged to include the Argonne and its western approaches within his sector, or to have shifted his sector east, giving the entire forest to the French Fourth Army, as Foch desired him to do after the battle had commenced. In a similar vein, I have already argued that the AEF should have launched a major offensive east of the Meuse.

A summary critique of the conduct of the Meuse-Argonne offensive itself is appropriate at this juncture, before, as they say, the smoke of battle clears from the field. The criteria for the performance of a modern armed force in the field is that it be able to shoot, move, and communicate. Inherent in that simplification is the ability to deliver fire effectively, to maneuver to destroy the enemy, to seize terrain, and to communicate in order to orchestrate both fire and movement. Judged by even these simple criteria, the performance of the First Army in the Meuse-Argonne must be given a fairly low rating. With respect to shooting, over four million artillery shells were expended in the contested area. However, the artillery was poorly employed. For a variety of reasons, human and natural, the artillery did not displace forward swiftly enough to continue giving support to the attacking infantry. While it was in position, it tended to move its rolling barrages forward too swiftly for the rate of infantry movement in difficult terrain and it continued to fire upon prearranged targets, rather than shifting to engage "targets of opportunity" discovered during the attack. The artillery used too few forward observers, firing often by map coordinates. This limited its support of attacking infantry. Infantry and artillery commanders can be faulted for their infrequent use of smoke to screen movements, and their reluctance to use poison gas to disable enemy artillery and reserves. Pershing was very anxious to use gas in order to break the enemy's defenses and allow for the open warfare he desired.[44] In his study "Gas Warfare in World War I," Rexmond Cochrane concluded that, until the 1 November offensive, American corps and lower commanders did not use gas to support their attacks. He believed that the commanders feared retaliation by gas fired by the enemy, and declined to use persistant gasses because they feared these gases would injure their troops as they advanced.[45] But the Germans were already using gas against the Americans—the most effective use of gas during the entire war, according to Liddell Hart.[46] Cochrane also showed that the AEF did not employ smoke efficiently. Smoke was not delivered in sufficient volume nor for periods long enough to provide effective screening. Commanders had no experience with either gas or smoke and used them poorly, according to Cochrane.[47] These criticisms were echoed by Charles Heller in his study "Chemical Warfare in World War I." Heller believed that American revulsion at the use of poison gas resulted in our being unprepared to engage in chemical warfare when we joined the war. Heller told of the poor training provided the personnel of the 1st U.S. Gas Regiment, and the departure of the unit for France "without gas masks."[48]

A major problem affecting all others was the failure to maintain communications, front-to-rear and especially rear-to-front. In military organizations, then and now, the responsibility for maintaining communications is upon the higher headquarters to establish and maintain contact with its lower unit headquarters. In the Meuse-Argonne, commanders were often out of contact with their subordinates. Thus they did not maintain control of the battle nor give good, continuing support to their units in attack. The higher headquarters were much too far in the rear to appreciate the conditions encountered by the fighting troops and commanders. Reliance on long telephone lines, laid across the ground as units advanced, pinned higher commanders to their headquarters, while the movement of troops, animals, and vehicles across the wires and the bursting of artillery often knocked out the wire connections. Radios, called "wireless," were heavy, unreliable, and of limited range in the rugged terrain and wet weather.

Major headquarters used motor messengers, air delivery of messages, and carrier pigeons. Units moving in battle used flares to signal for support. But in general units sent messengers back and forth. These often as not got lost or were turned back by encounters with enemy personnel or fire. The result was that there was not much command influence during a fight; combat communications were a problem for all the armies at the time. Still, the Germans and the Allies controlled and supported their combat forces better than did the AEF, using the same state-of-the-art means. The difference appears to be related to experience in planning for interruptions and for using alternate means of communications.[49]

Insufficient attention was given to solving the problem of moving supplies over no man's land, despite the recurrence of this problem throughout the campaign. Combat units frequently had to send guides to the rear to find and lead food and ammunition supply parties to their units. I scanned some 5,000 responses of veterans of World War I to a questionnaire sent to them by the U.S. Army Military History Institute. Nearly half mentioned being hungry during the fighting because their food supplies did not come forward. I have summarized the comments of 728 of these veterans who took part in the Meuse-Argonne campaign upon a number of subjects; the summary is listed in Appendix 10. I will comment upon these in this critique.[50]

A great many of the veterans commented about the lack of resupply of water. Although it rained frequently, water sources were often under fire of the enemy; some sources had been poisoned or polluted and, again, water supplies did not get forward regularly. Many of the veterans complained of being sick or wounded and of not being promptly evacuated from the fighting. Those who could walk usually made their way to aid stations in the rear. Many had to wait until the attack moved forward and aides could get to them. Many died waiting.

These problems could have been partly resolved by prior planning for automatic resupply and evacuation of wounded by returning supply parties. Knowing that the soldiers were going to be in intensive combat, resupply of ammunition, food, and other expendables should have been started forward as soon as the attackers jumped off. Supplies should have been stocked well forward, even if some were destroyed by fire. Some of these procedures were taken by the AEF late in the war, but not enough attention was given to these problems.

We know that influenza was a great problem in the AEF in France. A great many of the veteran respondees complained of dysentery, and most complained of being cold, wet, lice-infested and otherwise ill. While being cold and wet is a natural condition for a soldier in battle, treatment for illness, even by the medical standards of those days, was rather primitive in the AEF. Dr. Claude Moore, former surgeon at the AEF General

Hospital in Langres, France, remembers that the normal treatment of a wounded man was to clean the wound, sew up the opening, and hope for the best. The treatment for influenza and other respiratory diseases was to pump out the lungs where there was fluid accumulation, then give the patients rest. Medical troops dealing with influenza cases wore gauze masks. However, according to Dr. Moore, it was the cold and somewhat drier weather of December that helped to end the influenza epidemic shortly after the Armistice.[51]

I also criticize commanders at all levels for failure to employ reserves properly during the Meuse-Argonne campaign. Commanders appeared to utilize their reserves more to redeem failures, plugging the reserves behind units that were pinned down by fire, than to exploit successes by extending a successful advance. This option was limited by the restricted terrain and the narrow zone, but much more could have been done in the employment of reserves to outflank and turn enemy positions. Until very late in the offensive, commanders did not properly employ close-support weapons, such as machine guns, trench mortars, and direct-fire artillery, in conjunction with the maneuver of attacking infantry. These weapons were positioned by commanders to support the beginning of an attack; then they were not ordered forward to continue support.

Failure to use natural cover and concealment in approach to enemy defenses, infrequent movement and attack under cover of night—these failings also are charged to AEF commanders. General Mark Clark, commenting about the tactics of the AEF, in which he served, said, "Each division was given a narrow sector, and it was just massed infantry stuff." General Theodore Conway remembered that General Omar Bradley and other veterans of the World War, in postwar discussions, often expressed criticism of the tactics employed by the AEF.[52]

The combat training of the AEF has already been reviewed herein. In summary, I believe such training was misdirected. It was not based upon effective tactics, and the training that was provided did not emphasize those combat techniques that would prepare a soldier to kill and to remain alive on a modern battlefield. The failure of the AEF to enunciate a sound, relevant tactical doctrine led to faulty, incomplete training for soldiers and their leaders. Allan Millett stated, "This uncertain emphasis denied small-unit commanders the training necessary to provide fire support to attacking units, and to develop fire and maneuver."[53] Donald Smythe stated, "The key weapon in World War I was not the rifle, but the machine gun which killed many, and artillery which killed more. Against them, the American infantryman pitted raw courage, enthusiasm, inexperience, guts, some support from his auxiliary arms, and his own blood."[54] Pershing and his AEF trainers were correct in their criticism of the Allied leaders and soldiers for their failure to emphasize rifle marksmanship;

they were incorrect in declaring the rifle to be the most effective weapon for the war they were preparing to fight. This failing must be placed clearly on the shoulders of John J. Pershing, not only because he was the commander in chief of the AEF, but also because he promulgated an erroneous doctrine and demanded adherence to it. Pershing took satisfaction in noting (in *My Experiences*) that the French finally admitted that he was right in emphasizing open warfare and the importance of the rifle.[55] However, Donald Smythe stated that Pershing's research assistant for *My Experiences* could not find any statement to that effect by a French leader; neither could Smythe.[56] Of Pershing's doctrine, Liddell Hart said, "He thought he was spreading a new gospel of faith when actually it was an old faith exploded. That was the one flaw in the great structure he had built. It may even be said that he omitted but one factor from his calculations—German machine guns—and was right in all his calculations but one—their effect."[57]

Whatever the pressures upon the U.S. authorities and upon their general in the field, there was insufficient reason to send a man into battle untrained in his basic weapon. Of the 514 veterans of the Meuse-Argonne who commented upon training in response to the MHI questionnaire, nearly half spoke of poor training and many specifically stated that they had not been trained in using the weapon they were given in France. Smythe cited a pithy summary on this matter by the American military author Harvey DeWeerd: "The AEF learned to fight through bitter experience, not through any legerdemain with the rifle."[58] That's the sum of it! Wish I'd said that.

The author Richard Goldhurst, in his biography of Pershing, *Pipe Clay and Drill,* recorded that Pershing attempted, until the end of the war, to find ways to employ cavalry in an attack—this effort despite the terrible casualties that Allied cavalry had taken on the few occasions when they were committed, mounted, against machine guns in defense. Pershing's request for two cavalry divisions for the AEF was quietly pigeonholed by General March; that request did not come to light until many years after the war.[59] Pershing and his "old army" associates were deprecatory about the value of the tank in warfare. It is true that tanks at that time were blind monsters, underpowered and frequently disabled. Pershing thought that their value was in assisting the advance of infantry by clearing barbed wire obstacles. Pershing did detail Colonel Samuel D. Rockenbach to establish a tank corps in the AEF; he also complained that he had too few tanks to support the infantry. But he did believe that the tank had a limited role. Pershing was an accomplished horseman, as were most of his associates. After the war, he solemnly dedicated a plaque in the War Department building to the memory of the horses and mules who died in the war.[60]

This attitude—love of the horse and disdain for its replacement, the tank, continued in the army until well into World War II. General Dwight Eisenhower recorded the fact that in 1920 he was forced to recant statements he had made in an article that he had co-authored with then Colonel George Patton on the importance of the tank in future warfare. Eisenhower was told by the chief of the infantry branch that he would refrain from any statement contrary to existing doctrine, which limited tanks to support of infantry, or face court martial.[61] The purpose of citing these tactical precepts regarding cavalry and its successor arm, the tank, is to show that there was a mind-set on the part of General Pershing and his senior officers that changed very little, despite a great deal of bloody experience on the western front.

The prejudice against the tank was expressed by the old army officers equally against the airplane. Perhaps this was because the early advocates of air power were brash young men who tended to view themselves as, literally, "above" the ground officers whom they supported. Pershing formed an air service and directed that it be employed in combat; he gave little attention, however, to the employment of this arm, certainly less than did the Germans opposing him. General Mark Clark made the comment, "German bombardments by air-dropped bombs played havoc with columns in approach and with the organization of the rear area."[62] Pershing's lack of attention to the employment of air power may have been the result of his experiences in Mexico, where most of the aircraft employed in chasing Villa crashed or were otherwise disabled. Because the staffs of the divisions and corps gave little attention to air support, it tended to operate as an independent element, engaging in bombardments of the enemy's rear, in pursuit, and in observation. Thus, the close association of air with the advance of the ground troops was not established in the AEF.[63] It was very well established across the line in the German armies. In Pershing's defense, it must be admitted that the airplane, like the tank, was not a very reliable weapons system in that war. Its effectiveness and its role were growing rapidly in the last years of the war, and its potential should have been more appreciated by the command of the AEF. It is often stated that generals train their troops to fight the previous war. I regret that I must judge Pershing to be at least partially guilty of that failing.

A few summary comments are necessary on the subject of American leadership. This is a difficult task, for I believe that "leadership," like "love," is easier to recognize and appreciate than it is to analyze. Most of the authors who commented to me on this subject agreed that American leadership was somewhat better than the Allies credited it with being. Edward Coffman made the point that the Allied analysis of new American officers coming into the theater was likely very self-serving, but that it was probably to some extent correct. "They were the experienced leaders and we were not," he stated.[64] Irving B. Holley Jr. agreed that the Americans were probably far less capable than were the Allied officers at the time the AEF arrived in theater. "The whole generation of professional American Army officers, Holley stated, "came out of an animal-powered era. Thus, their appreciation for the application of the industrial revolution to the battlefront took some time to develop."[65] General Theodore Conway stated that it was undoubtedly true that the Allies downgraded American leadership even before it had had a chance to demonstrate its capability.

> From the European point of view," he stated, "we in the United States have always been thought of as amateurs in military affairs. This is the result of the fact that our nation has not chosen, until after World War II, to retain a large standing army; thus, our officer corps has not had direct experience with leading major military organizations.[66]

At this point in my critique, I feel I should balance out my generally critical comments on American officership. In response to my queries on leadership in the AEF, Irving Holley, who has had considerable military experience, stated that the regular army officers did rather well, all things considered.

> They built an AEF staff from scratch into a sophisticated staff organization by the end of 1918. . . . This could be done only by men who were well-grounded professionals with a good deal of ability to begin with. What they lacked was specific experience with the kinds and scale of problems they encountered in France. This they acquired on the run.[67]

Holley's comment was expanded upon by Timothy Nenninger, in his text *The Leavenworth Schools and the Old Army*. Nenninger concluded that training provided by the military school system paid off later in France.[68] Without withdrawing any of my criticisms, I can agree with Holley and Nenninger. The creation of a modern theater of war—training, fighting, and sustaining a force (which grew quickly to two million men, requiring a million tons of supplies and materiel per month) was a nearly impossible task.[69] That it was accomplished at all, however fragile the structure of the AEF, was little short of a miracle. Credit must go to the small cadre of Regular Army officers and non-commissioned officers who directed much of this effort, and I give credit here to the old army schools as well. Their graduates did learn relatively modern army command and staff techniques. However, an old army limerick keeps coming to my mind as I write and rewrite this section:

> Here's to the brave Captain White,
> The pride of this institution,
> Who went out like a light,
> In his very first fight,
> Following the school solution![70]

Recognizing that established doctrine did not always conform to reality, Nenninger noted that Leavenworth graduates in the AEF "exhibited too much self confidence, too great a belief in the rationality of warfare, and too high expectations of what the combat troops could accomplish . . . [this] compounded the problems that arose from the dichotomy between reality and doctrine."

Nenninger quoted Frederick Palmer, the war correspondent:

> Regular as well as reserve officers who had never been in action were to prove again that no amount of study of the theory of war, invaluable as it was, may teach a man how to keep his head in handling a thousand or three thousand men under fire. West Point cadet drill, Philippine jungle and "paddy" dikes, Leavenworth Staff School, army post routine, and border service had no precedent of experience for the problems of maneuver which they [the AEF] now had to solve.[71]

Nenninger also stated his conclusion: "Clearly, the AEF learned to fight by fighting, not because of Pershing's insistence on open warfare or because the prewar Leavenworth had expounded the proper tactical doctrine."[72]

Certainly there were leaders of vision and high intelligence in the AEF. George Marshall, Douglas MacArthur, Charles Summerall, John Hines, Hunter Liggett, and Hugh Drum come to mind. They saw the doctrinal and operational errors; they just did not have the time to make significant changes during the fighting. Billy Mitchell was something of a visionary, but he was right about the role of airpower in future war. Though he was a bit of a nuisance to the senior officers, he came up with a number of plans to restore maneuver to the modern battlefield. Harvey DeWeerd stated that Mitchell had even gained Pershing's approval, in concept, to air drop the soldiers of the 1st Division from a fleet of multipassenger airplanes (each soldier with a single parachute) behind enemy lines, in conjunction with a motorized ground attack.[73]

A judgment of the leaders in the AEF who were not regulars is more difficult to make. Many of the senior officers of the National Guard and National Army divisions were regulars. Some of the National Guard officers were too old, physically unfit, and/or not competent to lead at the level of the rank they held. This was also the condition of some of the senior regular officers whom Pershing rejected or dismissed. Those officers newly minted by the preparedness camps, the Reserve Officers' Training Corps, Student Army Training Corps, and Officer Training Camps and Schools suffered from insufficient training and lack of pertinent experience. Those technical and administrative experts and doctors appointed to military rank to coordinate, primarily, the logistical support of the AEF, brought an expertise that was sorely needed and generally did a great job. If forced, I would rate the regular officers and noncommissioned officers as the best two groups of leaders in the AEF; those of the prewar National Guard next best, and those leaders who held National Army rank only as the last. The regulars were criticized as being too stiff, not only in manner but in problem solving; the others were criticized as being, in varying degrees, unqualified and unmilitary.[74] I can think of perhaps sixty exceptions to the group ratings I have made, and I guess there are thousands. If fired upon on this matter, I will retreat!

It is to the credit of our people and our way of life that, when challenged, our nation brought forth a great number of citizens who were innovative, able to improvise, self-confident, and success-oriented—the raw material for effective military leadership. To my observation, many amateurs in military leadership, after some training and experience, have done as well as professionals on the battlefield. What they lack in military knowledge and experience they make up for by a greater degree of innovation and experimentation than many of the professional military leaders. The key problem is the time required for the knowledge and experience to be gained; if military experience must be gained during battle, the cost of such on-the-job-training can be expressed in high casualties among those being led.[75]

Peter Simkins, in discussing the BEF, stated that the National Army officers joining the AEF were probably similar in socioeconomic background to the young officers of Kitchener's Army; they were graduates of the British public (read private) school system, who marched into battle with enthusiasm, intelligence, and not much leavening experience.[76] I believe that the American officers in the AEF came from a broader spectrum of our society; yet there was a resemblance, as noted by Simkins.

The regular army officers in the AEF did look with disdain upon the officers from other components. This was only natural: they were the professionals; the others were less so. There was a marked dislike between the Regular and National Guard officers. For the regulars, the ranks held by officers of the guard, possibly higher than that of a regular of the same age, was a source of irritation. For the guard officers, with long unit and regional association, their second-class status was insulting. Liggett gave a fairly balanced analysis of the officers in the AEF from all sources. He found a mix of abilities among regulars and the others. An officer deemed unfit to lead in the AEF was sent before a fitness board in the town of Blois, France. The board would reassign him or send him home as unfit. The town was called "Blooey" in the AEF, Liggett said; being sent there meant one's status had "gone Blooey" according to the slang of the AEF.[77]

From their common trial-by-fire in the Meuse-Argonne, officers of the

AEF from all sources developed friendships and mutual respect, which offset, to some extent, the ill feelings between them because of their different sources of commission. By the end of the war, Pershing himself had come to appreciate the contributions of the Guard and National Army divisions and leaders. By the time he became chief of staff of the army, Pershing favored a relatively small Regular Army, one of whose major tasks would be to train a larger, civilian reserve force.[78]

I have been very critical of the leadership of the AEF. I should state that I am also critical of my own leadership. In the later wars, I lost a lot of men in battle; some of the losses were due to poor judgment on my part. These losses are a painful memory.

As in all wars, the soldiers of the AEF criticized their officers as a group and blamed them for failings in leadership. Interesting to note is the fact that many of the AEF veterans who commented upon leadership in responses to the MHI Questionnaire, most of them privates, had a high regard for the officers and noncommissioned officers under whom they served directly. Of 523 veterans of the Meuse-Argonne who commented on leadership (not all did), only 22 made derogatory remarks; most of these said their leaders lacked experience. The remaining 501 responses were positive; most told of a respect and affection for their unit leaders and admiration for their abilities.[79] Again, one could discount the comments of these aged veterans as having been mellowed by time. Nevertheless, the number of favorable responses speaks well for the human-relations aspect of the leadership of the AEF.

When I undertook this study, I wanted to avoid commenting upon General Pershing's leadership. I did so out of a concern that such ratings, if laudatory, are usually dismissed as patronizing; if critical, they call into question the judgment of the rater and any animus against the rated or his group that may be attributed to the rater. Frank Vandiver saw Pershing in heroic stature; a strong, dedicated leader, venerated by his soldiers, his nation and our Allies.[80] And so he was. Donald Smythe was more critical of Pershing, faulting him for his stubbornness and inflexibility. Smythe concluded, however, that, given the tremendous challenges he faced, Pershing performed as well as could any other American military leader.[81] The historian T. Harry Williams found Pershing to have been to obstinate and self-centered.[82] B. H. Liddell Hart credited Pershing with great strength of will, but faulted him for an aloofness, a coldness of manner, "lacking in personal magnetism which can make men lay down their lives gladly."[83] I concur with these criticisms: Pershing was venerated; he was not loved by his men! James Stokesbury rated Pershing as the equal of Foch or Haig, when the limits under which he operated are considered.[84] The British author John Terraine acknowledged such limits on Pershing; yet he questioned Pershing's capacity as a leader in a coalition.[85] John

Toland saw Pershing as a stubborn, solid leader with a reasonable leadership capability. Toland, as well as Theodore Ropp, questioned the ability of any analyst or historian to rate leaders on a qualitative scale.[86] Russell Weigley faulted Pershing's tactical concepts and his judgment.[87] Trevor Dupuy rated Pershing the equal of Haig, but judged both to be of lesser attainments than either Foch or Ludendorff.[88] Allan Millett saw Pershing as equal in Leadership to any of his Allied contemporaries.[89] Edward Coffmann credited Pershing with great organizational ability and with the ability to select capable subordinates; but he (Coffman) found Pershing to be no great strategist or tactician.[90]

I have come to believe that I cannot roundout the story of the Meuse-Argonne campaign without commenting on Pershing's leadership. I will do so directly: Mindful of the short period of this campaign and of the unfairness of evaluation by hindsight, I evaluate Pershing with empathy. Pershing was a strong leader. His strength and forcefulness were certainly needed during this period; otherwise, the American effort might have been diffused. He certainly was a bold commander, forceful and relentless in attack despite high casualties and little progress. His manner was cold and taciturn, although those close to him said he could be warm and personable. Donald Smythe believed that had the German offensives of 1918 gone all the way to the Loire River, with Pershing still refusing to amalgamate his forces with those of the Allies, he would likely have been relieved. But the offensive did not reach the Loire. As Smythe said, "Pershing was right in believing that the Allies could hold without the widespread amalgamation of American units; they did!"[91]

So agreeing, I rate Pershing's leadership as too narrow, too self-centered, too authoritarian, somewhat vain, lacking in flexibility and innovativeness, and bound by tradition and experience to the extent that he was unable to master the requirements of the modern battlefield. Pershing's insistence on controlling the AEF Headquarters, the First Army, and the services of supply overloaded his span of effective control, strained him physically, and prevented him from evaluating the failures of the offensive and determining new tactics and new procedures for support and sustenance of the AEF. Had the fighting continued into 1919, a thorough reorganization of the AEF would have been necessary, in my opinion. The historian David Trask concurred with my judgment in this matter and added that the management of the AEF was so bad that Pershing may well have been relieved had the war continued.[92] In his review of Pershing's *My Experiences,* Liddell Hart accused Pershing of so writing history as to show that all of his decisions were correct and appropriate.[93] On balance, however, Liddell Hart saw in Pershing "a man who has rare moral courage, driving force, bold vision, constructive power, and an ability to rise above professional prejudices in selecting his instruments."[94] I agree with Liddell Hart's analysis except on the question of Pershing's "ability to rise above professional prejudices." I have given this some thought and done some rereading about Pershing. I must judge him to have been rather provincial and biased. A man of strong opinions, he did not tolerate dissenting views well. In fairness to Pershing, it must be stated that the tenor of military leadership in his era was very authoritarian.

Pershing's machinations against the chief of staff of the army, General Peyton C. March, revealed a pettiness in his nature. DeWeerd judged Pershing's final report as commander-in-chief to have been of little value as a guide for the future. "To insist that the 'rifle is the master of the battlefield' in a day when the pace of technical advancement foreshadowed the possibility of fleets of monster tanks and swarms of dive bombers was to invite military stagnation," said DeWeerd.[95] However, DeWeerd agreed with and quoted Liddell Hart on Pershing:

> There was, perhaps, no other man who would or could have built the structure of the American Army on the scale he planned. And without that army the war could hardly have been saved and could not have been won.[96]

No question: Pershing put his stamp on the AEF. Those closest to him felt ennobled by that association. He was certainly a role model for a commander-in-chief as was noted by Smythe.[97] He was respected, even by those who did not like him. He was America's hero. I find in him many admirable traits; his failings—no worse than those of other great men. But were I a draftee in 1918 at the foot of Montfaucon, ordered to attack directly into machine-gun fire, I might think less of Pershing. I will end my analysis of Pershing on that uncertain note.

While our allies questioned and deprecated American leadership, they were unanimous in praise of the American soldiers, both amateur and professional. Certainly the Allies saw these men as fresh reinforcements for their depleted forces; but they found in the "Yank" more than they had expected. British Marshal Haig was particularly generous in his compliments concerning the abilities of the Americans with the BEF—their morale, their stamina, and their competitiveness. Other Allied commanders and observers spoke similarly.[98] The AEF veterans who responded to the MHI questionnaire spoke well of the Allied soldiers with whom and beside whom they served. They were critical of the food provided by the Allies, particularly of sour French wine and British "hardtack." Some, particularly those who stayed overseas after the armistice, made complaints and uncomplimentary remarks about the French people. But they had very few complaints regarding their associations with the "Tommy" and "Poilu." The comment by former Second Lieutenant Waldo Moore of the 109th Field Artillery is typical: "I had a high opinion of all the troops from those countries with which I had contact, particularly the British, French and Belgian."[99] The "Yanks" gave even more praise to the soldiers from the British Dominions; they felt a greater kinship with the Australians and Canadians than they did with the Europeans.[100]

Mindful of the intense hatred of the "Hun" during the war, I was surprised by the high ratings that the American veterans who responded gave to the enemy soldiers, particularly the Germans. Former private Ira Lacey of Battery B, 107th Field Artillery, said, "The Germans must have been pretty good fighters . . . the cost in lives that it took to defeat them." Of the 378 veterans who commented about the enemy, only twenty-nine had negative comments; twenty-two said the enemy were fairly good soldiers, while the other 227 described the Germans as good soldiers, good fighters.[101] It is probable that less commendatory statements would have been made about the enemy had the U.S. veterans endured four years of war on the western front, as did the Allied soldiers.

Some lessons may be deduced from this war regarding the problems of coalition warfare. For three years of war prior to America's entry into the conflict, the Allies suffered from the inability to gain unity of command over the forces on the western front. From the Battle of the Frontiers in August 1914 until the Battle of Caporetto in the fall of 1917, the Allies had seen their common aims frustrated by the unique aims and purposes that each member of the alliance considered separately paramount. During the fighting on the Marne in 1914, the French suspected that the British might fall back on the Channel—and the Germans focused their drives on the juncture of the British Expeditionary Force and the French armies to lead to that result. Later, the French openly stated that the British were withholding a substantial portion of their combat power from the western front to retain and expand their colonial empire, and this was apparently true. The British, on the other hand, suspected that the French were not committing all of their manpower to the defense of their own country, while they were encouraging the British to commit the last of their manpower to the defense of France.[102] Earlier, I told of British reservations about accepting orders from the Allied high command. Defending the British attitude, Peter Simkins stated that it was not appreciated by the French and others that Great Britain was keeping the sea lanes open, bottling up the German fleet, and fighting, nearly alone, in the Middle East and Africa against the Central Powers.[104]

It was this combination of suspicious allies that the United States joined in April 1917. Almost immediately, the Allies contested with each other for American manpower, and each whispered suspicions to American political and military leaders regarding the other. The French stressed the point that the Americans were in France and could learn the most from their associations with the French on the battlefield in which they would all fight. They also stressed long-term political associations, going back to the French commitments during the American Revolution. The British made the point that our troops would find a common language with the British and share a commonality of culture. The British desired the establishment of an American Army in association with the BEF, while the French suspected that they were doing exactly that. The French complained regarding the number of American replacements being trained with the British as a result of their having been transported to France in British ships, and the British complained when Pershing attempted to withdraw those troops placed with them for training; the British had assumed the U.S. troops would remain indefinitely. Thomas Lonergan (former lieutenant colonel, general staff, AEF) in his text *It Might Have Been Lost* cited documents from British and French archives that prove, as he saw it, that both sides were making desperate attempts to procure American manpower for their armies, at the same time that each attempted to prevent the other from gaining American reinforcements. Lonergan's sources can hardly be contested; his conclusions seem to be correct.[105] On the other hand, the Allies can hardly be faulted. During the German offensives of 1918, the AEF had a million men in France, at least another million in the United States who could be sent—and the Allies were fighting "with their backs to the wall."

The problems that the United States experienced in this, our first modern wartime coalition, were repeated with varying intensities of problem and pattern in World War II with the same allies in Europe. The designation in World War II of a "combined allied command" for the invasion of Europe, and General Dwight Eisenhower's success in directing multinational forces and leaders, give hope for successful coalition operations, should NATO be called to the field in future war. However, it is in the nature of partners in coalitions of "sovereign" powers to distrust each other and to give less than full assistance when it is not in their clear self-interest to do so. It is also a characteristic of a coalition of sovereign nations to be slow in decision making, and to fail to obey decisions of the combined command that seem to some of the members to be unwise. These experiences are relevant to our defensive associations today and for the foreseeable future.

From the Armistice until today, the importance of the AEF contribution to Allied victory on the western front is debated. Colonel John Elting (military historian and author) credited the Americans with having played a major role in stopping the 1918 German drives, and thought that their reinforcement of the Allies' forces was the decisive element in the final Allied offensive. Edward Coffman reflected the opinion of many historians on both sides of the ocean that it was the appreciation of U.S. reinforcements, current and projected, which caused Ludendorff to give up the fight.[107] As to the significance of the Meuse-Argonne campaign itself, the AEF commanders and staff believed it was the most decisive action on the western front.[108] One could as well argue, as did Correlli Barnett, that the British and French actions in stopping the German offensives of 1918, and the Allies' later advances were more significant.[109] However, the leader of the forces which fought the Americans and their Allies, General Ludendorff, said, "The American infantry in the Argonne won the war."[110]

The matter of the American contribution to the victory became a subject of contention in the press upon the publication of Pershing's *Experiences* in 1931. The *New York Times* selected the British military commentator B. H. Liddell Hart, to review the text. I mentioned earlier that Liddell Hart was rather critical of the work. He stated that the American battlefield contribution was an important one, but hardly the most decisive.[111] Hart's views prompted rebuttals in letters to the editor of the *New York Times*. Thomas M. Johnson of New York City cited Prince Max of Baden, General Ludendorff, and General Groener on the enemy's side, who stated that the Meuse-Argonne was the most critical point along the front.[112] Wendell Westover, former infantry captain in the AEF, took on Liddell Hart for criticizing Pershing's insistence on forming an American Army. Slashing at Hart for "rank deception," Westover stated that the German reserves were known to have concentrated against the American drive, while the British forces, filled with "war torn veterans and last resort infants" were hardly doing "great offensive deeds."[113] This last provoked a response from Liddell Hart. Citing figures to prove the sacrifices and achievements of the BEF and the British people, Liddell Hart defended his position on the relative merits of the campaigns of the BEF and the AEF, and huffily restated his experience in battle (a matter alluded to derogatorily by Westover).[114] From this vantage point in time, Liddell Hart seems to have got the better of the argument. His judgment—that the American reinforcement, in toto, was vital to victory, but that the American military commitment in the Meuse-Argonne was not the most decisive action—seems to be reasonable.

As recently as 1983, this matter came up again in the press. John Giles, founder and president emeritus of The Western Front Association (an active group, centered in England, who study and memorialize the events of the First World War), wrote to me about a contretemps concerning credit for hastening the departure of the Germans from the western front. In his letter he enclosed a clipping from *The London Daily Telegraph* of 3 August 1983, in which a British reader who had been in World Wars I and II, stated that he was fed up with the carping against the Americans. He wanted to record his opinion that the Americans had won the First World

War for the Allies. Giles answered in *The Telegraph* to the effect that had the war gone into 1919, the Americans would have had to bear the brunt of the fighting and could then have been considered to have won the war for the Allies—but it just did not turn out that way.[115] I agree with Giles.

I conclude that the Meuse-Argonne campaign was "a decisive action." It contributed to the Allied victory but it was not the only nor the most decisive offensive of the war. For the Americans, it was a hard-won victory—won only in the last stages and at a great cost in lives. It was a victory produced mostly by improperly trained leaders and soldiers, and it was won by determination, esprit, and the exhaustion of the enemy. The victory was a tribute to the vitality and strength of the United States when sorely tried. The losses should have served as a lesson of the price of military unpreparedness. That lesson was not learned.

After the Great War, U.S. military and civil leaders attempted to establish a permanent military structure that would keep the nation strong in time of peace. Secretary Baker and General March argued for a large, modern standing army. Pershing, commenting that "our traditions are opposed to the maintenance of a large standing army," proposed a smaller Regular Army, with a major commitment to train large, well-equipped civilian reserve organizations. Both Baker's and Pershing's proposals called for "universal military training for all males at age nineteen."[116] But the American people and their Congress would have none of it. By the National Defense Act of 1920, a Regular Army of 288,000 was authorized; appropriations allowed for only 200,000. In response to the public's mood, Congress reduced funds in successive years. By the end of Pershing's tour as army chief of staff in 1924, the active army was down to 110,000. The American people were disillusioned with their European allies and with the political results from the war in which they had sacrificed their young men and spent their money. Isolationism was running strong; equally strong was antimilitarism.[117]

What lessons were learned from the war? From their wartime experiences, the French were to adopt the "Maginot-line strategy," in which near total reliance was placed upon a strong defensive line on their eastern border. The British, horrified by their disastrous experiment in land warfare on the continent of Europe, relied again on their navy and looked to an indirect approach to any future threat from the continent. The postwar politics of England were increasingly dominated by a clique which held that military threats could be defused by diplomatic negotiations. The United States slammed the door on European affairs, at least for a time. Our solution to modern war was international disarmament, and nearly domestic disarmament as well. We had no warfighting strategy worthy of the title. The German military alone among the major powers, forged an offensive strategy from the very edge of developing technology: swift, deep penetration of an enemy's defenses by the combined "blitzkrieg" of massed tanks supported by fighter aircraft.

The American people had every reason for concluding that their noble effort to save the Allies had been in vain. American participation in the Great War did not "make the world safe for democracy." The elites in the Allied nations had no intention of surrendering power to the lower classes; the democracies that were formed in Europe by the peace treaties were short-lived—most giving way to dictatorships. The American public, too, shrank away from Woodrow Wilson's grand design for international order and peace. Finally, it became apparent that the war had not really been won; the "war to end all wars" had only postponed some international struggles that were building again in the 1930s.[118]

But I argue that America's entry into World War I was both necessary and inevitable—necessary to defeat worldwide aggression, at least on the seas, which if successful would have posed great problems for the United States. Our step into the Great War was inevitable, the assumption of a role in international leadership made necessary by our growing economic power in an increasingly interdependent and dangerous world. However much we may have wished to isolate ourselves, there was no turning back. The world of the twentieth century would not allow America to be secure in isolation. The historian C. Vann Woodward characterized this change in U.S. affairs as "the passing of the Age of Free Security."[119] The author Daniel Smith said in *The Great Departure: The United States and World I*: "World War I marked a great departure for the United States, from the less demanding world of the past into the more dangerous but challenging world of the twentieth century."[120] It would take another generation and another world war for America to understand and accept the thankless role of world leadership and to arm herself adequately to exercise that role.

In a hollow framed by the hills of Romagne, France, facing the heights on which the Kriemhilde defenses were anchored, an American cemetery was established in 1919. This is the resting place for fourteen thousand Americans who died during the Meuse-Argonne offensive. It is a well-landscaped, carefully tended shrine, a memorial for those who made the supreme sacrifice. French schoolchildren still visit the graves, and many plots are decorated with fresh flowers. A visitor may muse on the luck, or the lack of it, that brought these men here instead of home in victory. Luck does discriminate in any war. But some—no, many of these men lie here because they were committed to battle with insufficient training, poor tactics, and inadequate leadership. Of all that the United States gave to the Allied cause in the Great War, these young men were our most precious

The United States Military Cemetery at Romagne, France. *(From author's collection.)*

resource. Their unfulfilled lives, their hopes and dreams can only be imagined—and the loss remembered for all time. General Pershing dedicated this cemetery in 1919. I leave this narrative with the final words he spoke: "And now, dear comrades, farewell. Here, under the clear skies, on the green hillsides and amid the flowering fields of France, in the quiet hush of peace, we leave you forever in God's keeping."[121]

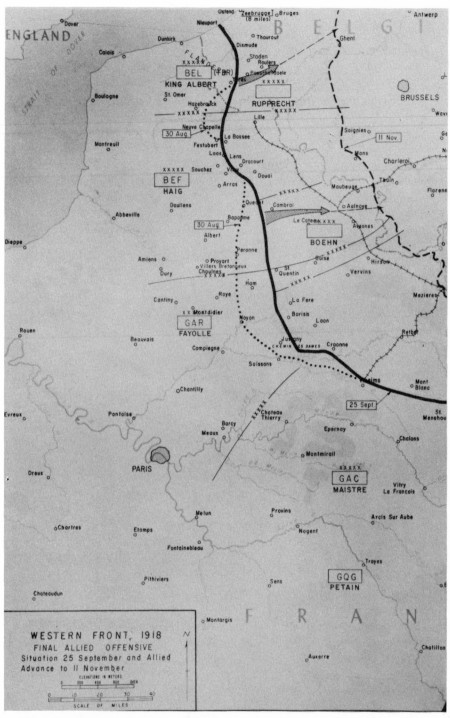

Map 8. The Western Front, 1918. *(From Department of History, United States Military Academy, map to accompany interim text,* **The Great War.** *West Point: U.S.M.A., 1979.)*

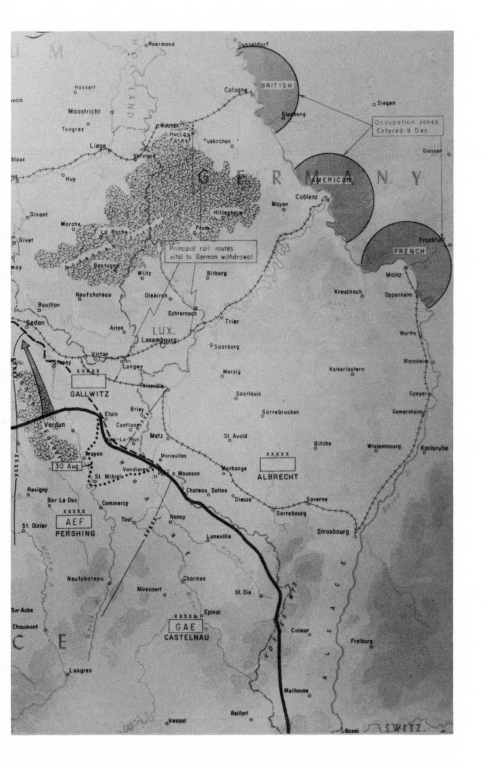

Roermond
Dusseldorf
Hasselt
BRITISH
Cologne
Siegen
Maastricht
Tongres
Siegburg
Occupation zones
Entered 9 Dec
Aachen
Liege
Verviers
Hurtgen Forest
Euskirchen
Giessen
Huy
G E R M A N Y
AMERICAN
Dinant
Mayen
Coblenz
Marche
Hillesheim
Givet
La Roche
Prum
Principal rail routes
vital to German withdrawal
FRENCH
Frankfurt
Bastogne
Wiltz
Bitberg
Mainz
Neufchateau
Diekirch
Kreuznach
Oppenheim
Bouillon
Echternach
LUX.
Trier
Sedan
Arlon
Luxembourg
Worms
Saarburg
Virton
Longwy
Merzig
Mannheim
Kaiserlautern
XXXXX
Thionville
Saarlouis
Speyer
GALLWITZ
Briey
Saarburg
Etain
Sarrebrucken
Gemersheim
Verdun
Conflans
Bitche
Metz
St. Avold
Wissembourg
Karlsruhe
30 Aug
Vandieres
Marieulles
Morhange
ALBRECHT
St. Mihiel
Pont a Mousson
Revigny
Chateau Salins
Bar Le Duc
Commercy
Dieuze
Saverne
Nancy
Sarrebourg
St. Dizier
AEF
Toul
PERSHING
Luneville
Strasbourg
Charmes
Neufchateau
Mirecourt
St. Die
Sur Aube
Epinal
Chaumont
GAE
Colmar
CASTELNAU
Freiburg
Langres
Mulhouse
Belfort
Vesoul
Basel
SWITZ.

APPENDIX 1
DEFINITIONS OF MILITARY TERMS,
ABBREVIATIONS, AND SYMBOLS

AEF = American Expeditionary Forces. The land forces, Army and Marines, which the United States sent to France in World War I.

BEF = British Expeditionary Force. The land force of British and Colonial troops which Great Britain sent to France.

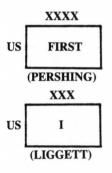 = The United States First Army, commanded by General Pershing. The four X's over the rectangle indicate an Army, consisting of a number of corps. The U.S. is used when foreign armies are also shown.

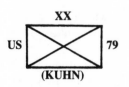 = The United States First Corps (corps are designated by Roman numerals), commanded by General Liggett. A corps consists of a number (variable according to mission) of divisions. Three X's over the rectangle indicate a corps.

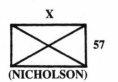 = The United States 79th Infantry Division, commanded by General Kuhn. An infantry division consisted of 28,000 personnel; its infantry combat units were two infantry brigades (8500 men each). The name of the commander is also shown after the title where the name is significant.

= The 57th Infantry Brigade (Gen. Nicholson).

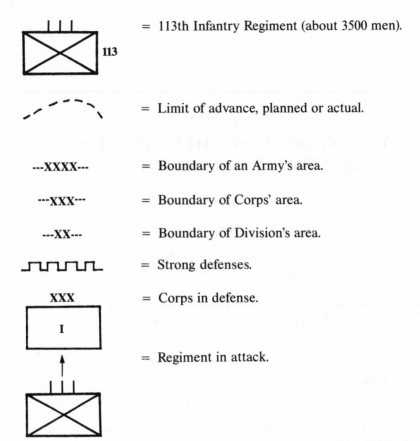

= 113th Infantry Regiment (about 3500 men).

= Limit of advance, planned or actual.

= Boundary of an Army's area.

= Boundary of Corps' area.

= Boundary of Division's area.

= Strong defenses.

= Corps in defense.

= Regiment in attack.

Objective = A geographical area to be attacked and seized.

Objective line, Phase Line, Maneuver Line = Lines drawn on a map to control the movement of attacking units by order (e.g. "move to" "hold at").

TO&E = The Table of Organization and Equipment which shows the personnel, weapons, and other equipment allocated to a unit, broken out by subunits and sections.

LOC = Line of Communications. The route along which an organization communicates with its supporting elements in its rear and with higher headquarters and support, and by which it receives support and supply.

Strategy = The plan for the employment of military forces in major groupings to place them in a favorable position for battle.

Tactics = The disposition and maneuver of units on a battlefield. Higher Tactics refers to the maneuver of major forces beyond a single battle area.

Turning or Outflanking = The act of moving an attacking unit around the sides or flanks of a defender to the extent that he is forced to withdraw or fight at a disadvantage.

Fire and Movement/maneuver = Directing the fires of weapons upon a defensive position to prevent return fire while moving a unit to attack the position or move around it.

Final Protective Fires/Lines = Fires of weapons from defensive positions which are preset along a single line, to be fired together when the position is under assault/attack.

Company Grade Officers = Lieutenants and Captains: Field Grade = Majors, Lieutenant Colonels, and Colonels; General Officers = all Generals.

Beaten/Killing Zone = That area, usually prearranged, where the fires from defensive weapons are concentrated.

Barrage = The coordinated firing of a number of artillery pieces or mortar weapons so that the projectiles land at the same time in a selected area.

Interdictory Fire = The employment of weapons to deny an area to enemy usage.

APPENDIX 2
TIME SPENT IN TRAINING AND COMBAT

```
Divi-      1917                              1918
sion Jul Aug Sep Oct Nov Dec Jan Feb Mar Apr May Jun Jul Aug Sep Oct N

1st  000000000000000/////////////////////////XXXXXXXXXXXXXXXXXXXXXXXXXX
2d   ooooooooooooooooo00000000000000000000///////////XXXXXXXXXXXXXXXXXXXX
26th       oooooooooooo000000000000///////////////////XXXXXXXXXXXXXXX
42d        ooooooooooo0000000000000//////////////////XXXXXXXXXXXXXXX
41st       ooooooooooooo0000000000000000000000000000000000000000000000000
32d        oooooooooooooooooooooooooo000000000000///////XXXXXXXXXXXXXXX
3d             ooooooooooooooooooooooo////////XXXXXXXXXXXXXXXXXXXX
77th         ooooooooooooooooooooooooooo000000000//////XXXXXXXXXXX
5th            ooooooooooooooooooooooooo0000/////////XXXXXXXXX
27th         ooooooooooooooooooooooooooooooo00000000XXXXXXXXXXXXXXXXX
35th         ooooooooooooooooooooooooooooooo000000//////XXXXXXXXX
82d          ooooooooooooooooooooooooooooooo00000///////XXXXXXXXX
4th               oooooooooooooooooooooo0000000XXXXXXXXXXXXXXX
28th         oooooooooooooooooooooooooooooooooo00000000XXXXXXXXXXXXXX
30th            boooooooooooooooooooooooooooooo000000XXXXXXXXXXXX
33d          ooooooooooooooooooooooooooooooooooo000000000000//XXXXXXX
80th          ooooooooooooooooooooooooooooooooo000000000000/XXXXXXX
78th         ooooooooooooooooooooooooooooooooooo0000000000XXXXXXXXX
83d          oooooooooooooooooooooooooooooooooooo00000000000000000
92d             ooooooooooooooooooooooooooooooooo0000000/////////
89th         ooooooooooooooooooooooooooooooooooooo00000////XXXXXXX
90th         oooooooooooooooooooooooooooooooooooooo00000///XXXXXXX
37th         oooooooooooooooooooooooooooooooooooooo000//////XXXXXX
29th   oooooooooooooooooooooooooooooooooooooooo00///////XXXX
91st       oooooooooooooooooooooooooooooooooooooooo000000//XXXXX
76th   oooooooooooooooooooooooooooooooooooooooooooo00000000000000
79th       oooooooooooooooooooooooooooooooooooo000000//XXXXX
6th          ooooooooooooooooooooooooooooooo00000////////
36th       oooooooooooooooooooooooooooooooooooo000000XXXXXX
85th         oooooooooooooooooooooooooooooooooooooooo00000000000000
7th              ooooooooooooooooooooooooooooo000000////
81st       oooooooooooooooooooooooooooooooooooooooo00000/////
88th       oooooooooooooooooooooooooooooooooooooo0000//////
40th         ooooooooooooooooooooooooooooooooooooooo00000000000
39th         oooooooooooooooooooooooooooooooooooooo0000008000
87th         ooooooooooooooooooooooooooooooooooooo000000000
86th         ooooooooooooooooooooooooooooooooooooo00000000000
84th         oooooooooooooooooooooooooooooooooooooo00000000
34th   ooooooooooooooooooooooooooooooooooooooooooo0000000
38th      oooooooooooooooooooooooooooooooooooooooooooo00000
31st      oooooooooooooooooooooooooooooooooooooooooooooo0000
8th              ooooooooooooooooooooooooooooooooooooooooooo0
```

ooooo Organization or entry on active duty until arrival in France.
00000 Arrival in France until entering the line.
///// In the line; quiet sector.
XXXXX Active combat.

From: Final Report of Assistant Chief of Staff G-1 to Commander-in-
      Chief, American Expeditionary Forces, 22 April 1919 (NA RG 120,
      Folder 29) 32.

176

APPENDIX 3
STATUS OF DIVISIONS ON THE WESTERN FRONT, 11 NOVEMBER 1918

Armies	Divisions on Line			Divisions in Reserve			Total
	Fresh	Tired	Total	Fresh	Tired	Total	Avail.
United States	4	12	16	3	11	14	30
France	19	17	36	19	53	72	108
Great Britain	5	24	29	6	29	35	64
Belgium	3	1	4	2	1	3	7
Italy	1	0	1	0	1	1	2
Portugal	0	0	0	2	0	2	2
TOTAL ALLIES	32	97	144	32	95	127	213
Germany/ Austria	47	97	144	2	39	41	185

NOTE: American divisions are approximately twice the size of those of other nations.

(From *Final Report of A C of S, G-3 to CINC AEF,* 2 July 1919 [NA, RG 120, Series 274], 88.)

APPENDIX 4
DIVISION DAYS ON THE LINE IN FRANCE

Division	Quiet Sector	Active Sector	QUIET	ACTIVE	TOTAL DAYS
1st	127	93	/////////////XXXXXXXXX		220
26th	148	45	///////////////XXXXx	193	
42d	125	39	/////////////XXXX	164	
2d	71	66	///////XXXXXXx	137	
77th	47	66	/////XXXXXXx	113	
5th	71	32	///////XXX	103	
82d	70	27	///////XXX	97	
35th	92	5	/////////x	97	
32d	60	35	//////XXXx	95	
3d	0	86	//////////	86	
89th	55	28	//////XXX	83	
29th	59	23	//////XXx	82	
28th	31	49	///XXXXX	80	
90th	42	26	////XXx	68	
37th	50	11	/////X	61	
33d	32	27	///XXx	59	
27th	0	57	XXXXXx	57	
30th	0	56	XXXXXx	56	
92d	51	2	/////x	53	
79th	28	17	///Xx	45	
4th	7	35	/XXXx	42	
6th	40	0	////	40	
78th	17	21	//XX	38	
7th	31	2	///x	33	
81st	31	0	///	31	
91st	15	14	/Xx	29	
88th	28	0	///	28	
36th	0	23	XXx	23	
80th	1	17	Xx	18	

///// Quiet Sector
XXXXX Active Combat

From: Final Report of Assistant Chief of Staff G-3 to Commander-in-Chief, American Expeditionary Forces, 2 July 1919. (NA RG 120, Series 274)9.

APPENDIX 5
DISTANCE ADVANCED AGAINST FIRE

Division	Distance	Miles
77th	XXXXXXXXXXXXXXXXXXXXXXXXXXXXXXXXXXXXXXXXXXXXXx	44.5
2d	XXXXXXXXXXXXXXXXXXXXXXXXXXXXXXXXXXXXXXXx	37.5
42d	XXXXXXXXXXXXXXXXXXXXXXXXXXXXXXXXXXX	34
1st	XXXXXXXXXXXXXXXXXXXXXXXXXXXXXXXX	32
89th	XXXXXXXXXXXXXXXXXXXXXXXXXXXXXX	30
3d	XXXXXXXXXXXXXXXXXXXXXXXXXx	25.5
80th	XXXXXXXXXXXXXXXXXXXXXXXx	23.5
26th	XXXXXXXXXXXXXXXXXXXXXXX	23
32d	XXXXXXXXXXXXXXXXXXXXXx	22.5
33d	XXXXXXXXXXXXXXXXXXXXXx	22.5
91st	XXXXXXXXXXXXXXXXXXXXX	21
37th	XXXXXXXXXXXXXXXXXXX	19
30th	XXXXXXXXXXXXXXXXXXx	18.5
5th	XXXXXXXXXXXXXXXXXX	18
90th	XXXXXXXXXXXXXXXXX	17
4th	XXXXXXXXXXXXXXX	15
78th	XXXXXXXXXXXXX	13
36th	XXXXXXXXXXXXX	13
79th	XXXXXXXXXXXX	12
82d	XXXXXXXXXXx	10.5
35th	XXXXXXXX	8
27th	XXXXXXX	7
28th	XXXXXX	6
92d	XXXXX	5
29th	XXXX	4
91st	XXXx	3.5
7th	x	.5
6th		0
88th		0

From: Final Report of Assistant Chief of Staff G-3 to Commander-in-Chief, American Expeditionary Forces, 2 July 1919. (NA RG 120, Series 274) 7.

APPENDIX 6
AWARDS FOR VALOR, AGGREGATED BY DIVISION

Division	Medal of Honor	Distinguished Service Cross	Oak Leaf Cluster	Total
2d	7	673	13	693
1st	2	415	3	420
3rd	2	328	2	332
30th	12	307	-	319
26th	2	269	5	276
32d	-	250	-	250
42d	2	239	4	245
77th	6	202	3	211
33d	9	202	-	211
5th	2	197	-	199
27th	6	161	2	169
29th	3	159	-	162
4th	-	159	-	159
91st	4	143	1	148
89th	9	137	-	146
28th	1	138	4	143
78th	1	116	-	117
82d	2	94	-	96
90th	-	88	-	88
79th	-	88	-	88
35th	2	85	1	88
93d	1	69	-	70
37th	-	52	-	52
80th	-	50	-	50
36th	2	39	-	41
7th	-	37	-	37
81st	-	23	-	23
92d	-	22	-	22
6th	-	15	-	15
88th	-	1	-	1

NOTE: Oak Leaf Cluster means a second award of the same decoration. (From: *A C of S, G1, Final Report to CINC AEF,* 22 April 1919 [NA, RG 120, Folder 29], 11.)

APPENDIX 7
CASUALTIES, AGGREGATED BY DIVISION

Division	Casualties	Total
2d	CCCCCCCCCCCCCCCCCCCCCCCCCCCCCCCCCCCCCCCCCCCCCCCCCCCC	25,232
1st	CCCCCCCCCCCCCCCCCCCCCCCCCCCCCCCCCCCCCCCCCCCCCCCCC	23,496
3d	CCCCCCCCCCCCCCCCCCCCCCCCCCCCCCCCCCCCCCCCC	18,468
28th	CCCCCCCCCCCCCCCCCCCCCCCCCCCCCCCCCCCCC	17,003
42d	CCCCCCCCCCCCCCCCCCCCCCCCCCCCCCCCCCC	16,107
26th	CCCCCCCCCCCCCCCCCCCCCCCCCCCCCCCCCC	15,619
4th	CCCCCCCCCCCCCCCCCCCCCCCCCCCCCCC	14,255
32d	CCCCCCCCCCCCCCCCCCCCCCCCCCCCCC	14,040
77th	CCCCCCCCCCCCCCCCCCCCCCCCCCCCC	12,361
27th	CCCCCCCCCCCCCCCCCCCCCCCCCCc	11,446
30th	CCCCCCCCCCCCCCCCCCCCCCCCC	11,158
5th	CCCCCCCCCCCCCCCCCCCCC	9,981
33d	CCCCCCCCCCCCCCCCCCC	9,379
89th	CCCCCCCCCCCCCCCCCC	8,838
82d	CCCCCCCCCCCCCCCCC	8,467
78th	CCCCCCCCCCCCCCCCc	8,282
90th	CCCCCCCCCCCCCCCC	8,090
35th	CCCCCCCCCCCCCCCC	8,025
79th	CCCCCCCCCCCCCCC	7,670
80th	CCCCCCCCCCCCCC	6,864
91st	CCCCCCCCCCCCCC	6,524
29th	CCCCCCCCCCCCCc	6,226
37th	CCCCCCCCCCCCCC	5,946
36th	CCCCC	2,735
7th	CCCC	1,838
92d	CCCC	1,697
81st	CCC	1,102
6th	C	679
88th		99

NOTE: Total casualties included killed in action,
wounded, and evacuated for illness.

From: Final Report of Assistant Chief of Staff, G-3 to Commander-
in-Chief, American Expeditionary Forces, 2 July 1919. NA,
RG 120, Series 274) 33.

APPENDIX 8
PRISONERS OF WAR, AGGREGATED BY DIVISION

Division	Prisoners of War	Total
2d	PPPPPPPPPPPPPPPPPPPPPPPPPPPPPPPPPPPPPPPPPPPPPPPPPPP	12,026
1st	PPPPPPPPPPPPPPPPPPPPPPPPPPPP 6,469	
89th	PPPPPPPPPPPPPPPPPPPPPP 5,061	
33d	PPPPPPPPPPPPPPPPPP 3,987	
30th	PPPPPPPPPPPPPPPP 3,848	
26th	PPPPPPPPPPPPPp 3,148	
4th	PPPPPPPPPPPP 2,756	
91st	PPPPPPPPPp 2,412	
27th	PPPPPPPPPp 2,357	
5th	PPPPPPPPPp 2,356	
3d	PPPPPPPPP 2,240	
29th	PPPPPPPPp 2,187	
32d	PPPPPPPPp 2,153	
90th	PPPPPPPp 1,876	
80th	PPPPPPP 1,813	
37th	PPPPPP 1,495	
42dh	PPPPPp 1,317	
79th	PPPPp 1,077	
28th	PPPp 921	
82dh	PPPp 845	
35th	PPP 781	
77th	PPP 750	
36th	PP 549	
78th	PP 432	
81st	p 101	
7th	69	
92d	38	
6th	12	
88th	3	

From: Final Report of Assistant Chief of Staff, G-3 to Commander-in-Chief, American Expeditionary Forces, 2 July 1919. (NA RG 120, Series 274) 8.

APPENDIX 9
CONSOLIDATION OF PERFORMANCE
FACTORS

Division	Total of Indicators
2d	IIIIIIIIIIIIIIIIIIIIIIIIIIIIIIIIIIIIIIIIIIII
1st	IIIIIIIIIIIIIIIIIIIIIIIIIIIIIIIIIIIIIII
3d	IIIIIIIIIIIIIIIIIIIIIIII
26th	IIIIIIIIIIIIIIIIIIIII
42d	IIIIIIIIIIIIIIIIIIII
32d	IIIIIIIIIIIIIIIIII
77th	IIIIIIIIIIIIII
5th	IIIIIIIIIIIIII
30th	IIIIIIIIIIIIII
89th	IIIIIIIIIIIII
4th	IIIIIIIIIIII
33d	IIIIIIIIIIII
91st	IIIIIIIIII
90th	IIIIIIIIII
28th	IIIIIIIII
27th	IIIIIIII
78th	IIIIIII
29th	IIIIIII

APPENDIX 10
RESPONSES OF 728 VETERANS OF THE MEUSE-ARGONNE CAMPAIGN TO ARMY SERVICE EXPERIENCES QUESTIONNAIRES

Criterion	# Responses	Yes/Good	OK/Fair	No/Poor	Comment
Training	514	12	16	486	Lack of time.
Leadership	503	467	14	22	Leaders cared.
Discipline	429	358	34	27	Hard but fair.
Weapons	371	40	2	329	German's better.
Equipment	316	39	25	252	Allied issue.
Food	431	21	54	346	Bad, insuff.
Supplies	319	10	28	281	Transp. Problems.
Health	380	16	44	320	Wet, flu, cooties.
Morale	467	375	53	39	High, except no supplies.
Allies	251	210	30	11	OK except food
Enemy	378	327	22	29	Good soldier.
Fellow soldiers	481	415	44	22	Great friends.
Value of service	427	413	10	4	Proud to serve; no pension.

NOTE: It is likely that far more of the 6700 respondees to the MHI Questionnaire actually participated in the Meuse-Argonne Campaign. Of the 5,000 responses scanned by this author, only 728 could be identified as having participated in the fighting.

(Figures were collected by author from the Responses of veterans of World War I to Army Service Experiences Questionnaires and request for memorabilia made by U.S. Army's Military History Institute; with permission of the director and staff of that Institute.)

NOTES

CHAPTER 1. EUROPE CHOOSES WAR

1. Barbara W. Tuchman, *The Guns of August* (New York: Macmillan, 1962) conveys well the emotional stimuli to war that swept Europe at that time.

2. A Polish banker turned military analyst, Ivan Bloch, published in 1898 a six-volume study, *The Future of War in Its Technical, Economic, and Political Relations,* trans. R. C. Long, (Boston: Doubleday and McClure, 1899). This treatise accurately forecast huge casualties from modern weapons and mass armies equipped by industrialized societies. The text so shocked the czar that it prompted him to call the first Hague Peace Conference in 1899. Bloch himself lectured the delegates on the slaughter that could be effected by automatic weapons and explosive artillery shells. Neither his efforts nor those of the conferees appears to have prevailed against the appeals of war. See Theodore Ropp, *War in the Modern World* (New York: Collier, 1962), 218–220.

3. For greater explication of these martial developments, see Bernard and Fawn Brodie's *From Crossbow to H-Bomb* (New York: Dell Books, 1962), 137–153.

4. Naval developments, such as the screw propeller and turret gunnery, are not covered in this summary of land fighting. The military applications of the internal combustion engine will be taken up later.

5. Trevor N. Dupuy, *The Evolution of Weapons and Warfare* (New York: Bobbs-Merrill, 1980), 288, 289.

6. Ropp, *War in the Modern World*, 215–221.

7. Bloch, *The Future of War*, xvi, xli.

8. Ropp, *War in the Modern World*, 221–227.

9. The elan of the intelligentsia for war is exemplified by quotations from poets of that time in *The Great War*, James B. Agnew et al. (West Point: Unites States Military Academy, 1979), 443ff.

10. Robert Leckie, *The Wars of America*, vol. 2 (New York: Harper and Row, 1968), 76.

11. Like the armies of the Entente powers, the Germans had regarded the machine gun as a general support weapon, assigning two to each front line battalion. The wars of the early twentieth century, however, convinced the Germans of the effectiveness of the machine gun as a forward support weapon. They formed jäger (hunter) companies, with six machine guns each, to operate with rifle units. The armies of the Entente did not increase their machine gun strength until after the frontier battles of 1914. See John Ellis, *The Social History of the Machine Gun* (New York: Pantheon Books, 1975), 113–116.

12. Vincent Esposito, ed., *The West Point Atlas of American Wars*, vol. 2 (New York: Praeger, 1959) gives a succinct and graphic summary of these war plans and their execution, maps and text 2–6.

13. One of the many excellent accounts of the German offensive and the First Battle of

the Marne is John Keegan, *Opening Moves: August 1914* (New York: Viking Press, 1971); also Cyril Falls, *The Great War, 1914–1918 (First World War)* (London: Longman's 1960), 79ff.

14. In the nineteenth century, the Prussian military philosopher Karl von Clausewitz announced the superiority of the defensive form of war (although he did prescribe a counteroffensive as a requisite to victory). Karl von Clausewitz, *vom Kriege*, (Berlin, 1832; trans. J. J. Graham, 1908; pub. by Pelican Books, Hammondsworth, England as *Carl von Clausewitz: On War,* 1968.

15. *West Point Atlas,* maps and text 16–21.

16. Excellent accounts of the British-led campaign in the Dardanelles are Robert R. James *Gallipoli* (London: Longman's, 1965) and Alan Morehead's *Gallipoli* (London: Hamilton, 1956); a personal attempt at exculpation is General Sir Ian Hamilton, *Gallipoli Diary* (London: Arnold, 1920).

17. Luigi Villari, *The War on the Italian Front* (London: Unwin, 1932).

18. The strategic deadlock is well summarized by Hanson Baldwin in his pithy text, *World War I: An Outline History* (London: Hutchinson, 1963).

19. Ibid., 73.

20. Col. G. L. McEntee, *Military History of the World War* (New York: Scribners Sons, 1937), quoted by Baldwin, *World War I,* 79.

21. The British official history of the Great War is entitled *History of the Great War.* The history of the BEF is entitled *Military Operations France and Belgium,* James E. Edmonds, ed., 1917, 3 vols; 1918, 5 vols. (London: Macmillan, 1935–48). The French official history is État-Major de l'Armée, Service Historique, *Les Armées Françaises dans la grande guerre.* Volumes 5–7 are germane to this period (Paris: Imprimerie Nationale, 1923–38). The German official history is *Der Weltkrieg, 1914 bis 1918.* Volumes 1, 5–7 are germane to this period (Berlin: Reicharchiv, 1925).

22. A military account of the "face off" of the two great fleets is given in Commander Halloway H. Frost, *The Battle of Jutland* (Annapolis: U.S. Naval Institute, 1936). A good account of the controversies surrounding the conduct of the battle from a British viewpoint is given by Admiral Sir Reginald Bacon in *The Jutland Scandal* (London: Hutchinson, 1925).

23. An American account of the blockade and submarine warfare, critical of the British, is Thomas G. Frothingham, *The Naval History of the World War,* vol. 1, 3 vols. (Cambridge: Harvard University Press, 1925). A more reasoned account is Louis Guichard's *The Naval Blockade, 1914–1918* (Paris: n.p., 1930).

24. The U.S.M.A. text, *The Great War,* gives a good summary of these operations and their effects in chapter 4, "Deadlock and Attrition on the Western Front, 1914–1916."

25. Criticism during the years of attrition was strongest and most public in the capitals of the Entente powers; however, dissatisfaction at the highest levels did result in the relief of the heads of the British, French, Russian, and German armies in 1915, and again, for the French and Germans, after the disasters of 1916. After the war, a torrent of criticism came from the home front and the trenches, their authors newly released from the restrictions of censorship. See bibliography.

26. Baldwin, *World War I,* 49ff; Dupuy, T. N., *Weapons and Warfare,* 217–229.

27. C. S. Forester, *The General* (Boston: Houghton Mifflin, 1936).

28. Wilhelm Balck, *Development of Tactics—World War,* trans. Harry Bell (Fort Leavenworth: General Staff School Press, 1922).

29. Ibid., 71ff.

30. Captain G. C. Wynne, *If Germany Attacks: The Battle in Depth in the West* (London: Faber and Faber, 1940), 83ff.

31. Ibid. 85–104.

32. Maurice is quoted by H. A. DeWeerd (no small critic himself) in the foreword to DeWeerd's text, *Great Soldiers of Two World Wars* (New York: W. W. Norton, 1962), 14.

CHAPTER 2. 1917—THE YEAR OF HOPE AND DESPAIR

1. German strategy and its changes are presented in some detail in Fritz Fischer, *Germany's Aims in the First World War* (New York: W. W. Norton, 1961); another view is that of Hans Gatzke, *Germany's Drive to the West* (Baltimore: The Johns Hopkins University Press, 1950).

2. U.S.M.A., *The Great War,* 210–221; also Baldwin, *World War I,* 99–104.

3. D. F. Fleming, *The Origins and Legacies of World War I* (Greenwich: Fawcett, 1968), 270–277.

4. The taking of Vimy ridge by the Canadians cost 100,000 lives and set a record for slaughter in a war where high casualties had become routine (Fleming, *Origins and Legacies,* 277). For an intriguing account of the political-military discussions preceding this offensive, see Gen. Sir E. L. Spears, *Prelude to Victory* (London: Cape, 1930).

5. The "first" battle of the Aisne was a prelude to the Allied "race to the sea," which occurred in September 1914.

6. U.S.M.A. Text, *The Great War,* 210ff, 207–222. For an account of the causes and effects of the French mutinies, see Richard M. Watt, *Dare Call It Treason* (New York: Simon and Schuster, 1963).

7. U.S.M.A., *The Great War,* 222–227; also Baldwin, *World War I,* 102–104. For an indictment of the futility of this offensive, see Leon Wolff, *In Flanders Fields: The 1917 Campaign* (London: Longman's, 1958).

8. U.S.M.A., *The Great War,* 225, 226, 230–233.

9. The best account of the confusing political-military maneuvers of this theater is Winston Churchill, *The Unknown War* (New York: Scribner's Sons, 1932), 353ff. The insertion of Lenin into the Russian political arena was a masterstroke on the part of the Germans; Lenin's presence had much to do with Russia's surrender and much more to do with postwar troubles for the Allies and for Germany.

10. *West Point Atlas,* map and text 43.

11. A good account of the new German offensive tactics (the so-called "hutier tactics") was given by Erwin Rommel in *Infantry Attacks,* trans. G. E. Kidde (Washington: GPO, 1944), 168–207.

12. *West Point Atlas,* map and text 41.

13. Villari, *War Italian Front,* 126ff. For a detailed study of the disaster at Caporetto, see Cyril Falls, *Caporetto 1917* (London: Weidenfield, 1965).

14. *West Point Atlas,* maps and text 52–56.

15. Allied shipping losses (largely British) were 868,000 tons in 1915; 1,236,000 tons in 1916; and two million tons during the first four months of 1917 (Fleming, *Origins and Legacies,* 276). A good account of the controversy over the convoy system is Arthur Marder, *From Dreadnaught to Scapa Flow,* vol. 2 of 5 vols. (New York: Oxford University Press, 1961–1970), 134–159.

16. Most authorities agree concerning the tremendous material and capital (loan) reinforcement provided by the U.S. before and after it became a belligerent.

CHAPTER 3. AMERICA SENDS AN ARMY TO FRANCE

1. Wilson's statement was paraphrased by Robert Leckie in *The Wars of America,* 2:75–76.

2. Ibid, 2:76.

3. Oliver L. Spaulding (Col., U.S. Army), *The United States Army in War and Peace* (New York: G. P. Putnam & Sons, 1937), pp. 406–408.

4. Leckie, *The Wars of America*, 2:78–104.

5. Tuchman writes interestingly of this crisis in her book, *The Zimmerman Telegram* (New York: Dell, 1958).

6. Leckie, *The Wars of America*, 104–106.

7. Daniel R. Beaver, *A Progressive at War: Newton D. Baker and the American War Effort, 1917–1919* (Ph.D. diss., Northwestern University, 1962), Preface.

8. Ibid., preface. also Maurice Matloff, ed., *American Military History* (Washington: GPO, 1973), 372–373.

9. Department of the Army, *The Army Lineage Book, Vol. II, Infantry* (Washington: GPO, 1953), 34–39, 60, 61.

10. Spaulding, *The U.S. Army*, 410.

11. Paul S. Bond (Col., U.S. Army) and Col. Clarence O. Sherrill, *America in the World War: A Summary of the Achievements of the Great Republic in the Conflict with Germany* (Menasha, Wis.: Collegiate Press, 1921), 47–53.

12. Ibid., 47–49.

13. Ibid., 52–55.

14. Richard Goldhurst, *Pipe Clay and Drill* (New York: Thomas Y. Crowell, 1977), 254–259. The attitude of the Allies regarding the capabilities of America's military leadership are well summarized in an unpublished thesis by Major James W. Rainey, *The Training of the American Expeditionary Forces in World War I* (Philadelphia: Temple University, 1981), 15, 16.

15. Edward M. Coffman, *The War to End All Wars* (New York: Oxford University Press, 1968), 47.

16. Josiah B. Miller, "Development of Departmental Direction of Training. . . ." (Washington: Dept. of Army, n.d.), 1, 2.

17. Ray Stannard Baker, *Woodrow Wilson: Life and Letters; Facing War, 1915–1917* (New York: Doubleday, 1937), 490–506; also Arthur S. Link, *Woodrow Wilson and the Progressive Era, 1910–1917* (New York: Harper, 1935), 277–282.

18. House was quoted by Rainey, *The Training of American Forces*, 11.

19. Ibid., 12.

20. Baker, *Woodrow Wilson*, 507.

21. In his *Reminiscences*, General Douglas MacArthur (New York: McGraw-Hill, 1964), 46, 47, said Funston had been selected to lead the AEF. There is no reliable evidence to support MacArthur's recollection.

22. Peyton C. March, *The Nation at War* (Garden City: Doubleday, 1932), 247–48.

23. Ibid., 249.

24. Frank E. Vandiver, *Black Jack: The Life and Times of John J. Pershing*, vol. 2, (College Station: Texas A&M Press, 1977), 695.

25. At the risk of killing yet another pleasant myth, it must be reported that Pershing did not utter the words, "Lafayette, we are here!" He was present at a review of the 16th Infantry Regiment on the 4 July 1917 at Lafayette's tomb when those words were uttered by a quartermaster colonel. See Matloff, ed., *American Military History*, 273.

26. "Final Report of Assistant Chief of Staff for Operations (G-3) to Commander in Chief, AEF," 2 July 1919. National Archives, Records Group 120, Series 274, 7. Hereafter, these archival groups records will be referred to by the notations "NA" and "RG."

27. Ibid., 8.

28. The identities of those in the picture are:
Left to right, standing: (1) Col. Benjamin Alvord, A.G. of AEF; (2) Maj. Robert Bacon, A.G. Dept.; (3) Lt. Col. George S. Simonds, War Dept. Inf.; (4) Col. Charles P. Summerall, W.D. Artillery; (5) Maj. Alvin B. Barber, Gen. Staff, AEF. (g-1); (6) Lt. Col. John Barker, Gen. Staff, AEF; (7) Lt. Col. Dwight E. Aultman, W.,D. Artillery; (8) Lt. Col. Fox Conner,

Gen. Staff, AEF (G-3); (9) Col. William S. Graves, W.D.G.S.; (10) Maj. Gen. John J. Pershing, C-in-C, AEF; (11) Maj. Arthur L. Conger, Gen. Staff, AEF (G-2); (12) Col. Chauncey B. Baker, Q.M.C.; (13) Lt. Col. Hanson E. Ely, W.D.; (14) Lt. Col. James G. Harbord, Chief of Staff, AEF; (15) Col. Mark L. Hersey, W.D.; (16) Lt. Col. Sherwood A. Cheney, Engineers, W.D.; (17) Lt. Col. Edward D. Anderson, Gen. Staff, W.D.; (18) Maj. Marlborough Churchill, AEF, Field Artillery.

Left to right, sitting: (1) Maj. Morris E. Locke, W.D., Artillery; (2) Maj. Nelson E. Margetts, A.C.C., AEF; (3) Lt. Col. Kirby Walker, Cav. W.D.; (4) Lt. Col. John McA. Palmer, G.S., AEF (G-3); (5) Lt. Col. Dennis E. Nolan, G.S. AEF (G-2); (6) Capt. Martin C. Shallenberger, ADC, AEF; (7) Capt. William O. Reed, Cav. AEF (G-2); (8) Maj. Hugh A. Drum, G.S., AEF; (9) Capt. Jas. L. Collins, ADC, AEF; (10) Maj. Robert H. Dunlap, Marine Corps, Washington; (11) Maj. Frank Parker, Cav. AEF.

Source of Photo: Copy from U.S. Army Signal Corps Photo #94307, held in the Archives of the Military History Institute, Carlisle Barracks, Pennsylvania.

29. *AC of S G-3, Final Report,* 8, 9.

30. Matloff, ed., *American Military History,* 374–375.

31. Rainey, *Training of AEF;* also *Final Report of AEF G–3,* 12.

32. Report of the Chief of Staff, U.S. Army to the Secretary of War, 1919 (Annual Reports, War Department, Washington: GPO, 1920), 18–19.

33. War Department General Order No. 53, 27 May 1918 (NA RG 94).

34. Edward M. Coffman, *The Hilt of the Sword: The Career of Peyton C. March* (Madison: University of Wisconsin Press, 1966), chap. 5.

35. Historical Division, U.S. Army, *The United States Army in the World War, 1917–1919,* 17 vols. (Washington, GPO, 1948) 3:38, 39.

36. Coffman, *Hilt of Sword,* 48–51.

37. Ibid., 60, 61.

38. Ibid, 58, 59; also Donald Smythe, *Pershing: General of the Armies* (Bloomington: University of Indiana Press, 1986), 56, 167, 168.

39. John J. Pershing, General of the Armies, *My Experiences in The World War,* 2 vols. (New York: Stokes, 1931), 1:103; *Final Report of G-3,* 45, 46; Matloff, *American Military History,* 382, 383.

40. Pershing, *My Experiences,* 1:100–110, 128, 129.

41. A detailed presentation of the organization, growth, and problems of the AEF logistics system is in Johnson Hagood, *The Services of Supply* (New York: Houghton Mifflin, 1927).

42. Pershing, *My Experiences,* 1:28, 29, 150–154.

43. Rainey, *Training of AEF,* 1–16.

44. Ibid; also Pershing, *My Experiences,* 1:150–154.

45. Letter to the author from Maj. Gen. Irving B. Holley Jr., professor of history, Duke University, author of the text, *General John M. Palmer: Citizen Soldiers and the Army of a Democracy* (Westport, Conn.: Greenwood Press, 1982).

46. George S. Pappas (Col., U.S. Army), *Prudens Futuri: The U.S. Army War College, 1901–1967* (Carlisle: USAWC, 1967), 89. Pappas argued that 30 percent of general officers serving at the time of the Armistice were War College graduates. He also quoted Maj. Gen. Hugh Scott (chief of staff in 1917) as to the tremendous demand for War College graduates for high-level command and staff positions.

47. Rainey, *Training of AEF,* 16.

48. Cable 228–S, 19 October 1917, Pershing to Adjutant General, War Department, quoted in *The United States Army in the World War, 1917–1919,* 14:316.

49. Pershing, *My Experiences,* 1:151–152.

50. See the program for training for the 1st Infantry Division, issued by headquarters,

American Expeditionary Forces, in October 1917, reproduced in vol. 14, *The United States Army in the World War,* 304; also, Pershing, *My Experiences,* 1:152–154.

51. War Department Document No. 394, *Infantry Drill Regulations, United States Army, 1911* (Washington: GPO, 1911); the revisions to the *Infantry Drill Regulations* are reviewed in a text published by the United States Infantry Association, *Infantry Drill Regulations, United States Army 1911, With Changes One to Eighteen* (Philadelphia, J. B. Lippincott, 1917).

52. Russell F. Weigley, *History of the United States Army* (New York: Macmillan, 1967), 391. In a letter to the author dated 11 March 1983, Weigley referred again to the obtuse thinking of Pershing (and his associates) and to their lack of clarity in strategy training and doctrine.

53. Rainey, *Training of AEF,* 28–30, quoted Kennedy and gave his own summary.

54. War Department Document No. 583, *Instructions on the Offensive Conduct of Small Units* (Washington: GPO, 1917); this document is a translation of a French document printed and distributed by the War Department in May 1917 and by AEF Headquarters in August 1917; it contained the standard French pessimism: "infantry of itself has no offensive power against obstacles defended by fire . . . reinforcement of riflemen . . . will simply increase the losses." A War Department "translation notice" reinforced this pessimism by stating that "recent developments confirmed the power of the machine gun and the inability of infantry forces to capture or break through modern entrenchments unless heavily supported by massive artillery fire" (Ibid., 5–9).

55. This memorandum to the AEF chief of staff was provided the author by Colonel William R. Griffiths, a longtime student of the AEF in World War I in a letter dated 2 March 1983. The authenticity of the memo from the American chief of training was verified by reference to the National Archives, RG 120, Folder 695–B. Griffiths is the author of "Coalition for Total War: Field-Marshall Sir Douglas Haig and Entente Military Cooperation, 1916–1918" (M.A. Thesis, Rice University, 1920).

56. Memorandum, Lt. Col. H. A. Drum to the assistant chief of staff G-3, 18 May 1918. This memorandum, including summary comments from American division commanders in France, is reprinted in *The United States Army in the World War,* 2:406–412.

57. Ibid., 412.

58. *U.S. Army in World War,* 3:131.

59. Weigley made this point in a letter to me dated 11 March 1983. Weigley averred that there was "a good deal of confusion in Pershing's mind" as to just what was meant by "open warfare" tactics. Allan Millett voiced the same opinion in a letter dated 18 February 1983.

60. GHQ, AEF, "Combat Instructions," dated 5 September 1918. NA, RG 120, Series 248.

61. Russell F. Weigley, *The American Way of War: A History of U.S. Military Strategy and Policy* (New York: MacMillan, 1973), 202.

62. Rainey details this personnel turbulence and its effects on training in his work, *The Training of AEF,* Part 2.

63. Ibid., 139.

64. E. S. Wallace, ed., *The Twenty-Eighth Division: Pennsylvania's Guard in the World War,* 5 vols. (Pittsburgh: Twenty-eighth Division Publishing Co., n.d.), 5:52, 54, 55.

65. Weigley, *History of the United States Army,* 371–375.

66. Pershing, *My Experiences,* 1:266.

67. Ibid.

68. Rainey, *Training of AEF,* 69.

69. Vandiver, *Black Jack,* 2:772; Pershing, *My Experiences,* 1:151–152.

70. Rainey, *Training of AEF,* 73–76.

71. Pershing, *My Experiences,* 1:264–265.

72. Memo, Assistant Chief of Staff G–5 to the Chief of Staff, AEF, dated 27 August 1917. Subject: School Project for American Expeditionary Forces. NA, RG 120, Series 230, Folder 211.

73. Ibid. This plan was approved by Gen. Pershing for immediate execution, the order signed by Col. J. C. Harbord, Chief of staff, on 31 August 1917.

74. Rainey cites one directive that required that nine of the division's twelve infantry battalion commanders attend staff school at Langres. (See *Training of AEF,* 208–213, 240.)

75. Weigley, *History of the Army,* 392.

76. Rainey, *The Training of AEF,* 226.

77. Ibid., 219–225.

78. Ibid., 227–229.

79. Final Report of Assistant Chief of Staff G–5 (Training) to Commander in Chief AEF, 2 July 1919, NA, RG 120, Series 274, 2. Numerical totals summarized by this author.

80. AEF Document No. 251, "Program of Training for the 1st Division," dated 6 October 1917, NA, RG 120, Series 331.

81. Rainey, *Training of AEF,* 246, 247.

82. Ibid., 253–259.

83. Ibid., 253–259.

84. Ibid., 259–266.

85. Ibid., 266–270.

86. Weigley stated his agreement with Rainey's thesis (he was thesis advisor to Rainey) in a letter to this author dated 11 March 1983.

87. Dr. Jay Luvaas, author of many military texts (e.g., *The Military Legacy of the Civil War* (Chicago: University of Chicago Press, 1959)), offered this opinion in a letter to this author dated 13 April 1983. Ropp states that all U.S. leaders were inexperienced and desperately overworked. Letter to author, 15 February 1983.

88. Gen. Theodore J. Conway (U.S. Army, Ret.) is currently a doctoral candidate at Duke University, writing a dissertation on the U.S. Army in the postwar I period. He expressed these opinions in a letter to this author dated 6 March 1983.

89. Letters from Gordon Brook-Shepherd (9 March 1983); Correlli Barnett (12 March 1983); Michael Howard (23 February 1983); Brian Bond (22 February 1983); and John Terraine (25 February 1983).

90. Letter from Dr. James L. Stokesbury (Acadia University), 12 March 1983. Stokesbury is author of the text, *A Short History of World War I* (New York: Morrow, 1981); also Dr. A. J. M. Hyatt (Univ. of Western Ontario), who has written on Canadian participation in World War I; letter to author dated 21 April 1983. Both expressed the opinion that American aggressiveness and adaptability made up quickly for their lack of training and experience.

91. MHI WWI Questionnaire; MHI archives.

CHAPTER 4. THE AMERICANS MOVE INTO THE LINE

1. Barrie Pitt, *1918: The Last Act* (New York: Ballantine Books, 1962), Prologue.

2. Two excellent texts on American participation in the Supreme War Council are David F. Trask, *The United States in the Supreme War Council: American War Aims and Inter-Allied Strategy, 1917–1918* (Middletown: Wesleyan University Press, 1961) and Frederick Palmer's text, *Bliss, Peacemaker: The Life and Letters of General Tasker Howard Bliss,* (New York: Dodd Mead, 1934).

3. A colorful account, recently published, of the last year of war is John Toland's *No Man's Land: 1918—the Last Year of the Great War* (New York: Doubleday, 1980).

4. Pershing, *My Experience,* 1:202–217.

5. *AC of S G–3, Final Report to CINC, AEF*, 17.

6. Ibid.

7. Pershing, *My Experiences*, 1:78, 256.

8. Frederick Palmer, *Bliss, Peacemaker*, 227–239.

9. *AC of S G–3, Final Report*, 18–22. See also Pershing, *My Experiences* 1:254–257.

10. For a complete and emotional tale of British attempts to "latch on" to U.S. manpower to save their own, see T. C. Lonergan's *It Might Have Been Lost: A Chronicle from Alien Sources of the Struggle to Preserve the National Identity of the AEF* (New York: Putnam's Sons, 1929).

11. *AC of S G–3, Final Report*, 2:22.

12. Pershing, *My Experiences*, 1:311–316.

13. Matloff, *American Military History*, 385–386.

14. *AC of S G–3, Final Report*, 23.

15. Matloff, *American Military History*, 385–387.

16. The "Paris Gun" was a specially cast, long-range German artillery piece which could fire a shell 75 miles.

17. Matloff, *American Military History*, 385–387.

18. Ibid., 388–389.

19. Toland, *No Man's Land*, 95.

20. Ibid.

21. Pershing, *My Experiences*, 1:360–363.

22. Pershing, *My Experiences*, 1:365; Foch, in his memoirs, remembers the commitment as more absolute than does Pershing. See *The Memoirs of Marshal Foch*, Col. T. Bentley Mott, trans., (New York: Doubleday, 1931), 270.

23. Pershing, *My Experiences*, 1:366–367.

24. Ibid.

25. Pershing, *My Experiences*, 2:7–13; Foch, *Memoirs*, 307–309.

26. Coffman, *The Hilt of the Sword*, 70–75.

27. Pershing, *My Experiences*, 2:20–21.

28. Pershing, *My Experiences*, 2:28–29; Coffman, *The Hilt of the Sword*, 71–72; Vandiver, *Black Jack*, 2:367.

29. Pershing, *My Experiences*, 2:31.

30. Ibid., 32–34.

31. Matloff, *American Military History*, 389–391; Baldwin, *World War I*, 143, 144.

32. Matloff, *American Military History*, 390–392.

33. Letter, John Toland to author, 18 February 1983.

34. Letter, Don Lawson to author, 4 March 1983.

35. Letter, William Griffiths to author, 2 March 1983.

36. Coffman, *Hilt of the Sword*, 71–74.

37. Ibid., 80–83.

38. Ibid., 84.

39. Pershing, *My Experiences*, 2:79, 80.

40. *AC of S G–3, Final Report*, 48.

41. Ibid.

42. Coffman, *Hilt of the Sword*, 86, 87.

43. Ibid.

44. Coffman, *The Hilt of the Sword*, 75, 111–115.

45. Baldwin, *World War I*, 144–146; *AC of S G–3, Final Report*, 45–47.

46. Matloff, ed., *American Military History*, 392–393.

47. *West Point Atlas*, vol. 2, Map 66; Matloff, ed., *American Military History*, 392–394.

48. John J. Pershing, *Report of General John J. Pershing, U.S.A., Commander-in-Chief,*

American Expeditionary Forces, HQ, AEF, 20 November 1918. Library of Congress (LOC) Documents Division, HQ AEF, 1922.

49. Hunter Liggett, Maj. Gen., USA, *Ten Year Ago in France* (New York: Dodd, 1928), 89ff; and Lt. Gen. Robert L. Bullard, USA, *American Soldiers Also Fought* (New York: Longman's, 1936), 64ff.

50. Toland, *No Man's Land,* 314–331.

CHAPTER 5. THE FIRST AMERICAN OFFENSIVE—ST. MIHIEL

1. Foch, *Memoirs,* 369–371.

2. Ibid., 372–374.

3. Erich von Ludendorff, *Erich von Ludendorff's Own Story August 1914–November 1919* (New York: Doubleday, 1929), 2:326.

4. *West Point Atlas,* Maps 66, 67.

5. Matloff, ed., *American Military History,* 396; *West Point Atlas,* Map 67. With respect to exploitation, the British had earlier taken heavy casualties in attempting to exploit with horse cavalry. The tanks were too blind and subject to break down to operate in an independent, fast-moving role.

6. Pershing, *My Experiences,* 2:175; see also *United States Army in the World War, 1917–1919,* 8:1–9.

7. Figures taken from *AC of S G–3, Final Report,* 58; also Bond and Sherrill, *America in War,* 110.

8. *U.S. Army in the World War,* 8:10–15.

9. R. E. Dupuy and T. N. Dupuy, Cols., U.S. Army, Ret., *The Encyclopedia of Military History* (New York: Harper and Row, 1970), 940, 947, 959, 982.

10. American Battle Monuments Commission, *A Guide to the Battle Fields in Europe* (Washington: GPO, 1927), 68–69.

11. AEF Assistant Chief of Staff G–2 Study 191–30.8, "Analysis of German Defensive System in St.-Mihiel Salient," dated 18 August 1918. NA, RG 120, Series 191.

12. U.S.M.A., *The Great War,* 289–290.

13. Central to this planning and to that for the Meuse-Argonne campaign, was Lt. Col. George C. Marshall, of later military and diplomatic fame. Marshall wrote memoirs of this period through 1919. In later years, distressed by the arguments in print of his World War I mentors, he declined to publish any memoirs and directed that those from World War I be destroyed. After his death in 1959, his widow found a copy and authorized the Army to publish it. It was published in 1976 as *Memoirs of my Services in the World War* (Boston: Houghton Mifflin, 1976).

14. Marshall, *Memoirs,* 131–133; AEF G–3 Report, 59ff.

15. Larry I. Bland, ed., *The Papers of George Catlett Marshall: Vol. I, The Soldierly Spirit, December 1880–June 1939* (Baltimore: The Johns Hopkins University Press, 1981), 152–155.

16. These troop density figures were developed by this author from personnel data earlier cited and a study of the area, including that area east of the Meuse. While the specific figures may be subject to refutation, the tendency of the AEF planners to press too many troops into an attack is clear.

17. U.S.M.A., *The Great War,* 289–290.

18. *AC of S G–3, Final Report,* 15, 21; Bland, *Papers of Marshall,* 157–160.

19. Pershing, *My Experiences,* 2:215–219.

20. Pershing, *My Experiences,* 2:243–255, recounts the contretemps with Foch as a bitter disagreement. Foch, *Memoirs,* 395–401 smooths the whole matter over with a few

sentences regarding a friendly give-and-take discussion on the new strategy. However, the record of this discussion supports Pershing. *U.S. Army in the World War,* 8:38–40.

21. Pershing, *My Experiences,* 2:246, 247.

22. Ibid., 2:247.

23. *AC of S G–3, Final Report,* 47–49.

24. *U.S. Army in the World War,* 8:47.

25. For Haig's reasoning see Robert Blake, ed., *The Private Papers of Douglas Haig, 1914–1919* (London: Wiedenfeld, 1952), 325. Foch records his judgments in *Memoirs,* 389–401.

26. James Stokesbury, *A Short History of World War I,* (New York: William Morrow, 1981). Stokesbury is a professor of history at Acadia University, Canada. He expressed the opinion I have quoted in a letter dated 12 March 1983 in response to questions from me on World War I.

27. Among those who commented to this effect were John Keegan, Forrest Pogue, Russell Weigley, Gordon Brook-Shepherd, Correlli Barnett, and T. N. Dupuy. See Bibliography: Interviews and Correspondence.

28. Pershing, *My Experiences,* 2:260, 261.

29. *U.S. Army in the World War,* 8:177–180.

30. Ibid., 291–300.

31. von Ledebur is quoted in Barry Gregory's *Argonne* (New York: Ballantine Books, 1972), 78.

32. Matloff, ed., *American Military History,* 396–398; *West Point Atlas,* Map 68.

33. William Matthews, and Dixon Wecter, *Our Soldiers Speak* (Boston: Little Brown, and Co., 1943) 303.

34. GHQ AEF, Assistant Chief of Staff for Operations, G–3, "Situation Report 12 Hours, 13 September 1918" NA, RG 120, Series 137. Hereafter, Situation Reports will be identified as "Sit. Rep.," showing the headquarters and the date. The story on big feet is in Pershing, *My Experiences,* 2:268.

35. Pershing, *My Experiences,* 2:266, 267.

36. GHQ AEF Sit. Rep., 14 September 1918.

37. *U.S. Army in the World War,* 8:258.

38. Pershing, *My Experiences,* 2:269–271; the information on the Metz controversy is taken from the U.S.M.A., *The Great War,* 290.

39. Quotation taken from Matloff, ed., *American Military History,* 398.

40. Pershing, *My Experiences,* 2:270.

41. Bullard, *American Soldiers,* 91.

CHAPTER 6. THE AEF ACCEPTS THE CHALLENGE: THE MEUSE-ARGONNE

1. Douglas W. Johnson, *Battlefields of the World War—Western and Southern Fronts: A Study in Miliary Geography* (New York: Oxford University Press, 1921) 339–406. Johnson's description in his text on Military Geography was verified and expanded by this author's reconnaissance of the area.

2. The description of these defenses was taken from Frank Vandiver's *Black Jack,* 2:955–956; J. F. C. Fuller's *Decisive Battles of the U.S.A.* (London: Harper, 1942). 383–384; The American Battle Monument Commission's *Guide,* 116–117; and Pershing's own account, *My Experiences,* 2:281–283.

3. Vandiver, *Black Jack,* 2:956.

4. Marshall, *Memoirs,* 137–138; Bland, *Papers of Marshall,* 1:160.

5. Marshall, *Memoirs*, 148–149; Pershing, *My Experiences*, 2:284–285.

6. Ibid., 149–156.

7. Ibid.

8. Letter, Forrest Pogue to author, 5 April 1983. Pogue is the author of the text, *George C. Marshall: Education of a General* (New York: Viking Press, 1963) among his many writings.

9. Pershing, *My Experiences*, 2:285, 286; Johnson Haygood, *The Services of Supply* (New York: Houghton Mifflin, 1927) 320, 335–337.

10. Pershing was quoted by Lieutenant General (then Major General) Robert L. Bullard in his text *American Soldiers also Fought*, 89.

11. Secret Order, Headquarters French Second Army, 21 September 1981; NA RG 120, Series 268. First Army Field Order No. 20, 20 September 1918; *U.S. Army in the World War* 9:4, 47, 82–87. Pershing's views were expressed in *My Experiences*, 2:292–294.

12. Ibid.; also Toland, *No Man's Land*, 408; Fairfax Downey, *Sound of the Guns* (New York: David McKay, 1955), 231.

13. *AC of S G–3, Final Report*, 79–81. Comments on training status are in Bullard, *American Soldiers*, 91, 92 and Rainey, *Training of AEF*, 262–378.

14. Marshall, *Memoirs*, 143.

15. Matloff, *American Military History*, 399; "Estimate of the Situation No. 235," Group of Armies von Gallwitz, 16 September 1918, *AC of S G–3, Final Report*, 80.

16. Donald Smythe advised about German foreknowledge of the coming American attack in the Meuse-Argonne in his text *Pershing, General of the Armies* (Bloomington: University of Indiana Press, 1986), 194, 195. Hubert Essame also stated that the Germans learned of the attack from French deserters; see his *Battle for Europe, 1918* (New York: Charles Scribner's Sons, 1972), 168.

17. Von Gallwitz's statement is in George Viereck, ed., *As They Saw Us* (New York: Doubleday, 1929), 239, 240. Bullard, *American Soldiers*, 93, 94.

18. This description is a collage taken from the American Battle Monuments Commission (BMC) texts *Summary of Operations in the World War* (Washington: GPO, 1944) prepared for each of the divisions in the AEF. Hereafter, these texts will be referred to as *BMC summary, —— Division*. See also Dale van Every, *The AEF in Battle* (New York: Appleton, 1928); Barry Gregory *Argonne* (New York: Ballantine Books, 1972); Liggett, *AEF: Ten Years Ago in France;* Bullard *American Soldiers Also Fought;* Robert Maddox, "The Meuse-Argonne Offensive" *American History Illustrated*, April 1975; Laurence Stalling, *The Doughboys: The AEF in World War I* (New York: Harpers and Row, 1963); Frederick Palmer, *America in France* (Westport, Conn.: Greenwood Press, 1981); and John Toland, *No Man's Land*.

19. "Estimate of Strength, Capabilities, and Combat Value of American Forces by the German Supreme Command, 1917–1918," unpublished staff study, 1935, United States National War College Library, Fort McNair, Washington, D.C. Also Viereck, *As They Saw Us*, 286–287, 294–295, 297–298.

20. Viereck, *As They Saw Us*, 50–51, 296–297; Liggett, *AEF: Ten Years Ago*, 250–251.

21. First Army Sit. Rep., 9 A.M. 26 September 1918. NA, RG 120, Series 137.

22. First Army Sit. Rep., 12:30 P.M. NA, RG 120, Series 770.

23. BMC Summary, 33rd Division, 28, 29.

24. BMC Summary, 80th Division, 20–23.

25. BMC Summary, 4th Division, 52, 53.

26. BMC Summary, 79th Division, 13–15.

27. BMC Summary, 37th Division, 12, 13.

28. BMC Summary, 91st Division, 14–16.

29. BMC Summary, 35th Division, 14–16.

30. BMC Summary, 28th Division, 35, 36.

31. Pershing, *My Experiences,* 2:295–297; First Army Sit. Rep., 4 P.M., 26 September 1918. NA, RG 120, Series 137; BMC Summary, 77th Division, 16–19.

32. This description is taken, in part, from an article by Major Elbridge Colby, "The Taking of Montfaucon," *Infantry Journal* (March–April, 1940) 1–14, and one by Colonel Conrad H. Lanza, "The Battle of Montfaucon," *Field Artillery Journal* (issues of May–June, July–August, November–December 1933, and July–August 1934).

33. Hoffman's statement is in his response to a questionnaire sent to him by the U.S. Army's Military History Institute (MHI) at Carlisle Barracks, Pennsylvania, 315th Infantry Regiment folder, 79th Division, MHI archives.

34. Colby, "Taking Montfaucon," 7.

35. Ibid.

36. V Corps Sit. Rep., 1040 A. M., NA RG 120, Series 137.

37. V. Corps Operations Report, 26 September 1918; NA RG 120, Series 137. Hereafter, operations reports will be called *Op. Rep.*

38. AEF Headquarters Daily Communique, 26 September 1918; NA RG 120, Series 137.

39. Colby, "Taking Montfaucon," 8,9.

40. Ibid., 9.

41. Ibid., 9; *BMC Summary, 4th Division,* 12–14.

42. Colby, "Taking Montfaucon," 10,11.

43. First Army Sit. Rep., 7:30 P.M., 26 September 1918; NA RG 120, Series 137.

44. Colby, "Taking Montfaucon," 11.

45. Ibid., 12.

46. Ibid., 13.

47. First Army Sit. Rep., 4:30 A.M., 27 September 1918. I Corps Op. Rep., 26 September 1918; III Corps Op. Rep. 26 September; V Corps Op. Rep., 26 September; division Op. Reps., same period. NA RG 120, Series 137, 271.

48. Pershing, *My Experiences,* 2:296, 297; Viereck, *As They Saw Us,* 32, 33, 238, 239.

49. Bullard, *American Soldiers,* 94; Maddox, "Meuse-Argonne," 26.

50. Liggett, *AEF, Ten Years Ago,* 180; Bullard, *American Soldiers,* 92. Essame, *Battle,* 169.

51. Viereck, *As They Saw Us,* 239–243.

52. *BMC Summary, 4th Division,* 54, 55.

53. *BMC Summary, 37th Division,* 14, 15.

54. *BMC Summary, 91st Division,* 14–21.

55. *BMC Summary, 35th Division,* 14–20.

56. BMC Summary, 28th Division, 46, 47.

57. Daniel R. Beaver, *Newton D. Baker and the American War Effort, 1917–1919* (Lincoln: University of Nebraska Press, 1967), 195; Smythe, *Pershing,* 197–199.

58. Beaver, using several sources, estimates combat casualties at between 45,000 and 50,000 for the four days of September. Beaver, *Newton D. Baker,* 195.

59. First Army Op. Reps., 28–29 September 1918; NA RG 120, Series 271; AEF G–3 memo. "Study of the Situation Considering the Defensive Plan," 29 September 1918; NA RG 120, Series 270.

60. Smythe, *Pershing,* 200, 201.

61. I Corps and V Corps Op. Reps., 1 October 1918; NA RG 120, Series 271; *BMC Summary, 1st Division,* 64; *3d Division,* 59; *32d Division,* 37; *91st Division,* 23.

62. Beaver, *Newton D. Baker,* 196; Smythe, *Pershing,* 200; Essame, *Battle,* 173–195.

CHAPTER 7. THE TEST OF BATTLE: FIGHTING THROUGH TO VICTORY

1. MHI WWI Questionnaire; MHI archives.

2. AEF G–3 Memo, "Defensive Plan," 29 September; AEF G–3 Memo, "Study of the

Changes in Zone of Action of Corps," 29 September 1918; NA RG 120, Series 270.

3. Pershing, *My Experiences*, 2:327; Charles E. Heller, "Chemical Warfare in World War I," Leavenworth Papers No. 10, Fort Leavenworth, Kansas: U.S. Army Command and General Staff College, September 1984.

4. Pershing, *My Experiences*, 2:311ff.

5. Ibid., 303.

6. Smythe, *Pershing*, 200, 201; Essame, *Battle*, 173, 174; Toland, *No Man's Land*, 415.

7. Letter, Marshall Foch to General Pershing, 2 October 1918, *U.S. Army in the World War*, 2:619.

8. Pershing, *My Experiences*, 2:chaps 46, 47. Vandiver, *Black Jack*, 2:967, 968; Beaver, *Newton D. Baker*, 197, 198; Falls, *Great War*, 357.

9. MHI WWI Questionnaire; MHI archives.

10. Pershing, *My Experiences*, 2:327ff.

11. AEF AC of S G–3, *Final Report*, 81; First Army Op. Rep., 4 October, reported POWs' statements on defense orders of German Supreme Command; NA, RG 120, Series 271.

12. *AEF G–3, Final Report* 82, 83.

13. David M. Kennedy, *Over Here: The First World War and American Society* (New York: Oxford University Press, 1980), 204.

14. Pershing, *My Experiences*, 2:321–322.

15. BMC Summary, 4th Division, 63, 64.

16. BMC Summary, 80th Division, 20, 30.

17. III Corps Op. Reps., 4, 5, 6 October 1918; NA, RG 120, Series 271; *AEF G–3, Final Report*, 81.

18. BMC Summary, 3rd Division, 62, 63.

19. V Corps Op. Reps., 4, 5 October 1918; NA, RG 120, Series 271; BMC Summary, 32nd Division, 38–43.

20. BMC Summary, 1st Division, 9, 10; 28th Division, 67, 68.

21. I Corps Op. Reps., 2, 3, 4, 5 October 1918; NA, RG 120, Series 271.

22. Matthews, *Our Soldiers Speak*, 305.

23. James M. Merrill, *Uncommon Valor* (New York: Rand McNally, 1964), 326–330. Also Matthews, *Our Soldiers Speak*, 306.

24. Merrill, *Uncommon Valor*, 330–335.

25. Letter, Edwin Randall to author, 3 August 1983.

26. Pershing admits this total of casualties in *My Experiences*, 2:328.

27. MHI WWI Questionnaire; MHI Archives.

28. Vandiver, *Black Jack*, 2:968–969.

29. MHI WWI Questionnaire; MHI Archives.

30. Pershing, *My Experiences*, 2:299–304; Ludendorff, *Ludendorff*, 2:404.

31. First Army Field Order No. 33, 1 October 1918, *U.S. Army in the World War*, 9:191–192.

32. First Army Field Order No. 20, Pershing, *My Experiences*, 2:289–293.

33. First Army Field Order No. 39, 5 October 1918, *U.S. Army in the World War*, 9:215.

34. BMC Summary, 28th Division, 13, 14; 33rd Division, 35–38.

35. Vandiver, *Black Jack*, 2:969–970; 33rd Division Op. Reps., 8, 9, 10 October 1918; NA, RG 120, Series 271. Pershing, *My Experiences*, 2:331–333.

36. BMC Summary, 28th Division, 63–69; 82nd Division, 25–27.

37. Pershing, *My Experiences*, 2:327–334; I, III, V Corps Op. Reps., 8, 9, 10, 11 October 1918, NA, RG 120, Series 271; *AC of S G–3, Final Report*, 81–82; 1st Division Op. Reps., 8, 9, 10, 11 October 1918, NA, RG 120, Series 271.

38. BMC Summary, 1st Division, 77, 78; 5th Division, 27, 28; 80th Division, 35, 36.

39. *AC of S G–3, Final Report*, 82; Bullard, *American Soldiers*, 107.

40. MHI WWI Questionnaire; MHI archives.

41. *AC of S G–3, Final Report,* 82; Pershing, *My Experiences,* 2:327, 328; Smythe, *Pershing,* 206, 207.

42. Pershing, *My Experiences,* 2:335.

43. Smythe, *Pershing,* 208, 209. Smythe also expressed his opinion of Pershing's condition at this time in an interview with me on 1 March 1985.

44. Vandiver, *Black Jack,* 2:972. Vandiver cites a memo of conversation between General Preston Brown and French Colonel de Chambrun at the Army War College, 2:30 P.M., 18 January 1920. Vandiver footnotes that a copy is in the Pershing Papers, Box 35. I hold a copy of the memo, but I believe the recollections of de Chambrun or possibly of Brown are in error.

45. Secretary Baker's statement is recorded by Richard O'Connor, *Black Jack Pershing* (New York: Doubleday, 1961), 316. Hereafter, to avoid confusion with Vandiver's text, O'Connor's text will be referred to by the short title *Black.* I gained Smythe's opinion in an interview on 1 March 1985. Pershing, *My Experiences,* 2:335, reports only a meeting with Foch at the time at which he (Pershing) discussed the reorganization of his armies. Foch, *Memoirs,* 432–442, states his defense of Pershing against demands by Clemenceau for his relief. Vandiver, however, believes that both Foch and Pershing failed to record the attempted relief of Pershing out of courtesy. Vandiver, *Black Jack,* 2:956, Note 86.

46. Vandiver, *Black Jack,* 2:973–975; Pershing, *My Experiences,* 2:335.

47. Charles C. Dawes, *A Journal of the Great War,* 2 vols. (Boston: Houghton Mifflin, 1921), 2:189.

48. Bliss is quoted in O'Connor, *Black,* 313.

49. Army Times Editors, *The Yanks are Coming: The Story of John J. Pershing* (New York: Putnam's Sons, 1960), 128.

50. Pershing, *My Experiences,* 335–339.

51. Smythe, *Pershing,* 214–216.

52. BMC Summary, 29th Division, 21; 33d Division, 41, 42.

53. BMC Summary, 42d Division, 61–65.

54. MHI WWI Questionnaire; MHI archives.

55. BMC Summary, 78th Division, 21; 3d Division, 83, 84; 5th Division, 31, 34; Pershing, *My Experiences,* 2:340, 341, 351, 352.

56. Pershing, *My Experiences,* 2:351, 352.

57. Beaver, *Newton Baker,* 202, 203.

58. Vandiver, *Black Jack,* 2:978, 970; Smythe, *Pershing,* 217–219; Heller, "Chemical Warfare", 83–90.

59. Letter, AEF Chief of Staff to Commanders, First and Second Armies, 22 October 118, *U.S. Army in the World War,* 2:364; Letter of Instructions to Commanding General, First Army, 21 October 1918; First Army Field Order No. 88, 27 October 1918, *U.S. Army in the World War,* 9:332, 333.

60. Vandiver, *Black Jack,* 2:978, 979; Pershing, *My Experiences* 2:372–374.

61. *AC of S G–3, Final Report,* 83.

62. Raymond C. Cochrane, "The Use of Gas in the Meuse-Argonne Campaign, September–November, 1918," Study Number 10, U.S. Army Chemical Corps Historical Office, Army Chemical Center, 87; Fairfax Downey, *Sound of the Guns: The Story of American Artillery* (New York: David McKay, 1955), 233.

63. Downey, *Sound of the Guns,* 233.

64. Ibid.

65. BMC Summary, 2d Division, 70, 71.

66. BMC Summary, 78th Division, 42, 43.

67. Smythe, *Pershing,* 226.

68. *AC of S G–3, Final Report,* 84, 85; Beaver, *Newton Baker,* 208, 209; First Army Field

Order No. 99, 3 November 1918; First Army Op. Rep., 4 November 1918, *U.S. Army in the World War,* 9:377–380.

69. Beaver, *Newton Baker,* 209.

70. Pershing, *My Experiences,* 2:378.

71. *Stars and Stripes,* 8 November 1918, 1.

72. First Army Op. Reps., 4, 5 November 1918, *U.S. Army in the World War,* 9:382–386; Pershing, *My Experiences,* 2:378–381; BMC Summary, 5th Division, 47; 79th Division, 24–32; 81st Division, 14–20.

73. BMC Summary, 2nd Division, 84–87; 89th Division, 31.

74. BMC Summary, 80th Division, 38–55.

75. BMC Summary, 78th Division, 20, 44, 45; 42nd Division, 76–78.

76. First Army Op. Reps., 6, 7, 8 November 1918; *U.S. Army in the World War,* 9:388–394; BMC Summary, 1st Division, 83, 84.

77. Viereck, *As They Saw Us,* 280–281.

78. Vandiver, *Black Jack,* 2:982, 983.

79. Pershing, *My Experiences,* 2:383–387; First Army Field Order No. 104, 7 November 1918; Memo, Chief of Staff, First Army, to deputy (1st Division out of Sector), 7 November 1918; *U.S. Army in the World War,* 9:481–482; BMC Summary, 1st Division, 85; 42nd Division, 88–91. Smythe, *Pershing,* 227, 228.

80. MHI WWI Questionnaire; MHI Archives.

81. Patton is quoted by Toland, *No Man's Land,* 557.

CHAPTER 8. IN RETROSPECT

1. Pershing, *My Experiences,* 2:chap. 51.

2. Bond and Sherrill, *America in the War,* 144–146; also Pershing, *My Experiences,* 389. Bond and Sherrill show a total of 63,000 prisoners of war captured by Americans on all fronts (page 145), while Pershing in his *Report to the Secretary of War,* 20 November 1918 (Washington, G.P.O., 1922), 23, cites a total prisoner of war count of 44,000.

3. Bond and Sherrill, *America in the War,* 146.

4. Ibid.

5. Kennedy, *Over Here,* 348–359.

6. *AC of S G–3, Final Report,* 87.

7. Ibid., 87.

8. Ibid.

9. Kennedy, *Over Here,* quotes French "Notes on American Offensive Operations," 200.

10. Kennedy, *Over Here,* quotes from the notes of a British War Cabinet meeting, 200.

11. Kennedy, *Over Here,* 200; also Smythe, *Pershing,* 112.

12. Letter to author from Correlli Barnett, 12 March 1983.

13. Interview with Peter Simkins, historian of the Imperial War Museum, London, England, on 13 May 1983.

14. MHI WWI Questionnaire; MHI Archives.

15. Letter to author from Trevor N. Dupuy, 15 February 1983.

16. Marshall's statement is quoted by O'Connor, *Black,* 354.

17. Letter to author from Allan R. Millett, 18 February 1983.

18. Charts are composed from data supplied in *AC of S G–3, Final Report,* as amplified by data from Bond and Sherrill, *America in the War.* See charts for specific sources.

19. The 77th had leadership problems from the division commander down the chain of

command. Pershing cited the 1st in general orders for excellence; he did not select any other division for such a unique rating. Smythe believes the 1st was Pershing's favorite, *Pershing*, 230. Many cite the 2d Division as first in performance. I would find it difficult to rank the 1st, 2d and 42d, all having performed well in combat, but I wouldn't rate the 77th as high as those three.

20. One recent attempt to quantify combat capabilities is in Trevor N. Dupuy's text, *The Evolution of Weapons and Warfare* (New York: Bobbs-Merrill, 1980). Dupuy has come closer in establishing combat value criteria than any other work I've seen. However, his work is criticized by many.

21. Smythe, *Pershing*, 237.

22. Letters to the author from Theodore Conway, 6 March 1983; from Edward Coffman, 4 February 1983; from Theodore Ropp, 15 February 1983; and from John Keegan, 30 March 1983. Keegan, *Six Armies in Normandy* (London: Sharp, 1982). Pershing's rejection of AEF comparisons is cited by John Palmer, *America in Arms* (New Haven: Yale University Press, 1941), 352.

23. Marshall, *My Service*, 13ff.

24. Smythe, *Pershing*, 82, 83, 161–166.

25. O'Connor, *Black*, 195; Pershing, *My Experiences*, 1:182–186, 321, 322, 388, 389; 2:180, 181.

26. Richard Goldhurst, *Pipe Clay and Drill—John J. Pershing: The Classic American Soldier* (New York: Thomas Crowell, 1977), 285, 286; Coffman, *The Hilt*, 81, 892, 104–117.

27. Letter, John Toland to author, 18 February 1983. Toland *No Man's Land* (Garden City, N.Y.: Doubleday, 1980).

28. Letter, Correlli Barnett to author, 12 March 1983.

29. Letter, James Rainey to author, 4 April 1983.

30. Letter, Gordon Brook-Shepherd to author, 9 March 1983. Brook-Shepherd, *November 1918: The Last Act of the Great War* (London: Collins, 1981).

31. Smythe, *Pershing*, 200, 217.

32. Letter, Edward M. Coffman to author, 4 February 1983.

33. Letter, Allan Millett to author, 18 February 1983.

34. Timothy Nenninger, *The Leavenworth Schools and the Old Army* (Westport, Conn.: Greenwood Press, 1978).

35. Letter, Weigley to author, 11 March 1983.

36. Letters, Ropp to author, 15 February 1983; I. B. Holley to author, 15 March 1983.

37. Harbord's statement is reported by Smythe, *Pershing*, 230.

38. Liggett's statement taken from U.S.M.A., *Great War*, 290; Rainey's opinion given in a letter to me, 14 April 1983.

39. Vierick, *As They Saw Us*, 31–33.

40. Pershing, *My Experiences*, 2:270.

41. Pershing, *My Experiences*, 2:243–250; Foch, *Memoirs*, 400, 401.

42. Bullard, *American Soldiers*, 79.

43. David Lloyd George and Winston Churchill were among British leaders who wanted a seaborne strategy.

44. Pershing, *My Experiences*, 1:205, 207.

45. Rexmond C. Cochrane, "Gas Warfare in World War I," Study Number 10, U.S. Army Chemical Corps Historical Studies, Army Chemical Center, Maryland, 75, 76.

46. Liddell Hart is quoted in Cochrane, "Gas Warfare," 76.

47. Cochrane, "Gas Warfare," 83–87.

48. Heller, "Chemical Warfare," 44, 87–90.

49. Smythe illustrates communications problems in *Pershing*, 197.

50. The appendix is my summary of comments from veterans whom I could definitely

associate with the Meuse-Argonne campaign. I am certain there are hundreds of others whose comments I could have included had I taken time to do more detailed research on these records.

51. Interview with Dr. Claude Moore, 16 June 1983.

52. Letter from General Mark Clark to author, 16 June 1983; letter from General Theodore Conway to author, 6 March 1983.

53. Allan Millett, *The General: Robert L. Bullard and Officership in the U.S. Army, 1881–1925* (Westport, Conn.: Greenwood, 1975), 247.

54. Smythe, *Pershing,* 235, 236.

55. Pershing, *My Experiences,* 1:153.

56. Smythe, *Pershing,* 235.

57. Basil Liddell Hart, *Reputations Ten Years After* (Boston: Little, Brown, 1928), 314, 315.

58. Smythe, *Pershing,* 235.

59. Goldhurst, *Pipe Clay,* 233, 234, 301.

60. Downey, *Sound,* 207.

61. Dwight D. Eisenhower, *At Ease: Stories I Tell to Friends* (New York: Doubleday, 1967), 173.

62. Letter from Clark to author, 16 June 1983.

63. Smythe, *Pershing,* 143, 144, 285.

64. Letter from Coffman to author, 14 February 1983.

65. Letter from Holley to author, 15 March 1983.

66. Letter from Conway to author, 6 March 1983.

67. Letter, Holley to author, 15 March 1983.

68. Nenninger, *Leavenworth Schools,* 149.

69. Figures are from Thomas G. Frothingham, *The American Reinforcement in the World War* (Freeport, N.Y.: Books for Libraries Press, 1971), 332–340.

70. This limerick was often recited in my presence to deride officers who came from military schools to their first combat experience.

71. Nenninger, *Leavenworth Schools,* 151.

72. Ibid.

73. Harvey A. DeWeerd, *Great Soldiers of Two World Wars* (New York: W. W. Norton, 1941), 365; see also Smythe, *Pershing,* 143, 144, 284, 285, for Mitchell's relations with other AEF officers.

74. Matloff, *American Military History,* 377; Liggett, *Ten Years Ago,* 255, 256.

75. The historian T. Harry Williams, *Americans at War: The Development of the American Military System* (New York: Collier Books, 1960), 135, found unique qualities in the American similar to my listing.

76. Interview with Peter Simkins, 13 May 1983.

77. Liggett, *Ten Years Ago,* 252–257.

78. Smythe, *Pershing,* 262, 263.

79. MHI WWI Questionnaire; MHI archives.

80. I have summarized Frank Vandiver's opinions on Pershing, expressed in Vandiver's two-volume biography of Pershing, *Black Jack.*

81. Smythe, *Pershing,* 238–244; also interview with Smythe, 1 March 1985.

82. T. Harry Williams, *The History of American Wars* (New York: Knopf, 1981), 402, 403.

83. Liddell Hart, *Reputations,* 314, 315.

84. Letter, James Stokesbury to author, 12 March 1983.

85. Letter, John Terraine to author, 21 February 1983.

86. Letter, John Toland to author, 18 February 1983; Theodore Ropp to author, 15 February 1983.

87. Letter, Russell Weigley to author, 11 March 1983.

88. Letter, Trevor Dupuy to author, 15 February 1983.

89. Letter, Allan Millett to author, 18 February 1983.

90. Letter, Edward M. Coffman to author, 14 February 1983.

91. Interview with Donald Smythe, 1 March 1985.

92. Interview with David Trask, 14 March 1983. Trask is the author of the text *The United States and the Supreme War Council* (Middletown: Wesleyan University Press, 1961).

93. *The New York Times Book Review,* 26 April 1931, 1.

94. Liddell Hart is quoted by DeWeerd, *Great Soldiers,* 185.

95. Ibid., 184.

96. Little Hart, *Reputations,* 316; DeWeerd, *Great Soldiers,* 186.

97. Smythe, *Pershing,* 244.

98. Pershing, *My Experiences,* 2:354; Kennedy, *Over Here,* 200.

99. MHI WWI Questionnaires; MHI archives. For totals, see Appendix 10. "Tommy" and "Poilu" were nicknames for the British and French soldiers, respectively.

100. Ibid.

101. Ibid.

102. Trask, *Supreme War Council,* chap. 4.

103. Ibid.

104. Interview with Peter Simkins, 13 May 1983.

105. Thomas Lonergan, *It Might Have Been Lost* (New York: C. P. Putnams, 1929).

106. Letter, John Elting to author, 14 May 1983.

107. Letter Edward Coffman to author, 14 February 1983.

108. *AEF G–3, Final Report,* 87.

109. Letter, Correlli Barnett to author, 12 March 1983.

110. Ludendorff is quoted by Smythe, *Pershing,* 237.

111. *The New York Times Book Review,* 26 April 1931, 1.

112. *The New York Times Book Review,* 24 May 1931, Letters to the Editor.

113. *The New York Times Book Review,* 10 May 1931, Letters to the Editor.

114. *The New York Times Book Review,* 2 August 1931, Letters to the Editor.

115. Letters, John Giles to author, 28 July 1983, 12 August 1983.

116. Smythe, *Pershing,* 261, 262.

117. Walter Millis, *Arms and Men: A Study of American Military History* (New York: Mentor Books, 1958), 214ff; Smythe, *Pershing,* 278, 279.

118. Millis, *Arms and Men,* 216, 217.

119. Woodward is quoted in the Preface of Daniel M. Smith, *The Great Departure: The United States and World War I, 1914–1920* (New York: J. Wiley and Sons, 1965).

120. Smith, *The Great Departure,* 201.

121. Smythe, *Pershing,* 259.

BIBLIOGRAPHY

ARCHIVAL MATERIAL

National Archives. There is a veritable gold mine of records of the American military effort in World War I in the old Army and Navy Division of the National Archives. For my research, the most valuable sources were:

Record Group (RG) 120. Records of the American Expeditionary Forces (AEF), 1917–1923. Approximately 18,000 linear feet, comprising orders, records, reports, memoranda, and studies collected from divisions, corps, armies, headquarters, and staff sections of the AEF and the supporting services of supply (SOS). A mimeographed inventory (NM–91) is available to researchers; it is a valuable guide to this extensive collection. Cartographic material (maps and photographs) are mostly in separate storage under the care of the cartographic and audio-visual branches of the archives. A guide to this material is in Franklin W. Burch's *Cartographic Records of the American Expeditionary Forces, 1917–1921,* Preliminary Inventory 165, National Archives.

Microfilm listings (Microcopy T–900) of the "Index to Correspondence of the Adjutant General, AEF Headquarters, 1917–1920." This extensive index is an excellent guide to specific orders and directives.

Microfilm bibliography (Microcopy T–619) "History of the U.S. Army Air Service, 1917–1919," compiled by Colonel Edgar S. Garrell, gives a complete listing of documents related to the development and employment of our air services.

RG 165. Records of the War Plans Division, War Department General Staff. These files also contain a collection of Austro-Hungarian and Germany military records of World War I as well as some records on Allied forces, British, French, and Italian.

RG 94. Records of the War Department, general and special staffs and the adjutant general for the period of World War I and earlier.

RG 177. Records of the chief of air service of the War Department for 1917–1922. These files also contain records for the chief of arms for the War Department for World War I and other periods.

RG 107. Records of the Office of the Secretary of War for World War I and some other eras.

RG 156. Records of the Ordnance Department, machine guns and artillery.

RG 166. Records of the War College Division (Historical Branch) General Staff of the War Department. Contains monographs and studies on the war and related matters.

The Congressional Library contains a large collection of published material for World War I, listed under the title "European War, 1914–1921." It also holds the personal papers of many of the luminaries of the period including some of the Pershing papers.

The Library of the National War College, Fort McNair, Washington, D.C., contains a wealth of studies and monographs on military operations in World War I and related matters.

The library of the Center of Military History of the Department of Army, Washington, D.C., contains a random collection of unpublished studies on World War I and related subjects.

The U.S. Army's Military History Institute at the U.S. Army War College, Carlisle Barracks, Pennsylvania, contains much unpublished material on World War I. An ongoing collection of over sixty-seven hundred responses of World War I veterans to Army Services Experience Questionnaires (World War I Research Project) is a rich source of personal observations awaiting scholarly exploitation. In this research effort, the collection (segregated by military organization) was reviewed to gain verification/refutation of official records and to add the color of personal narration of events. The responses of those 728 veterans who were found to have participated in the Meuse-Argonne were collated for determining group opinion on matters related to the campaign. The Army War College also holds a quantity of student monographs on World War I and related subjects. The U.S. Army's Command and General Staff College at Fort Leavenworth, Kansas, also holds a number of student monographs on U.S. participation in World War I.

The American Battle Monuments Commission produced a series of 69 volumes of photographs of the terrain of the Meuse-Argonne taken from vantage points to show the ground as viewed by the personnel of the AEF and their enemies. Each of the 1,396 photographs is accompanied by a 1:20,000 scale map, marked to show the location of the camera and the direction of the photograph. The series is entitled, *Terrain Photographs, American World War*. A copy of this collection is in the archives of the Military History Institute, Carlisle Barracks, Pennsylvania.

INTERVIEWS AND CORRESPONDENCE

Apostolico, Martin. Former corporal, U.S. Marine Corps, assigned to 2d Infantry Division during the Meuse-Argonne campaign. Interviewed on 12 April 1983.

Barnett, Correlli. British military historian; author of *The Swordbearers: Supreme Command in the First World War*. New York: William Morrow, 1964. Letter to author 12 March 1983.

Blumenson, Martin. American military historian; author of *The Patton Papers, 1885–1940*. 2 vols. Boston: Houghton Mifflin, 1972, and "The Outstanding Soldier of the AEF." *American History Illustrated* 1 (February 1967): 4–13, 50–54. Letter to author 12 March 1983.

Bond, Brian. *British Military Policy between the Two World Wars*. Oxford: Clarendon Press, 1980. Letter to author 22 February 1983.

Brook-Shepherd, Gordon. British journalist; author of *November 1918: The Last Act of the Great War.* London: Collins, 1981. Letter to author 9 March 1983.

Clark, Mark W. General, U.S. Army, (retired). Served in the AEF in World War I. Letter to author 16 June 1983.

Coffman, Edward M. American military historian; author of *The Hilt of the Sword: The Career of Peyton C. March.* Madison: University of Wisconsin, 1966; and *The War to End All Wars.* New York: Oxford University Press, 1968. Letter to author 14 February 1983.

Conway, Theodore J. General, U.S. Army, (retired), Ph.D. candidate; dissertation topic: "The U.S. Army Prepares for World War II." Letter to author 6 March 1983.

Dupuy, Trevor N. Colonel, U.S. Army, (retired). Military historian and analyst; author of *The Evolution of Weapons and Warfare.* New York: Bobbs Merrill, 1980, and with his father, Colonel R. Ernest Dupuy, *Brave Men and Great Captains.* New York: Harper & Brothers, 1955. Letter to author 15 February 1983.

Elting, John R. Colonel, U.S. Army, (retired). Military historian and analyst; author of *American Army Life.* New York: Scribner's Sons, 1982. Letter to author 14 February 1983.

Giles, John. Military historian and chairman emeritus of *The Western Front Association;* author of many studies on World War I. Letters to author 28 July, 12 August 1983.

Griffiths, William R. Colonel, U.S. Army. Military historian; coauthor of *The Great War.* West Point, N.Y.: United States Military Academy, 1979. Letter to author 2 March 1983.

Holley, Irving B. Major General, U.S. Air Force, (retired). Military historian; author of *General John M. Palmer: Citizen Soldiers and the Army of a Democracy.* Westport: Greenwood Press, 1982. Letter to author 15 March 1983.

House, Jonathan. Major, U.S. Army. Military historian; author of "John McAuley Palmer and the Reserve Components," *Parameters,* 12 (September 1982): 11–18.

Jewett, Richard L. Brigadier General, U.S. Army, (retired); has written on military logistics in World War I. Letter to author 31 August 1983.

Keegan, John. British military historian; author of *Opening Moves: August 1914.* New York: Viking Press, 1971, and *The Face of Battle.* New York: Viking Press, 1976. Letter to author 30 March 1983.

Lawson, Don. American writer; author of *The United States in World War I.* New York: Scholastic Book Services, 1963. Letter to author 4 March 1983.

Luvaas, Jay. American historian; author of *The Military Legacy of the Civil War: The European Inheritance.* Chicago: University of Chicago Press, 1959. Letter to author 13 April 1983.

Maddox, Robert J. American historian; author of "The Meuse-Argonne Offensive." *American History Illustrated* (April 1975): 22–31. Letter to author 29 March 1983.

Matloff, Maurice. American military historian; editor of *American Military History.* Washington: GPO, 1973. Note to author 4 April 1983.

Millett, Allan R. American historian; author of *The General: Robert L. Bullard and Officership in the United States Army, 1881–1925*. Westport: Greenwood Press, 1975, and *Semper Fidelis: The History of the United States Marine Corps*. New York: Macmillan, 1980. Letter to author 18 February 1983.

Moore, Claude. Former chief surgeon, Langres Base Hospital, AEF. Interviewed 22 March 1983.

Pogue, Forrest C. American historian; biographer of general of the army George C. Marshall. Letter to author 5 April 1983.

Pyle, David. Commander, Region 3, Veterans of World War I. Interviewed 12 April 1983.

Rainey, James W. Lieutenant Colonel, U.S. Army; author of "The Training of the American Expeditionary Forces in World War I." M.A. thesis, Temple University, 1981. Letter to author 4 April 1983.

Randle, Edwin H. Brigadier General, U.S. Army, (retired); rifle company commander in AEF in Meuse-Argonne. Letter to author 3 August 1983.

Ropp, Theodore. American historian; author of *War in the Modern World*. Durham, N.C.: Duke University Press, 1959. Letter to author 15 February 1983.

Simkins, Peter. Historian, British Imperial War Museum; writing a text on Kitchener's Army. Interviewed 13 May 1983.

Smythe, Donald. American historian; author of a two-volume biography of general of the armies John J. Pershing. Interviewed 1 March 1985.

Stokesbury, James L. Canadian historian; author of *A Short History of World War I*. New York: William Morrow, 1981. Letter to author 12 March 1983.

Terraine, John. British military historian; author of *To Win a War*. London: Sidgwick, 1978. *The Smoke and Fire*. London: Sidgwick, 1980. Letter to author 25 February 1983.

Toland, John. American writer; author of *No Man's Land*. New York: Doubleday, 1980.

Trask, David F. Chief historian, U.S. Army Center of Military History; author of *The United States in the Supreme War Council*. Middletown: Wesleyan University Press, 1961. Interviewed 14 March 1983.

Weigley, Russell F. American historian; author of *The American Way of War: A History of United States Military Strategy and Policy*. Bloomington: Indiana University Press, 1973, and *Towards an American Army: Military Thought from Washington to Marshall*. New York: Columbia University Press, 1962. Letter to author 11 March 1983.

SECONDARY SOURCES

Abrahamson, James L. *American Arms for a New Century*. New York: Free Press, 1982.

American Battle Monuments Commission (ABMC). *American Armies and Battlefields in Europe: A History, Guide and Reference Book*. Washington, GPO 1938.

———. *Summary of Operations in the World War*. 44 vols. Washington: GPO, 1944.

Aron, Raymond. *The Century of Total War*. Garden City, N.Y.: Doubleday, Doran, 1954.

Army Times Editors, *The Daring Regiments*. New York: Dodd, Mead, 1954.

Asprey, Robert B. *At Belleau Wood*. New York: Putnam's Sons, 1965.

Ayres, Leonard P. *The War with Germany: A Statistical Summary*. Washington, GPO, 1919.

Bacon, Eugene H., and C. Joseph Bernardo. *American Military Policy: Its Development Since 1775*. Harrisburg, Stackpole, Penn.: 1955.

Baker, Newton D. "America's Duty." *National Geographic* 31 (May 1917): 453–457.

———. "America's War Effort." *Current History Magazine of the New York Times* (August 1918): 229–232.

———. "Return of the Soldier." *Review of Reviews* 59 (February 1919): 143–144.

Baker, Ray Stannard. *Woodrow Wilson: Life and Letters*. Vol. 6, *Facing War: 1915–1917;* Vol. 7, *War Leader: April 6, 1917–February 28, 1918;* and Vol. 8, *Armistice: March 1–November 11, 1918*. Garden City, N.Y.: Harper & Brothers, 1937–1939.

Baker, Ray Stannard, and William E. Dodd, eds. *The Public Papers of Woodrow Wilson*. 6 vols. New York: Harper & Brothers, 1925–1927.

Balck, Wilhelm von. *Development of Tactics—World War*. Translated by Harry Bell. Leavenworth, Kan.: General Service Schools Press, 1922.

Baldwin, Hanson. *World War I: An Outline History*. London: Hutchinson, 1963.

Barnes, Harry E. *Genesis of the World War*. New York: Alfred Knopf, 1962.

Barnett, Corelli. *The Swordbearers: Supreme Command in the First World War*. New York: William Morrow, 1964.

Baruch, Bernard M. *American Industry in the War*. New York: Prentice-Hall, 1941. First printed in 1921 by Government Printing Office, Washington, D.C.

Beard, Charles A. *The Devil Theory of War*. New York: Vanguard Press, 1936.

Beaver, Daniel R. *Newton D. Baker and the American War Effort*. Lincoln: University of Nebraska Press, 1966.

Bernstorff, Johann H. von. *My Three Years in America*. New York: Scribners, 1920.

Blake, Robert, ed. *The Private Papers of Douglas Haig, 1914–1919*. London: Spottswood, 1952.

Bland, Larry I., ed. *The Papers of George Catlett Marshall*. Vol. 1, *The Soldierly Spirit, December 1880–June 1939*. Baltimore: Johns Hopkins University Press, 1981.

Bliss, Tasker H. "The Evolution of Unified Command." *Foreign Affairs* 1 (December 1922): 1–30.

———. "The Strategy of the Allies." *Current History* 29 (November 1928): 197–211.

Bloch, Ivan. *The Future of War in its Technical, Economic and Political Relations*. 6 vols. Translated by R. C. Long. Boston: Doubleday and McClure, 1899.

Blumenson, Martin. *The Patton Papers, 1885–1940*. 2 vols. Boston: Houghton Mifflin, 1972.

———. "The Outstanding Soldier of the AEF." *American History Illustrated* 1 (February 1967): 4–13, 50–54.

Bond, Brian. *British Military Policy between the Two World Wars.* Oxford: Clarendon Press, 1980.

Bond, Paul S., and Clarence O. Sherrill. *America in the World War.* Menasha, Wis.: Banta Pub. Co., 1921.

Brodie, Bernard, and Fawn Brodie. *From Crossbow to H-Bomb.* New York: Dell, 1962.

Brook-Shepherd, Gordon. *November 1918: The Last Act of The Great War.* London: Collins, 1981.

Broun, Heywood. *The AEF: With General Pershing and the American Forces.* New York: Harcourt, 1918.

Brown, L. Ames. "The General Staff." *North American Review.* (August 1917): 229–240.

Buchan, John. *A History of the Great War.* Boston: Houghton Mifflin, 1922.

Bullard, Robert Lee. *Personalities and Reminiscences of the War.* Garden City, N.Y.: Doubleday, Page, 1925.

———. *American Soldiers Also Fought.* New York: Longmans, Green, 1936.

Callwell, Sir Charles Edward. *Field Marshal Sir Henry Wilson, His Life and His Diaries.* 2 vols. New York: Scribners, 1927.

Carver, Sir Michael. *The War Lords.* Boston: Little, Brown, 1976.

Carnegie Endowment for International Peace. Preliminary History of the Armistice, Official Documents Published by the German National Chancellery by Order of the Ministry of State. New York: Oxford University Press, 1924.

Cate, James Lea. "The Air Service in World War I." *The Army Air Forces in World War II.* Edited by Cate and Wesley Frank Craven. Vol 1, Chicago: University of Chicago Press, 1948.

Chandler, David, ed. *A Guide to the Battlefields of Europe.* Philadelphia: Chilton, 1965.

Chambers, Frank P. *The War Behind the War, 1914–1918.* New York: Harcourt, Brace, 1939.

Chase, Joseph C. *Soldiers All: Portraits and Sketches of the Men of the AEF.* New York: Scribners, 1920.

Churchill, Allen L., Francis T. Miller, and Francis J. Roynolds. *The Story of the Great War: History of the European War from Official Sources.* 8 vols. New York: P. F. Collier and Son, 1916–1920.

Churchill, Winston S. *The Unknown War.* New York: Scribners, 1932.

———. *The World Crisis.* 4 vols. New York: Scribners, 1923–1929.

Clemenceau, Georges. *Grandeur and Misery of Victory.* New York: Harcourt, Brace, 1930.

Cochrane, Raymond C. "Gas Warfare in World War I." Study Number 10. *U.S. Army Chemical Corps Historical Studies.* Army Chemical Center, Maryland, 1958.

Coffman, Edward M. *The Hilt of the Sword: The Career of Peyton C. March.* Madison: University of Wisconsin, 1966.

———. "Conflicts in American Planning: An Aspect of World War I Strategy." *Military Review* (June 1963): 78–90.

———. *The War to End All Wars.* New York: Oxford University Press, 1968.

Colby, Eldridge. "The Taking of Montfancon." *Infantry Journal* (March–April 1940): 1–13.

Cramer, Clarence C. *Newton D. Baker.* Cleveland, Ohio: World Press, 1961.

Creek, George. *How We Advertised America.* New York: Harper & Brothers, 1929.

Crowder, Enoch H. *The Spirit of Selective Service.* New York: Century, 1920.

Crowell, Benedict, and Robert Forrest Wilson. *How America Went to War, An Account from Official Sources of the Nation's War Activities, 1917–1920.* 6 vols. New Haven: Yale University Press, 1921.

Crowell, J. Franklin. *Government War Contracts.* New York: Oxford University Press, 1920.

Crozier, William. *Ordnance and the World War.* New York: Scribners, 1920.

Cruttwell, Charles R. M. F. *A History of the Great War.* Oxford: The Clarendon Press, 1934.

Culver, Wallace W. "A Look Back at a Long Time Ago—World War I." *Officer Review,* (March 1984): 9–11.

Curti, Merle E. *The American Peace Crusade.* Durham, N.C.: Duke University Press, 1929.

Daniels, Jonathan. *The End of Innocence.* Philadelphia: J. B. Lippincott, 1954.

Daniels, Josephus. *The Wilson Era: Years of War and After, 1917–1923.* Chapel Hill: University of North Carolina Press, 1946.

Dawes, Charles G. *A Journal of the Great War.* 2 vols. Boston: Houghton Mifflin, 1921.

DeWeerd, Harvey A. *Great Soldiers of Two World Wars.* New York: W. W. Norton, 1941.

Dickinson, John. *The Building of an Army, A Detailed Account of Legislation, Administration and Opinion in the United States, 1915–1920.* New York: Century, 1922.

Dickman, Joseph T. *The Great Crusade: A Narrative of the World War.* Boston: Appleton, 1927.

Dreiziger, N. F., ed. *Mobilization for Total War: The Canadian, British and American Experience, 1914–1918, 1939–1945.* Waterloo, Canada: W.L.V. Press, 1984.

Dupuy, Trevor N. The Evolution of Weapons and Warfare. New York: Bobbs-Merrill, 1980.

———. *Brave Men and Great Captains.* New York: Harper and Row 1955.

Earle, Edward M., ed. *Makers of Modern Strategy, Military Thought from Machiavelli to Hitler.* Princeton: Princeton University Press, 1943.

Ebelshauser, G. A. *The Passage: A Tragedy of First World War.* Huntington, W. Va.: Griffin Books, 1984.

Edmonds, James E., ed. *Military Operations, France and Belgium.* 1917, 3 vols.; 1918, 5 vols. London: Macmillan, 1935–1948.

――――. *A Short History of World War I*. London: Oxford University Press, 1951.

Eisenhower, David. D. *At Ease: Stories I Tell to Friends*. Garden City, N.Y.: Doubleday, 1967.

Ellis, John. *The Social History of the Machine Gun*. New York: Random House, 1975.

Elting, John R. *American Army Life*. New York: Scribner's Sons, 1982.

Ely, Hanson E. "The Attack on Cantigny." *National Service* 7 (April 1920): 201–208.

Esposito, Vincent J., ed. *The West Point Atlas of American Wars*. New York: Praeger, 1959.

Essame, Hubert. *The Battle for Europe, 1918*. New York: Scribners, 1972.

――――. "Night Counter-Attack." *Military Review* (January 1962): 7.

Every, Dale van. *The AEF in Battle*. New York: Appleton, 1928.

Falkenhayn, Erich von. *The German General Staff and its Decisions, 1914–1916*. New York: Dodd, Mead, 1920.

Falls, Cyril. *The Great War*. New York: Putnam's Sons, 1959.

――――. *Caporetto, 1917*. London: Weidenfeld, 1965.

――――. *War Books: A Critical Guide*. London: Davies, 1930.

Ferro, Marc. *The Great War: 1914–1918*. Translated by Nicole Stone. London: Routledge, 1972.

Fleming, D. F. *The Origins and Legacies of World War I*. Greenwich, Conn.: Fawcett, 1968.

Foch, Ferdinand. *The Memoirs of Marshall Foch*. Translated by T. Bentley Mott. Garden City, Doubleday, Doran, 1931.

Foley, William. "Restraints in Gas Warfare." *Military Review* (October 1963): 23.

Foulois, Benjamin D. "Why Write a Book?" *The Air Power Historian* (April 1955): 17–35.

Fortescue, Sir John. *History of the British Army*. 13 vols. London: Macmillan, 1910—1935.

France. Etat-Major de l'Armee. Service Historique. *Les Armees Francaises dans la Grande Guerre*. Volumes 5–7 with annexes. Paris: Imprimerie Nationale, 1922.

Frothingham, Thomas G. *The American Reinforcement in the World War*. Garden City, N.Y.: Doubleday, Page, 1927.

――――. *The Naval History of the World War*. Cambridge: Harvard University Press, 1925.

Fuller, J. JF. C. *The Military History of the Western World*. New York: Funk and Wagnalls, 1954–1956.

――――. *Decisive Battles of the U.S.A.* London: Harper and Row, 1942.

Fussell, Paul. *Siegfried Sasson's Long Journey*. New York: Oxford University Press, 1984.

Ganoe, William A. *History of the United States Army*. Washington: GPO, 1924.

"General of the Armies Wins Another Victory." *Life,* 2 May 1938, 9–12.

"General Pershing in France." *Current History* 6 (July 1917): 6–11.

"General Pershing's Homecoming." *Current History* 11 (October 1919): 1–9.

Gershater, E. M. "Chemical Agents and Battlefield Mobility." *Military Review* (June 1963): 37.

Gibbs, Philip. *Now It Can Be Told*. New York: Harper & Brothers, 1920.

Giehrl, Hermann von. "Battle of the Meuse-Argonne." *Infantry Journal* 19 (August–September, October–November 1921): 131–138, 377–384, 534–540.

Goldhurst, Richard. *Pipe Clay and Drill—John J. Pershing: The Classic American Soldier*. New York: Thomas Y. Crowell, 1977.

Grattan, C. Hartley. *Why We Fought*. New York: Vanguard Press, 1929.

Graves, Robert. *Goodbye to All That. Garden City, N.Y.: Doubleday Anchor Books, 1929*.

Great Britain. Public Records Office. List 53. Alphabetical Guide to War Office and Other Military Records Preserved in the Public Records Office. London: PRO, 1931.

Great Britain. Public Records Office. List 28. *List of War Office Records*. London: PRO, 1908.

Gregory, Barry. *Argonne*. New York: Ballantine Books, 1982.

Griffiths, William R. "Coalition for Total War: Field-Marshall Sir Douglas Haig and Entente Military Cooperation, 1916–1918." MA. thesis, Rice University, 1970.

———. *The Great War*. West Point: U.S.M.A., 1979.

Gurney, Gene. *A Pictorial History of the United States Army*. New York: Bonanza Books, 1966.

Hagedorn, Herman. *The Bugle That Woke America*. New York: John Day, 1940.

———. *Leonard Wood, A Biography*. 2 vols. New York: Harper & Brothers, 1931.

Hagood, Johnson. *The Services of Supply*. Boston: Houghton Mifflin, 1927.

Hankey, Maurice. *The Supreme Command, 1914–1918*. 2 vols. London: Longman's, 1951.

Harbord, James G. *The American Army in France*. Boston: Little, Brown, 1936.

———. *Leaves from a War Diary*. New York: Dodd, Mead, 1925.

Heller, Charles E. "Chemical Warfare in World War I: The American Experience, 1917–1918." Leavenworth Papers No. 10. Fort Leavenworth, Kansas: U.S. Army Combat Studies Institute, September 1984.

Higham, Robin. *Official Histories*. Manhattan: Kansas State University Library, 1970.

———. *A Guide to the Sources of British Military History*. Berkeley: University of California Press, 1971.

Hill, Jim Dan. *The Minute Man in Peace and War*. Harrisburg, Penn.: Stackpole, 1964.

Hindenburg, Paul von. *Out Of My Life*. New York: Cassell, 1920.

Hodges, Arthur. *Lord Kitchener*. London: Thornton Butterworth, 1936.

Hoffman, Max. *The War of Lost Opportunities*. New York: International Pub., 1925.

Holley, Irving B. *Ideas and Weapons.* New Haven: Yale University Press, 1953.

———. *General John M. Palmer: Citizen Soldiers and the Army of a Democracy.* Westport, Conn.: Greenwood Press, 1982.

Hoover, Herbert. *The Memoirs of Herbert Hoover: Years of Adventure, 1874–1920.* New York: Macmillan, 1951.

House, Jonathan. "John McAuley Palmer and the Reserve Components." *Parameters* 12 (September 1982): 11–18.

Howard, Michael. *Studies in War and Peace.* New York: Viking Press, 1970.

———. *War in European History.* London: Oxford University Press, 1976.

Huntington, Samuel P. *The Soldier and the State.* Cambridge: Belknap Press of Harvard University, 1957.

Hurley, Edward M. *The Bridge to France.* New York: J. B. Lippincott, 1927.

Huston, James A. *The Sinews of War: Army Logistics 1775–1953.* U.S. Army Historical Series. Washington: GPO, 1966.

Infantry Journal. "Infantry in Battle." Washington: Infantry Journal, 1939.

Ironside, Sir Edmund. *Tannenburg.* Edinburg: Blackwood and Sons, 1933.

Jackson, Robert. *Fighter Pilots of World War I.* New York: St. Martin's Press, 1977.

James, D. Clayton. *The Years of MacArthur.* 2 vols. Boston: Houghton Mifflin, 1970–1985.

Joffre, Joseph. *Personal Memoirs.* 2 vols. Translated by T. Bentley Mott. New York: Harpers, 1932.

Johnson, Douglas. *Battlefields of the World War—Western and Southern Fronts: A Study in Military Geography.* New York: Oxford University Press, 1921.

Johnson, Ellis L. *The Military Experiences of General Hugh A. Drum from 1898–1918.* Wisconsin: University of Wisconsin Press, 1975.

Johnson, Thomas M. *Without Censor: New Light on our Greatest World War Battles.* Indianapolis, Ind.: Bobbs-Merrill, 1928.

Jusserand, Jean J. *What Me Befell.* Boston: Houghton Mifflin, 1933.

Keegan, John. *Opening Moves: August 1914.* New York: Viking Press, 1971.

———. *The Face of Battle.* New York: Viking Press, 1976.

Kennedy, David M. *Over Here: The First World War and American Society.* New York: Oxford University Press, 1980.

Keyes, Sir Roger. *The Naval Memoirs of Admiral of the Fleet Sir Roger Keyes.* Vol. 2, 1916–1918. London: Butterworth, 1935.

Kreidberg, Marvin A., and Merton G. Henry. *History of Military Mobilization in the United States Army, 1775–1945. Washington: GPO, 1955.*

Lasswell, Harold B. *Propaganda Techniques in the World War.* New York: Alfred A. Knopf, 1927.

Lawson, Don. *The United States in World War I.* New York: Scholastic Book Services, 1964.

Leckie, Robert. *The Wars of America.* Vol. 2. New York: Harper and Row, 1968.

Leland, W. G., and W. D. Mereness. *Introduction to the American Official Sources for the Economic and Social History of the World War.* New Haven: Yale University Press, 1925.

Liddell Hart, Basil H. *History of the World War, 1914–1918.* Boston: Little, Brown, 1935.

———. *Reputations Ten Years Later.* Boston: Little, Brown, 1928.

———. *Through the Fog of War.* New York: Random House, 1938.

———. "Pershing and His Critics." *Current History* (November 1932): 135–140.

Liggett, Hunter. *A.E.F.: Ten Years Ago in France.* New York: Dodd, Mead, 1928.

Link, Arthur S. *Woodrow Wilson and the Progressive Era, 1910–1917.* New York: Harper & Brothers, 1954.

Lloyd George, David. *War Memoirs of David Lloyd George.* 6 vols. Boston: Little, Brown, 1934.

Lockmiller, David A. *Enoch A. Crowder: Soldier, Lawyer and Statesman.* Columbia: University of Missouri Press, 1945.

Lonergan, Thomas C. *It Might Have Been Lost.* New York: G. P. Putnam's Sons, 1929.

Lossberg, Fritz von. *Meine Tatigkeit im Weltkrieg 1914–1918.* Berlin: Mittler, 1939.

Lowry, Edward G. "The Emerging Mr. Baker: A Pacifist who is in this war business 'to see it through.' " *Colliers Weekly,* 6 October 1917, 6, 7, 35, 36.

Lucas, Pascal. *The Evolution of Tactical Ideas in France and Germany during the War.* Translated by P. V. Kieffer. Fort Leavenworth, Kan.: Army Service Schools Press, 1925.

Ludendorff, Eric von. *Ludendorff's Own Story: August 1914–November 1918.* 2 vols. New York: Harper & Brothers, 1920.

Lupfer, Timothy T. "The Dynamics of Doctrine: The Changes in German Tactical Doctrine during the First World War." Leavenworth Papers No. 4. Ford Leavenworth: Command General Staff College, (July 1981).

Lutz, Ralph H., ed. *The Causes of the German Collapse in 1918.* by W. L. Campbell. Stanford, Calif.: Stanford University Press, 1934.

Luvaas, Jay. *The Military Legacy of the Civil War: The European Inheritance.* Chicago: Chicago University Press, 1959.

Lyddon, William G. *British War Missions to the United States, 1914–1918.* London: Oxford University Press, 1938.

MacArthur, Douglas. *Reminiscences.* New York: McGraw-Hill, 1964.

MacDonald, Charles B. "The Neglected Ardennes." *Military Review* (April 1963): 74.

MacDonald, Lyn. *Somme.* New York: Michael Joseph, 1984.

McEntee, Gerald L. *Military History of the World War.* New York: Scribners, 1937.

McLean, Ross H. "Troop Movements on the American Railroads during the Great War." *The American Historical Review* (April 1921): 464–488.

McMaster, John B. *The United States in the World War.* 2 vols. New York: Appleton, 1918, 1920.

Maddox, Robert. "The Meuse-Argonne Offensive." *American History Illustrated* (April 1975): 22–31.

Magnus, Philip. *Kitchener: Portrait of an Imperialist.* London: Arrow Books, 1958.

March, Francis A. *History of the World War*. Philadelphia: John Winston Co., 1921.

March, Peyton C. *The Nation at War*. Garden City, N.Y.: Doubleday, Doran, 1932.

Marder, Arthur J. *From Dreadnaught to Scapa Flow: The Navy in the Fisher Era, 1904–1919*. London: Oxford University Press, 1961.

Markey, John D. "That Was Pershing." *American Legion Magazine* (January 1949): 28.

Marshall, George C. *Memoirs of My Services in the World War, 1917, 1918*. Boston: Houghton Mifflin, 1976.

———. "Some Lessons in History." *Maryland Historical Magazine* (September 1945): 175–184.

Marshall, S. L. A. *The American Heritage History of World War I*. New York: The American Heritage Pub., 1964.

Matloff, Maurice, ed. *American Military History*. Washington: GPO, 1973.

Matthews, William, and Dixon Wecter. *Our Soldiers Speak*. Boston: Little, Brown, 1943.

May, Ernest R., ed. *The Ultimate Decision: The President as Commander in Chief*. New York: Braziller, 1960.

Merrill, James M. *Uncommon Valor*. Chicago: Rand McMally, 1964.

———. "Submarine Scare, 1918." *Military Affairs* (Winter 1953): 181–190.

Messenger, Charles. *Trench Fighting 1914–1918*. New York: Ballantine, 1972.

Meyer, Herman. *A Check List of the Literature and Other Materials in the Library of Congress on the European War*. Washington, GPO, 1918.

Miller, Josiah B. "Development of the Departmental Direction of Training and Training Policy in the United States Army, 1789–1954: Background for Twentieth Century Training 1899–1917." Draft manuscript, Office of the Chief of Military History, Department of Army, Washington, D.C., n.d.

———. "Development of Departmental Direction of Training and Training Policy in the United States Army, Revolutionary War to 1920." Draft manuscript, Office of the Chief of Military History, Department of Army, Washington, D.C., n.d.

Millett, Allan R. *The General: Robert L. Bullard and Officership in the United States Army, 1881–1925*. Westport, Conn.: Greenwood Press, 1975.

———. *Semper Fidelis: The History of the United States Marine Corps*. New York: Macmillan, 1980.

Millett, Allan R., and Peter Maslowski. *For the Common Defense: A Military History of the United States of America*. New York: Macmillan, 1984.

Millis, Walter. *Arms and Men: A Study of American Military History*. New York: G. P. Putnam's Sons, 1958.

———. *The Road to War: America, 1914–1917*. Boston: Houghton Mifflin, 1925.

Mitchell, William. *Memoirs of World War I, From Start to Finish of Our Greatest War*. New York: Random House, 1960.

———. *Our Air Force*. New York: E. P. Dutton, 1921.

———. "The Air Service at the Argonne-Meuse." *World's Work* 38 (September 1919): 552–560.

Moll, Kenneth L. "Writing on Water with a Fork." *Military Review* (August 1964): 29.

Morison, Elting E., ed. *The Letters of Theodore Roosevelt.* 8 vols. Cambridge: Harvard University Press, 1951, 1954.

————. *Admiral Sims and the Modern American Navy.* Boston: Houghton Mifflin, 1942.

————. *Turmoil and Tradition: A Study of the Life and Times of Henry L. Stimson.* Boston: Houghton Mifflin, 1960.

Mott, T. Bentley. *Twenty Years as a Military Attache,* Garden City, N.Y.: Doubleday, Doran, 1937.

Nagel, Fritz. *Fritz: The WWI Memoirs of a German Lieutenant.* Huntington, W. Va.: Griffin Books, 1984.

Nelson, Otto L. *National Security and the General Staff.* Washington: Infantry Journal Press, 1946.

Nenninger, Timothy K. *The Leavenworthh Schools and the Old Army: Education, Professionalism, and the Officer Corps of the United States Army, 1881–1918.* Westport, Conn.: Greenwood Press, 1978.

Newman, George P. *The German Air Force in the Great War.* London: Hodder and Stoughton, 1920.

O'Connor, Richard. *Black Jack Pershing.* New York: Doubleday, 1961.

Ormsby, Hilda. *France, A Regional and Economic Geography.* New York: E. P. Dutton, 1931.

Otto, Ernst. "The Battles for the Possession of Belleau Woods, June, 1918." *U.S. Naval Institute Proceedings* 54 (November 1928): 940–962.

Page, Arthur W. *Our 110 Days Fightings.* Garden City, N.Y.: Doubleday, Page, 1920.

Palmer, Frederick. *Bliss, Peacemaker: The Life and Letters of General Tasker Howard Bliss.* New York: Dodd, Mead, 1934.

————. *John J. Pershing: A Biography.* Westport, Conn.: Greenwood Press, 1948.

————. *Newton D. Baker: America at War.* 2 vols. New York: Dodd, Mead, 1931.

————. *Our Greatest Battle.* New York: Dodd, Mead, 1919.

————. "Looking Back on the World War." *World's Work* 53 (April 1927): 587–593.

Palmer, John M. *America in Arms: The Experience of the United States with Military Organization.* New Haven: Yale University.

————. "Reorganization of the War Department." *Army and Navy Journal* (27 August 1921): 1365.

Pappas, George. *Prudens Futuri: The War College, 1901–1967.* Carlisle, Pa.: U.S. Army War College, 1967.

Paxson, Frederic L. *American Democracy and the World War.* 3 vols. Boston: Houghton Mifflin, 1937, 1984.

————. "The Great Demobilization." *American Historical Review* 44 (January 1939): 237–251.

————. "The American War Government, 1917–1918." *American Historical Review* 26 (October 1920): 54–76.

Perkins, Dexter. *America and Two World Wars*. Boston: Little, Brown, 1944.

Pershing, John J. *My Experiences in the World War*. 2 vols. New York: Frederick Stokes Co., 1931.

———. "The Meuse-Argonne." *Foreign Service* 15 (August 1927): 6, 7.

———. "Our National Military Policy." *Scientific American* 127 (August 1922): 83, 142.

———. *Final Report of General John J. Pershing, Commander-in-Chief, American Expeditionary Forces*. Washington: GPO, 1920.

Pershing, John J., and Hunter Liggett. *Report of the First Army, American Expeditionary Forces: Organization and Operations*. Fort Leavenworth, Kan.: General Service Schools Press, 1923.

Pétain, Henri P. *Verdun*. New York: Dial Press, 1930.

Peterson, Horace C. *Propaganda for War*. Norman: University of Oklahoma Press, 1939.

Peterson, Horace C., and Gilbert C. Fite. *Opponents of War, 1917–1918*. Madison: University of Wisconsin Press, 1957.

Pierce, C. Fredericks. *The Great Adventure: America in the First World War*. New York: E. P. Dutton, 1960.

Pitt, Barrie. *1918: The Last Act*. New York: Ballantine Books, 1963.

Pogue, Forrest C. *George C. Marshall: Education of a General, 1880–1939*. New York: Viking Press, 1963.

———. *George C. Marshall: Ordeal and Hope, 1939–1942*. New York: Viking Press, 1966.

———. *George C. Marshall: Organizer of Victory, 1943–1945*. New York: Viking Press, 1973.

Preston, R. A., S. F. Wise, and H. O. Werner. *Men in Arms: A History of Warfare*. New York: Frederick Praeger, 1962.

Rainey, James W. "Training of the American Expeditionary Forces in World War I." M.A. thesis, Temple University, 1981.

Read, James M. *Atrocity Propaganda, 1914–1918*. New Haven: Yale University Press, 1941.

Reilly, Henry J. *Americans All, The Rainbow at War: Official History of the 42d Rainbow Division in the World War*. Columbus, Ohio: F. J. Heer, 1936.

Remak, Joachim. *The Origins of World War I, 1871–1914*. Hinsdale: Dryden Press, 1967.

Renn, Ludwig [Arnold von Golssenau]. *War*. London: Martin Secker, 1929.

Repington, Charles. *The First World War, 1914–1918*. 2 vols. Boston: Houghton Mifflin, 1920.

Reynolds, E. A. B. *The Lee-enfield Rifle*. New York: Anchor Press, 1969.

Riker, William H. *Soldiers of the States: The Role of the National Guard in American Democracy*. Washington: Public Affairs Press, 1957.

Risch, Erna. *Quartermaster Support of the Army: A History of the Corps, 1775–1959*. Washington: GPO, 1962.

Ritter, Gerhard. *The Schlieffen Plan*. New York: Frederick Praeger, 1958.

Rizzi, Joseph N. *Joe's War: Memoirs of a Doughboy.* Huntington, W.Va.: Griffin Books, 1984.

Robertson, Sir William. *Soldiers and Statesmen, 1914–1918.* 2 vols. London: Cassell, 1926.

Rommel, Erwin. *Infantry Attacks.* Washington: Combat Forces Press, 1956.

Root, Elihu. *The Military and Colonial Policy of the United States.* Cambridge: Harvard University Press, 1916.

Ropp, Theodore. *War in the Modern World.* Durham, N.C.: Duke University Press, 1959.

Rudin, Harry. *Armistice 1918.* New Haven: Yale University Press, 1944.

Ryan, Garry D. "Disposition of AEF Records of World War I." *Military Affairs* 30 (Winter 1966–1967): 212–219.

Rupprecht, Crown Prince of Bavaria. *Mein Kriegstagebuch.* 3 vols. Berlin: Mittler, 1919.

Russell, Thomas H. *America's War for Humanity.* New York: Walker, 1919.

Sabel, Walter R. "Christmas in the Meuse-Argonne." *National Tribune,* 23 December 1982.

Scott, Hugh L. *Some Memories of a Soldier.* New York: Century, 1928.

Scott, Emmett J. *The American Negro in the World War.* Cincinnati, Ohio: Central Pub., 1919.

Seymour, Charles. *American Diplomacy during the World War.* Baltimore: Johns Hopkins University Press, 1934.

———. *American Neutrality, 1914–1917.* New Haven: Yale University Press, 1935.

Seymour, Charles, ed. *The Intimate Papers of Colonel House.* 4 vols. Boston: Houghton Mifflin, 1926–1928.

Sharp, William Graves. *The War Memoirs of William Graves Sharp, American Ambassador to France, 1914–1919.* London: Constable & Co., 1931.

Slosson, Preston W. *The Great Crusade and After.* New York: Macmillan, 1930.

Smythe, Donald. *Guerrilla Warrior: The Early Life of John J. Pershing.* New York: Scribners, 1973.

———. *Pershing: General of the Armies.* Bloomington: University of Indiana Press, 1986.

———. "The Battle Pershing Almost Lost." *Army* 33 (February 1983): 50–55.

———. "John J. Pershing: A Study in Paradox." *Military Review* 49 (September 1969): 66–72.

———. "The Pershing-March Conflict in World War I." *Parameters* 11 (December 1981): 53–62.

Society of the First Division. *History of the First Division during the World War, 1917–1919.* Philadelphia: Lippincott, 1922.

Spaulding, Oliver. *The United States Army in War and Peace.* New York: G. P. Putnam's Sons, 1937.

Spears, Sir Edward. *Prelude to Victory.* London: Jonathan Cope, 1939.

Spector, Ronald. " 'You're Not Going to Send Soldiers Over There Are You?': The American Search for an Alternative to the Western Front." *Military Affairs* 36 (February 1972): 1–4.

Spencer, Samuel R. *Decision for War, 1917*. Ridge, N.H.: Richard Smith Pub., 1953.

Stallings, Laurence. *The Story of The Doughboys: The AEF in World War I*. New York: Harper & Row, 1963.

Stokesbury, James L. *A Short History of World War I*. New York: William Morrow, 1981.

———. "The Aisne-Marne Offensive." *American History Illustrated* (July 1980): 8–17.

Sullivan, Mark. *Our Times: The United States, 1900–1925*. Vol. 5, *Over Here, 1914–1918*. New York: Scribners, 1933.

Sunderman, James F. *Early Air Pioneers, 1862–1935*. New York: Franklin Watts, 1961.

Taylor, A. J. P. *A History of the First World War*. London: Berkley Press, 1959.

Tansill, Charles C. *America Goes to War*. Boston: Little, Brown, 1938.

Terraine, John. *The Western Front*. London: Lippincott, 1965.

———. *To Win a War*. London: Sidgwick, 1978.

———. *The Smoke and the Fire*. London: Sidgwick, 1980.

———. "The March Offensive, 1918." *History Today* 18 (April 1968): 234–243.

Toland, John. *No Man's Land: 1918—The Last Year of the Great War*. New York: Doubleday, 1980.

Trask, David F. *The United States and the Supreme War Council: American War Aims and Inter-Allied Strategy, 1917–1918*. Middletown, Conn.: Wesleyan University Press, 1961.

———. "Political-Military Consultation among Allies." *Army* (February 1983).

Tucker, George B. et al. *A History of Military Affairs in Western Society since the Eighteenth Century*. Ann Arbor, Mich.: Edwards Brothers, 1952.

Tuchman, Barbara. *The Guns of August*. New York: Macmillan, 1962.

———. *The Zimmerman Telegram*. New York: Dell Books, 1958.

Tumulty, Joseph P. *Woodrow Wilson as I Know Him*. Garden City, N.Y.: Doubleday, Doran, 1954.

United States Army War College, Historical Section. *The Genesis of the American First Army*. Washington: GPO, 1938.

———. *Order of Battle of the United States Land Forces in the World War: American Expeditionary Forces*. Washington: GPO, 1937.

United States Congress. *Congressional Record, 64th Congress, 2d Session; 65th Congress, Special Session, 1st and 2d Sessions; 66th Congress, 1st Session*. Washington: GPO, 1916–1919.

United States Congress, House of Representatives, Military Affairs Committee. *Army Reorganization Hearings, 66th Congress, 1st Session*. Washington: GPO, 1919.

———. *Increasing the Efficiency of the Military Establishment Hearings, 64th Congress, 2d Session*. Washington: GPO, 1916.

United States Congress, Senate Military Affairs Committee. *Army Reorganization Hearings.* 2 vols. Washington: GPO, 1917, 1918.

————. *Increasing the Military Establishment Hearings, 65th Congress, 1st Session.* Washington: GPO, 1917.

————. *Investigation of the War Department of the United States, December 1917–January 1918 Hearings, 65th Congress, 1st Session.* Washington: GPO, 1918.

————. *Preparedness for National Defense Hearings, 64th Congress, 2d Session.* Washington: GPO, 1916.

U.S. Department of the Air Force. *The U.S. Air Service in World War I.* Edited by M. Maurer. 4 vols. Washington: GPO, 1978.

U.S. Department of the Army. *Army Lineage Book, Volume 2: Infantry.* Washington: GPO, 1953.

————. Historical Division. *United States Army in the World War, 1917–1919.* Washington: GPO, 1948.

U.S. Department of State. *Papers Relating to the Foreign Relations of the United States, 1917.* Washington: GPO, 1926.

————. *Papers Relating to the Foreign Relations of the United States, 1917; Supplement 1, The World War.* Washington: GPO, 1926.

————. *Papers Relating to the Foreign Relations of the United States, 1917; Supplement 2.* 2 vols. Washington: GPO, 1932.

————. *Papers Relating to the Foreign Relations of the United States, 1918.* Washington: GPO, 1933.

————. *Papers Relating to the Foreign Relations of the United States, Supplement 1, The World War.* 2 vols. Washington: GPO, 1933.

United States Military Academy. *The Great War.* West Point: U.S.M.A., 1979.

United States War Department. *Annual Reports: 1917–1919.* Washington: GPO, 1917–1919.

————. *Annual Report of the Secretary of War, 1917, 1918, 1919.* Washington: GPO, 1917–1919.

Upton, Emory. *The Military Policy of the United States from 1775.* Washington: GPO, 1904.

Vagts, Alfred. *A History of Militarism.* New York: Meridian Books, 1959.

Vandiver, Frank E. *Black Jack: The Life and Times of John J. Pershing.* 2 vols. College Station: Texas A & M University Press, 1977.

————. *John J. Pershing and the Anatomy of Leadership.* Colorado Springs: United States Air Force Academy, 1963.

Viereck, George, ed. *As They Saw Us.* Garden City, N.Y.: Doubleday, Doran, 1929.

Waite, Robert G. L. *Vanguard of Nazism.* New York: Norton, 1969.

Wallace, E. S., ed. *The Twenty-Eighth Division: Pennsylvania's Guard in the World War.* Pittsburgh: 28th Div. Pub. Co., 1923, 1924.

Walworth, Arthur. *Woodrow Wilson.* 2 vols. New York: Longman's, 1958.

Watson, Mark. *Chief of Staff: Prewar Plans and Preparations.* Vol. 4, *United States Army in World War II.* Washington: GPO, 1950.

———. "Who Won the War? Still an Issue." *Baltimore Sun,* 25 September 1932, 1–3.

Watt, Richard. *Dare Call It Treason.* New York: Simon and Schuster, 1963.

Weigley, Russell F. *The American Way of War: A History of United States Military Strategy and Policy.* New York: Macmillan, 1973.

———. *The History of the United States Army.* New York: Macmillan, 1967.

———. *Towards an American Army: Military Thought from Washington to Marshall.* New York: Columbia University Press, 1962.

Western Front Association, The. *Stand To: The Journal of The Western Front Association.* Quarterly issues from 1980 to 1986. London: WFA.

Wetzell, George. *From Falkenhayn to Hindenburg-Ludendorff.* Translated by F. W. Merten. Washington: U.S. Army War College, 1935.

Whan, Vorin E., ed. *A Soldier Speaks: Public Papers and Speeches of General of the Army Douglas MacArthur.* New York: Frederick Praeger, 1965.

Wilhelm, Crown Prince of Germany. *My War Experiences.* London: Hurst and Blackett, 1923.

Williams, T. Harry. *Americans at War: The Development of the American Military System.* Baton Rouge: University of Louisiana Press, 1960.

Williams, Wythe. *The Tiger of France: Conversations with Clemenceau.* New York: Duell, Sloan and Pearce, 1949.

Willoughby, Charles A. *The Economic and Military Participation of the United States in the World War.* Forth Leavenworth, Kan.: The Command and General Staff School Press, 1931.

Woolcott, Alexander: "Them Damned Frogs." *North American* 210 (October 1919): 490–498.

Wolff, Leon. *In Flanders Field: The 1917 Campaign.* New York: Viking Press, 1958.

Wynne, Graeme C. *If Germany Attacks: The Battle in Depth in the West.* London: Faber and Faber, 1940.

———. "The Development of the German Defensive Battles in 1917, and Its Influence on British Defence Tactics." *Army Quarterly.* Pts. 1 and 2, 34 (April–July 1937): pt. 3, 35 (October 1937).

———. "The Hindenburg Line." *Army Quarterly.* 37 (October 1938–January 1939).

Yardley, Herbert O. *The American Black Chamber.* Indianapolis, Inc.: Bobbs-Merrill, 1931.

Young, Peter, ed. *The British Army, 1642–1970.* London: Kimber, 1967.

INDEX

Abbeville Conference, 66, 69

AEF. See *American Expeditionary Forces*

Africa: British Colonies, 165; German Colonies, 26

Aincreville, capture of, 133

Aire: river, 87; valley, 123

Airplanes: attitudes toward, 158; bombardments, 158; combined aviation element, 84; in support of AEF, 145; in support of 26 September attack, 96; in U.S. Army prior to war, 38

Aisne: Aisne-Marne, 62, 64, 73; Aisne-Vesle Line, 76; region, 115; river, 31, 73, 81, 93, 122, 152; Second Battle of, 31

Alexander, Gen. Robert, 99

Allenby, Gen. Edmund, 34, 59

Allies: advances of, 137, 152; amalgamation of Americans into armies of, 44, 61, 163–166; American attitude toward, 35; Americans with armies of, 135, 147; blockade by, 27; casualties, 63, 67, 144; their cause, 169; cavalry of, 157; coalition of, 31, 165; command of, 146, 165; contribution of, to war, 144, 145, 166, 167; and criticism of American leadership, 158, 159; and criticism of Pershing, 129, 130; and global situation, 24, 34; leadership of, 34; morale of, 33, 39; operations in 1914, 26; operations in 1915, 26; operations in 1916, 27; operations in 1917, 30–34; operations in 1918, 63–76, 114, 115, 126, 136, 137; performance of, compared with AEF, 155; and regard for American soldier, 146; and reinforcement request, 69; and strategies in postwar period, 169. *See also* Belgium; France; Great Britain; Italy; Russia

Amiens salient, 67, 68, 75

America: amalgamation of soldiers with Allies, 44, 61, 163–166; armed forces buildup, 37, 38, 40; cemetery, 169; contribution to war, victory, 39, 166, 167; entry into war, 36; militia system, 149; mobilization, 36, 37; neutrality, 35, 36; world leadership, 39, 40, 169. *See also* American Expeditionary Forces; War Department

American Expeditionary Forces: arrival in France of, 46; and "baptism of fire," 112; casualties, 50, 144, 155; commanders of, 40, 129–131, 156, 167; doctrine of, 47–51, 57, 58, 113, 122; directives of, 40, 41, 56, 80, 85, 90, 91, 117–119, 129, 135, 141; and enemy, 75–79, 88–90, 111, 115, 137, 138; evaluation of, 113, 130, 135, 146–49, 152, 156; General Hospital of, 155, 156; headquarters of, 46, 113, 150, 151, 157, 163; health of, 92, 129, 155; leadership of, 146, 153, 159–163; operations of, 67, 68, 84, 85, 93–143; organization of, 43, 46, 47, 66, 68, 69, 71, 83, 84, 114, 116; personnel of, 41, 44, 51, 52, 60–62, 64–66, 70, 71, 129, 135, 144; plans of, 76, 79–82, 90, 91, 94–96, 131, 141, 152; schools of, 54–58; staff of, 41–45, 49, 55, 56, 61, 69, 92, 108, 115, 122, 150; strategy of, 94, 151, 152; supply of, 62, 91, 92, 114, 115, 135, 155; training of, 39, 53–58, 113, 135; transportation of, 83, 84, 90–92, 111–113; veterans of, 164; weapons of, 76, 77, 113, 135

—First Army: St. Mihiel, 75–86; 26–29 September, 87–111; 4–10 October, 115–126; 14–30 October, 131–135; 1–11 November, 135–143

—Second Army: 76; east of Meuse, 130–141, 152

221

—I Corps: Chateau-Thierry, 68, 73; St. Mihiel, 84, 85; Aire Valley-Argonne Forest, 94–96, 98, 99, 119–126; Grandpre, 132, 133; to the Meuse, 136–141

—II Corps: 68, 80

—III Corps: activation, 68; Vesle, 73, Meuse, 93–99; Cunel, 116–126; Aincreville, 131–133; Woevre, Meuse, 136–139

—IV Corps: St. Mihiel, 84, 85; east of Meuse, 129

—V Corps: St. Mihiel, 84; Montfaucon, 94–110; Romagne, 116–127; Cote Dame Marie, 127–133; Barricourt, Meuse, 136–139

—Divisions: *1st,* 41, 55, 60, 62, 73, 85, 96, 111, 114, 126, 136, 141, 147–149, 160; *2d,* 63, 67, 73, 111, 136, 137, 138, 148; *3d,* 67, 72, 73, 94, 119, 131, 135, 136, 148, 149; *4th,* 73, 94, 97, 107, 109, 117, 119, 129, 135; *5th,* 126, 131, 135, 136, 139; *6th,* 135; *8th,* 122; *26th,* 62, 73, 85, 131, 149; *27th,* 68, 148; *28th,* 51, 73, 96, 99, 119, 120, 122, 147, 149; *29th,* 96, 133; *32d,* 68, 73, 94, 111, 119, 133, 135, 136, 149; *33d,* 94, 98, 133, 135; *35th,* 96, 99, 109, 111, 114; *36th,* 148; *37th,* 94, 99, 101; *42d,* 62, 72, 73, 126, 136, 141, 148, 149; *77th,* 73, 96, 99, 110, 111, 119, 120, 126, 133, 141, 148, 149; *78th,* 51, 133, 137, 141; *79th,* 94, 99, 101, 103, 107–111, 115, 129, 139; *80th,* 94, 99, 119, 126, 136, 139, 148; *81st,* 139; *82d,* 96, 126, 136; *89th,* 136; *90th,* 136; *91st,* 94, 99, 110, 111, 126; *92d,* 96

—Other Units: *8th* Brigade, 106; *84th* Brigade, 133; *157th* Brigade, 103, 107; *158th* Brigade, 107; *314th* Infantry Regt., 107; *316th* Infantry Regt., 107; *1st* Gas Regiment, 154; *313th* Infantry Regt., 103; *1st Battalion,* 308th Infantry Regt. (The Lost Battalion), 120

Andevaune, 137

Anglo-Belgian forces, 115

Apremont, 79, 94

Ardennes, 146

Argonne, 82, 114, 116, 139, 143, 153; forest, 58, 81, 87, 93, 94, 110, 123, 126, 153; hills, 126; ridges, 116

Arietal Farm, 119

Armentiers Pocket, 75

Armistice, 123, 133, 141, 143, 151, 156, 166

Arras, 76, 81

Artillery, 25, 26, 28, 29, 31, 32, 43, 63, 72, 75–77, 84, 93, 96–98, 99–105, 116–120, 123–126, 135–137, 145, 153, 154

Artois, 26

Attrition, 26, 116, 152

Australians, 165

Austria-Hungary: declares war, 25; forces of, 26, 27; operations of, 26, 31, 34

Baden, Prince Max von, 122, 123

Baker, Newton D., U.S. Secretary of War, 40, 44, 55, 64, 65, 72, 85, 115, 130, 168

Baker Board, 41, 43

Balck, Gen. Wilhelm, 28, 29

Baldwin, Hanson, 27

Balkan incident, 24

Baltic, the, 33

Bangalore torpedoes, 84

Bantheville, Bois de, 133

Bar-le-Duc, 91

Barnett, Correlli, 146, 150, 167

Barricourt, 136, 137; heights, 136, 139

Bar River, 139

Barrois Plateau, 87

"Beaten zone," 123

Beaumont, 27

BEF. *See* Great Britain

Belfort, 82

Belgium: 25, 26; Belgians driving on Brussels, 136; king of, 93

Belgrade, 25

Bell, Gen. George Jr., 98

Belleau Wood, 67

Bethincourt, 89

Binarville, 87, 94

"Black Day for the German Army," 76

"Black Jack." *See* Pershing

Bliss, Gen. Tasker M., 60, 61, 64, 65, 68, 130

Blitzkrieg, 34, 169

Bloch, Ivan, 24

Blois, France, 161

"Bodies for bullets," 116

Bolsheviks, 34

Bombon, 75, 130

Borne de Cornouiller, 139

Boult aux Bois, 136

Boureuilles, 89

Bourshes, 67

Bradley, Gen. Omar, 156

Bridges, Gen. G. T. M., 61

Brieulles, 94; Bois de, 110

Briey, 139
Britain (British). *See* Great Britain
Brook-Shepherd, Gordon, 150
Brown, Gen. Preston, 119, 131
Brusilov, Gen. Alexei, 33
Buck, Gen. Beaumont B., 131
Bullard, Gen. Robert, III, 68, 73, 85, 86, 94, 109, 129
Bulson, 141
Busigny, 93
Buzancy, 137; Buzancy-Stonne, 93

Cadorna, Gen. Luigi, 59
Cambrai, 33, 93; Cambrai-St. Quentin, 81
Cameron, Gen. George, 94, 129
Canadian forces, 31, 165
Cantigny, 67, 131
Caporetto, 34
Central Powers, 24, 26, 27, 32, 33, 35, 60, 74, 75, 144, 152, 165. *See also* Germany; Austria-Hungary
Chalons-Mezieres Road, 93
Chamberlain, Sen. George E., 44
Champagne, 26; Champagne-Marne, 73
Champigneulles, 137
Champ Mahaut, 99
Charlevaux Creek, 120
Charpentry, 110
Chateau-Thierry, 64, 67, 73
Chatel Chehery, 119
Chatillon, Bois de, 139
Chaumont, 45, 46
Chemical warfare, 30, 63, 98, 103, 111, 119, 135, 137, 154
Chemin des Dames, 31, 32, 62, 64
Cheppy, 99
Chiers River, 139
Cierges, 105; Cierges-Nantillois, 101
Clark, Gen. Mark, 156, 158
Clemenceau, Georges, Premier, 65, 66, 69, 83, 114, 130
Clery-le-Grand, 137
Cobb, Frank, 40
Cochrane, Rexmond, 154
Coffman, Edward, 69, 150, 158, 163, 166
Combined allied command, 166
Communications, 113
Congress. *See* United States
Connor, Gen. Fox, 50
Consenvoye, 123
Conway, Gen. Theodore, 57, 150, 156, 159

Convoy system, 34
Cote Dame Marie, 126, 133
Cote Lemont, Bois de la, 122
Craig, Harold, S/Maj., 115
Cronkhite, Gen. Adelbert, 99
Cuisy, Bois de, 103–106
Cunel, 87, 94, 116, 119, 133; Cunel heights, 106, 123; Cunel-Romagne heights, 123

Daly, Daniel, Sgt., 67
Dardanelles, 26
Dawes, Gen. Charles C., 130
DeWeerd, Harvey, 157, 160, 164
Dickman, Gen. Joseph, 85, 129
Distinguished Service Cross, 148
District of Columbia, 101
Douellens, 64
"Doughboys," 141
Downey, Fairfax, 137
Drum, Gen. Hugh A., 50, 90, 160
Dunkerque, 26, 80
Dun Sur Meuse, 137, 139
Dupuy, Trevor N., 24, 27, 147, 163

East Prussia, 26
Edwards, Gen. Clarence R., 131
"Eighty division program," 70
Eisenhower, Gen. Dwight, 158, 166
Ely, Gen. Hanson, 131
Elting, Col. John, 166
Engineer School, 54
England. *See* Great Britain
English Channel, 26, 62; ports, 46
Entente Powers, 26, 35
Epionville, 99, 110
Essame, Hubert, 97, 110, 113
Etain-Longuyon, 151
Etang River, 139
Etzel-Giselher Stellungen, 89, 98
Europe, 23, 24, 35, 41, 166, 168, 169; armies of, 25; European belligerents, 144; European militarism, 35; Europeans, 165
Exermont, 110

Falkenhayn, Gen. Erich von, 153
Falls, Cyril, 114, 115
Farnsworth, Gen. Charles, 99
Fays, Bois du, 119, 120
Filipinos, 40
Fiske, Col. Harold B., 49

Flanders, 32, 33, 64, 73, 80, 82, 84, 115, 122; group of armies of, 93
Fleville, 126
Foch, Marshal Ferdinand: appointed French military representative on Supreme War council, 59; appointed "Coordinator" of Allied armies, 63; Pershing offers American forces in France to, 64; his memoirs show ready agreement regarding need for American infantry, 65; urges utmost insistence on maximum U.S. infantry reinforcements, 69; states requirement for one hundred American divisions, 69; recommends, with Pershing's agreement, shipment of more U.S. combat troops, 70; confidently planning Allied counteroffensive, 73; urges British and French armies to attack, 76; agrees to formation of two American armies, 76; directs assignment of American divisions to French armies, 81; agrees to St. Mihiel and Meuse-Argonne offensives for American Army, 82; his plan for Allied general offensive, 92, 93; told by Clemenceau that American attack was stalled, 114; opines that Americans are learning, 114; demands American attack continue without interruption, 114; alleged to have attempted to relieve Pershing, 129; questions Pershing on Wilson's peace plans, 130; approves creation of two American armies, 130; attempts to turn American attack to west, 135; decisions on employment of American forces analyzed, 152, 153; rated in comparison with Pershing, 162, 163
Folie, Bois de la, 137
Forester, Charles S., 28
Forges, Bois de, 98, 99
Fort Leavenworth, 47
Fort McNair, 27, 43
Fosse, 136, 137
Franco-Prussian War, 25, 93
France: and military doctrine, 24; strategy of, 25; weapons of, to AEF, 38; American army in, 40, 41; military attaches of, to U.S., 52; attempts to reduce U.S. influence, 129, 130; cost of war to, 145; suspicions of, about allies, 165; association of French with Americans, 166; U.S. cemetery in, 170
—French Army: countered German drive,

26; at Verdun, 27; and recovery, 29; and Nivelle offensive, 31, 32; First Army, 32, 93; and staff organization adopted by AEF, 45; and command of U.S. units on line, 53; Fifth Army, 63, 64; and training of U.S. forces, 56, 57; unstable, 59; Sixth Army, 64, 73, 76; Tenth Army, 73; "bled white," 75; Third Army, 76; Second Army, 81, 93, 94, 114, 115; II Colonial Corps, 84, 93; French XVII Corps, 93, 123, 126, 133, 139; Fourth Army, 81, 82, 93, 94, 114, 126, 135, 137, 153; 5th Cavalry Division, 96; has honor of liberating Sedan, 141; report of, on AEF, 146; awards, compared to AEF, 149; and final operations, 167; and Maginot strategy, 168
Fresnes, 80; en Woevre, 129
Freya Stellung, 89, 135
Friedensturm, 72
Fuchs, Gen., 77
Funston, Gen. Frederick, 40

Gallwitz, Gen. Max von, 97, 110, 137, 141
Gas. See Chemical warfare
General Organization Project, 41
General Staff College, 54, 56
Germany: military system of, 24, 25; 1914 offensive of, 26, 27; changes in tactics of, 28, 29; 1917 strategy of, 30, 31; reaction of, to French and British attacks in 1917, 32, 33; operations of, in Russia, 33, 34; submarine warfare of, 35; offer to Mexico, 36; espionage of, in U.S., 36; divisions of, compared with AEF, 43; AEF threat to, 46; 1918 offensives of, 63, 64, 67, 68, 72, 73; forces of, at St. Mihiel, 77–79; withdrawal of, from St. Mihiel salient, 84; defenses of, in Meuse-Argonne, 88, 89, 96, 97, 98, 110, 111, 116; report of German tanks, 120; machine guns of, 122; artillery of, 123, 136; no slackening of defensive efforts of, 131; and loss of Kriemhilde defenses, 133; and use of gas on Americans, 135; and Kriegsmarsch, 137; hopeless situation of, in the west, 139; withdrawal of, to Meuse-Antwerp, 141; and armistice, 143; relative strengths of, 144, 145; and evaluation of post-Armistice situation, 146; and strategic situation in the west, 152; and control and support of forces, 155; and aerial bombardments, 158;

American rating of German soldier, 165; opinion of German leaders, 167; and analyses of future warfare, 168
Germont, 137
Gesnes, 110, 119
Giles, John, 167
Goethels, Gen. George, 71
Goldhurst, Richard, 157
Gondrecourt, 41
Gorze, 139
Goudy, Pvt. Wiley, 122
Grandpre, 94, 126, 133
Grant, Col. Walter, 90
Great Britain: mobilizes manpower, 24; declares war, 25; operation of, in the Dardanelles, 26; recovery of, from mistakes of 1914, 29; and dominance of the seas, 35; military personnel of, sent to U.S. to train army, 38; and transport for U.S. forces, 44, 57, 61, 62, 69, 70; and request for more American troops, 129; attempts to minimize American military effort, 130; cost of the war to, 145; English military organizations, 147; army officers of, compared to American officers, 161; and suspicions of allies, 165; and desire for an American army in Flanders, 166; and contribution to victory, 167, 168
—British Expeditionary Force: commitment of, 26; in area of the Somme, 27; leadership of, 28; and Ypres offensive, 32, 33; Second Army, 32; compared to AEF, 43; and lack of spirit, 49; attaches to U.S., 52; and command of U.S. units, 53; Third Army, 63, 76; and 1918 offensive, 75, 76, 80–83; First Army, 93; Fourth Army, 93; driving on Brussels, 136; evaluations of, 146, 149, 161, 164–168
Great War, the, 24, 27, 168, 169
Griffiths, Col. Williams, 68
Groves, Pvt. Frank, 58

Hagen Stellung, 89
Haig, Field Marshal Sir Douglas, 32, 33, 63, 64, 75, 76, 80, 114, 115, 146, 152, 162–164
Harbord, Gen. James G., 45, 71, 151
Harricourt, 137
Haucourt, 104
Haudiomont, 77
Heights of the Meuse, 87, 126, 139
Heller, Charles, 154

Hill 240, 119
Hill 255, 126
Hill 265, 119
Hill 272, 116, 126
Hill 282, 103
Hindenburg, Marshal Paul von, 60, 74, 122
Hindenburg Line, 31, 85, 115
Hines, Gen. John, 99, 129, 160
Hirschauer, Gen., 129
Hoffman, Priv. Robert, 101
Holley, Gen. Irving B., Jr., 47, 151, 158, 159
Hoover, Herbert, 39
House, Col. Edward M., 39, 61, 141
"Hun," 36, 165
Hutier, Gen. Oscar von, 34; Hutier tactics, 34, 60

Illiberalism at home, 40
Immigrants, 35
Imperial War Museum, 146
Indians, 40
Infantry Drill Regulations, 48
Infantry Journal, 147
Influenza ("flu"), 96, 113, 129, 135
Inspector General, AEF, 108
Isonzo region, 26, 27
Italy, 24, 31, 34; forces of, 27
Ivoiry, 104

Jerusalem, 34
Joffre, Marshal Joseph, 39, 61
Johnson, Gen. Evan, 107
Johnson, Thomas M., 167
Johnson, Gen. William, 99
Joint Note #12, 62
Joint Note #18, 64
Jure, Bois de, 99
Jutland, 27

Kaiser. *See* Wilhelm II
Keegan, John, 150
Kennedy, David, 49, 116, 145
Kerensky, Alexander, 33; government of, 34
Kernan, Gen. George, 71
Kerth, Col. Monroe, 90
Kitchener, Lord: Kitchener's Army, 161; Kitchener Divisions, 146, 147
Kriegsmarsch, 137
Kriemhilde Stellung, 89, 97, 109, 110, 112, 116, 123, 133, 169
Kuhn, Gen. Joseph, 99, 101, 103

La Besaca, 141
Lacey, Priv. Ira, 165
Lachausee, 141
Langres, 56, 156
La Tuilerie farm, 137
Lawson, Don, 67
Leavenworth: schools, 151, 160; graduates, 160
Leckie, Robert, 35
Ledebur, Gen. von, 84
Lenin, Nicholai, 34
Leningrad, 33
Les Esparges, 77–79; Esparges-Vigneulles, 84
Les Petites Armoises, 141
Liddell Hart, Basil H., 154, 157, 162, 163, 164, 167
Liggett, Gen. Hunter, 50, 68, 73, 85, 94, 109, 126, 130, 133, 135, 136, 151, 160, 161
Ligny-en-Barrois, 80
Lloyd George, David, 31, 34, 61, 63–66, 69, 80, 83, 115
Loire, 66; river, 163
London Daily Telegraph, 167
Lonergan, Lt. Col. Thomas, 166
Lorraine, 25, 46, 76, 101
Lossber, Gen. von, 28
"Lost Battalion, The," 120, 126
Ludendorff, Gen. Erich von, 32, 60, 62, 67, 68, 72, 73, 76, 84, 122, 133, 135, 152, 163, 167
Luneville, 63, 82
Lusitania, 36
Luvaas, Jay, 57
Lys River, 64, 93

McAndrews, Gen. James, 50
McArthur, Gen. Douglas, 45, 85, 133, 160
McMahon, Gen. John, 126, 131
Maistre, Gen. Paul, 141
Mantieulles, 139
March, Gen. Peyton C., 44, 45, 68, 71, 72, 157, 164, 168
Marne, 69, 165; river, 64, 65, 67; salient, 68, 72, 73, 76
Marseilles, 80
Marshall, Col. George C., 79, 90–92, 96, 106, 147, 150
Maryland, 101
Maurice, Gen. Sir Frederick, 29, 111
Max, Prince of Baden, 167

Meade, Camp, 101
Mediterranean, 34
Melancourt, 99, 101; Bois de, 103, 104
Messines Ridge, 31
Metz, 80, 89, 97, 151; Metz-Lille Railroad, 79; Metz-Sedan-Mezieres Railroad, 133; Metz-Thionville, 79
Meuse, 52, 81, 89, 114, 116, 119, 123, 129, 136, 139, 141, 143; west of, 152; east of, 152; Meuse-Antwerp, 141; Meuse-Argonne, 56, 86, 87, 90, 91, 94, 108, 112, 115, 119, 120, 143, 145, 147, 150, 153, 154–156, 161, 168; campaign, 93, 144, 149, 163, 167, 169; Meuse-Argonne veterans, 157; heights of, 87, 116, 119, 123, 125, 126, 133; river, 81, 87, 92–94, 99, 129, 137, 153
Mexico, 36, 40; border of, 40
Mezieres, 81, 82, 152; Mezieres-Sedan, 83
Michel Stellung, 79, 80, 84, 85
Middle East, 165
Military History Institute (MHI), 157; questionnaire of, 162, 164
Millett, Alan, 147, 151, 156, 163
Milly, 139
Milner, Lord Alfred, 70
"Miracle of the Marne," 26
Mitchell, Col. William, 84, 160
Mollieville Farm, 133
Montfaucon, 87, 89, 94, 98, 101, 104, 106, 108–110, 114, 164; Bois de, 99
Montmedy, 97
Montrebeau Woods, 110
Moore, Dr. Claude, 155, 156
Moore, 2d. Lt. Waldo, 165
Moranville, 139
Morrison, Gen. John F., 52
Moscow, 34
Moselle, 79, 80, 93, 115, 129, 139
Muir, Gen. Charles, 99, 129
Murphy, Sgt. Stephen, 113
Myers, Priv. Lawrence, 133

Nantillois, 99, 106, 110
National Defense Act: of 1916, 36, 37; of 1920, 168
National Guard, 36–38, 131, 144, 147, 149, 160, 161
Nenninger, Timothy, 151, 159, 160
Neville, Gen. Robert, 31; offensive of, 32
New York Times, 167
New York World, 40

North Atlantic Treaty Organization (NATO), 166

North Sea, 30

November 1918: The Last Act of The Great War, 150

Noyon salient, 31

Officers' candidate school, 54; at Langres, 56; at Mailly, 56; at San Samur, 56; Officer Training Camps and Schools, 160

Ogons, Bois de, 110, 119

Oise, 76

"Open warfare," 48, 50–53, 120, 157

Orlando, Vittorio, Prime Minister of Italy, 69

Oury, Col., 104, 105

Owen, Gen. von, 110

Palmer, Major Frederick, 160

"Pals Battalions," 147

Paris, 26, 114, 115

Passchendaele, 33

Patton, Lt. Col. George, 84, 96, 143, 158

Peace conferences, 130

Pershing, General John J.: appointed to command of AEF, 40; arrival in France, 41; cables War Department to plan sending one million men, 41; directs Baker Board to work with his staff, 41; decides on artillery for AEF, 43; complains of noncooperation on part of War Department, 44; disapproves of General Officer List of War Department, 45; promoted to four-star general, 45; approved AEF staff organization, 45; gains approval of American Sector in France, 46; relies on training of soldier as marksman, 47; announces "open warfare" doctrine, 48l; expresses disagreement with Allied tactics, training, 50; complains of poor training of replacements, 52; divides responsbility for training between War Department and AEF, 52, 53; establishes AEF schools system, 54–56; places training of replacement units and personnel entirely under AEF, 57; continues to insist upon full training program, 59, 60; responds to Allied pressure for expediting commitment of American units to combat, 61; "Six Division Plan" for British agreed to by Pershing, 62; offers all American units in France to Foch, 64, 65; acknowledges acrimony at Sarcus Meeting, regarding U.S. troops for support of Allies, 65, 66; demands formation of American Army, 66; agrees to temporary commitment of American divisions to stop German advance, 67; demands improvement in censorship, 68; agrees to Allied proposals for shipping Americans to France on 1 June 1918, 69, 70; gains Allied agreement for early formation of American Army, 70; disputes with War Department over eighty-division program, 70, 71; rejects detachment of SOS from his command, 71; complains about commanding manner of Chief of Staff, 72; describes performance of American divisions in Allied counteroffensive as "excellent," 73; again requests formation of American First Army, 76; receives St. Mihiel mission, 76; requests major support effort from Allies, 76, 77; receives most of support requested, 80; objects to Foch's plan to limit St. Mihiel attack; divides American forces, 80–82; agrees to take Meuse-Argonne mission, 84; executes limited St. Mihiel attack, 84, 85; expects to take Montfaucon in one day, 89; agrees that First Army's mission is attrition of enemy, 93; assumes responsibility for sector, 93; approves attack plan for 26 September, 94; assumptions wrong in all respects, 94; directs 79th Division to advance without delay, 106; states in *Experiences* that initial advance was rapid, 109; does not commit reserves, 109; agrees to go into defensive posture, 111; brings experienced divisions from St. Mihiel, 111; conducts furious schedule of visits, critiques, 114; rejects Foch's plan to again divide American forces, 114; criticism of logistical tangle by Clemenceau, others, 114, 115; instructs commanders to use smoke, 116; directs French XVII Corps to attack Heights of Meuse, 123; approves temporary defense posture for First Army, 126; creates Second Army; appoints Liggett to command First, 129; alleged attempt by Foch to relieve Pershing, 129, 130; conference with Foch at Bombon, 13 October, 130; conducts visits and provides guidance to commanders, 131; relieves some commanders, 131, 132;

and provides guidance to commanders, 131; relieves some commanders, 131, 132; directs continuation of attack, 131, 132; comments upon proposals for armistice, 133, 134; rejects Foch's directive to turn First Army to west; agrees to resumption of offensive on 1 November, 135; sets no limits on advance, 136; orders pursuit continued, 139; announces agreement with "unconditional surrender" demand upon Germans, 141; orders Sedan taken, 141; comes close to relief by U.S. authorities, 141; criticized for premature formation of U.S. army, 146; challenges Haig on criticism of AEF, 146; rejected comparison of U.S. divisions, 150; selection of narrow, obstructed well defended zone criticized, 152; his strategy, doctrine criticized, 153; his desire to use gas, and problems, 154; his emphasis on rifle, disregard of machine gun criticized, 156, 157; his prejudice against tank and airplane, 158, 159; came to appreciate Guard and Reserve, 162; his leadership evaluated, 162–164; his machinations against March criticized, 164; put his stamp on AEF, 164; publication of *Experiences,* 167; as Army Chief of Staff, 168; dedicates cemetery, 170

Pétain, Marshal Henri, 32, 62, 63, 75, 76, 80, 85, 89
Petrograd, 34
Philippine jungle, 160
Piave River, 34
Pirate guns, 133
Pogue, Forrest, 92
"Poilu," 32, 165
Pont-a-Mousson, 77
Pratt, Lt. Col. Merritt, 58
"Preparedness program," 36
Pripet marshes, 33
Prisoners of war, 86, 108, 149, 150
Progressive movement, 35
Provisional Government of Russia, 33
Prussia, 25

Rainey, Maj. James, 39, 47, 49, 51, 55, 56, 150, 151
Randle, Gen. Edwin, 120
Rapallo, 59
Rappes, Bois de, 131

Read, Gen. George W., 68
Reading, Lord, 61
Regneville, 84, 87, 89
Regular Army, 37, 38, 47, 144, 147, 149, 159, 162, 168
Reims, 72
Remilly, 141
Reserve Officers Training Corps, 160
Retraining School, 54
Richene Hill, 123
Rifle: Lee-Enfield, 96; Mauser, 96; Springfield, 38, 43
Roberts, Pvt. Norman, 85
Rockenbach, Col. Samuel, 157
"Rock of the Marne," 72
Romagne, 87, 94, 131, 133, 169; Bois de, 126
Roosevelt, Theodore, 40
Root, Elihu, 43
Ropp, Theodore, 24, 57, 150, 151, 163
Ross, Sgt. Fred, 113
Russia, 25, 30, 34; offensive of, 27, 33; Russo-Japanese War, 24, 40

Saar, 79
St. Juvin, 116
St. Mihiel: 81, 85, 86, 90, 91, 94, 101, 147, 151; campaign of, 50, 76, 152; salient of, 75, 79, 81, 83
Schlieffen, Count Alfred von, 25; plan of, 25
Sedan, 89, 93, 136, 141, 144
Seiser, Pvt. Edmund, 58
Selective Service Act, 37
Selle, 129
Septsarges, 99, 105, 106
Serbia, 25
Services of Supply (SOS), 46
Shock troops (divisions), 60, 63
Showman, Capt. Frank W., 147
Sibley, Cpl. William, 52, 122, 143
Siegfried-Hindenburg Line, 76
Simkins, Peter, 146, 147, 161, 165
Sims, Adm. William, 34
"Six Division Plan," 62, 80
Smith, Daniel, 169
Smythe, Donald, 97, 111, 130, 150, 156, 157, 162, 163, 164
Socialists, 35
Soissons, 31, 68, 73
Sommauthe, 139
Somme, 27, 62, 63, 122, 146

Souilly, 93, 96
Stars and Stripes, 139
Stenay, 131, 139
Stokesbury, James, 57, 83, 162
Stonne, 87, 141
Submarine tactics, 36
Suez, 26
Suippe River, 92, 93
Summerall, Gen. Charles P., 129, 133, 160
Summers, Cpl. Herbert, 129
Supreme War Council, 59, 61, 62, 64, 65, 67–69
Sweezy, Col., 101, 104, 105
Switzerland, 26, 30

Tank, 30, 33, 38, 84, 96, 145, 157, 158
Tannenberg, 26
Telegraph, 168
Terraine, John, 162
Thiaucourt, 80, 85
Tokyo, 40
Toland, John, 67, 150, 162, 163
"Tommy," 164
Toul, 62
Trask, David, 163
Traub, Peter, 99
Trench warfare, 50, 52, 56; trench units, 73, 77
Trentino, 27
Triple Alliance, 24, 25
Trotsky, Leon, 34
Tuilerie, Bois de, 101, 108
Turks, 34

United States: Army, Military Historical Institute, 155; Army War College, 37, 43, 47, 52; Congress, 36, 43, 44, 148, 168; end of isolationism of, 169; expenditures of, on war, 145; influence of, on peace settlement, 130; joins Allied coalition, 165, 166; Military Academy, 40; military missions of, 43; reinforcements from turned tide of war, 167; slammed door on European affairs, 168; War Department of, 37–39, 41, 43, 44, 47–49, 52, 53, 61, 62, 65, 66, 68–71,

101, 113, 114, 129, 130, 150. *See also* America; American Expeditionary Forces

Vandiver, Frank, 41, 129, 162
Varennes, 89, 99
Vauquois, 89, 99, 101
Vaux, 67; Vaux-en-Dieulet, 139
Verdun, 27, 46, 63, 77, 79, 87, 96, 101, 122, 153
Verrieres, 137, 141
Versailles, 69
Very, 99
Vesle River, 73
Veterans of Meuse-Argonne campaign, 162
Vienne-le-Chateau, 89
Vigneulles, 84, 85; Vigneulles-Regneville, 81, 82
Villa, Pancho, 40, 158
Ville devant Chaumont, 139
Villemontry, 139, 141
Villers, 141
Vosges, 60

Washington, 36
Weigley, Russell, 48, 51, 57, 151, 163
Western Armies, 23
Western Europe, 167
Westover, Capt. Wendell, 167
Weygand, Gen. Maxime, 114, 130
Whittlesey, Maj. Charles, 120
Wilhelm II, Kaiser, 35, 36
Williams, T. Harry, 162
Wilson, Gen. Sir Henry, 59
Wilson, Woodrow, President, 35–37, 39, 40, 60, 64, 65, 69, 123, 129, 130, 141, 145, 169
Woevre, 7, 141, 152
Wood, Gen. Leonard, 40
Woodward, C. van, 169
World War I, 156, 169
World War II, 33, 158, 159, 166
Wynne, Capt. Graeme C., 28

Yank, 164
Ypres, 32, 33, 113